COMBAT LOADED

Joseph G. Dawson III, General Editor

COMBAT LOADED

Across the Pacific on the USS *Tate*

THOMAS E. CREW

Texas A&M University Press
College Station

Library of Congress Cataloging-in-Publication Data

Crew, Thomas E., 1957–
  Combat loaded : across the Pacific on the USS Tate / Thomas E. Crew — 1st ed.
    p. cm. — (Texas A&M University military history series ; no. 108)
  Includes bibliographical references and index.
  ISBN-13: 978-1-58544-556-1 (cloth : alk. paper)
    1. Tate (Ship). 2. World War, 1939–1945—Naval operations, American. 3. World
War, 1939–1945—Regimental histories—United States. 4. World War, 1939–1945—
Campaigns—Pacific Ocean. 5. World War, 1939–1945—Transportation—United States.
I. Title. II. Series: Texas A&M University military history series ; 108.
  D774.T39C74 2007
  940.54'5973—dc22

                                                            2006014330

To all of the U.S. combat veterans whose stories remain untold.

CONTENTS

ILLUSTRATIONS

Map P.1. USS Tate *(AKA-70), Theater of Major Operations. Courtesy Chris Robinson.*

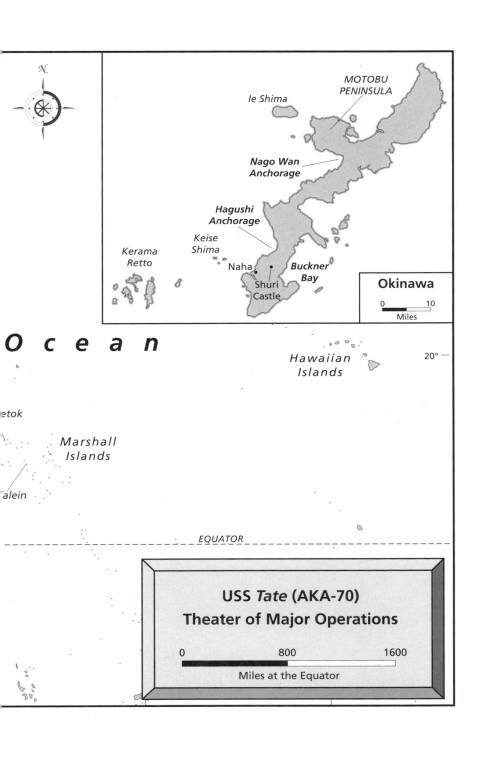

N

le Shima

MOTOBU PENINSULA

Nago Wan Anchorage

Hagushi Anchorage

Keise Shima

Kerama Retto

Naha

Buckner Bay

Shuri Castle

Okinawa

0   10
Miles

O c e a n

Hawaiian Islands

20°

etok

Marshall Islands

alein

EQUATOR

USS *Tate* (AKA-70)
Theater of Major Operations

0   800   1600
Miles at the Equator

PREFACE

ONE OF THE TRADITIONS of my baby-boomer childhood was my father giving me a navy haircut while I sat on a wooden bench in our basement. In the short time it took to buzzcut my brother and me, Dad often treated us to a story about his World War II service in the Pacific. Hanging on the wall near where we lost our hair was a framed shellback certificate he had earned when his ship crossed the equator. Decorating the margin were magnificent sea creatures, bare-bosomed mermaids, and a raging King Neptune stating that the USS *Tate* (AKA-70) had entered his royal domain on a "Secret Mission of War." My father downplayed this phrase, which preyed heavily on my young imagination, by saying things like "We were hauling beef and toilet paper in the Pacific."

In 1988 I found myself crossing the equator for the first time as my shipmates dipped me in garbage, flogged me with wet hoses, and abused me in ways the uninitiated can never appreciate. During that sleepless night, I thought back with pride to my father's wartime shellback stories. After winning the drag beauty contest and being crowned Queen of the Wogs, I realized that my father had left out many of the saltier details of this classic seafaring rite of passage. Years later, when casually researching *Tate,* I discovered that much of the ship's history was on the verge of being lost forever. Like the tale of the equator crossing, my father's war stories had often omitted many relevant details. Through a combination of the fog of war, the characteristic detachment of veterans, a professionalism that makes men reluctant to speak of themselves, and the overwhelming scope of the events in the Pacific, this story remained hidden.

Tate was an attack cargo (AKA) ship whose mission was to use its boats to land amphibious assault troops in enemy territory and then supply them with combat cargo. Commonly referred to as transports, the AKAs and slightly bigger attack transports (APAs) were the largest of the many types of World War II amphibious warships. After that war, the transports that were not scrapped, mothballed, or sold into commercial service continued to serve into the Vietnam era in much the same fashion as they had in World War II. Even after significant modernization, they retained their close-in, hit-the-beach reputation until advances in technology dictated a transformation to amphibious assault ships with over-the-horizon capability.

The numerous accounts by the U.S. Navy, U.S. Army, U.S. Coast Guard, and U.S. Marine Corps in World War II relative to amphibious operations rarely weave together the experiences of the different military cultures. Usually there is a sharp transition in these stories at the point when the troops land, making it sound almost as if they were dropped off and forgotten. This is not the truth, but it is a notion sustained by the dearth of World War II literature devoted to joint amphibious operations from the perspective of an individual ship or organizational unit. Most of the studies focus on individual battles and campaigns or their contribution to the doctrinal evolution of amphibious warfare. This story describes amphibious warfare from the perspective of a single attack cargo ship, *Tate,* a ship built as part of an energized war economy and manned predominantly by mobilized civilians. Any deficiencies in the hastily constructed *Tate* and her quickly trained crew needed resolving in just a few short weeks before sailing across the Pacific. A ship affectionately referred to by its crew as the Hot Tater, it carried into battle the humorous image of three steaming baked potatoes on its smokestack. Yet, *Tate* was a ship like every other ship that has sailed to war. At its rails, men stood gazing at the seemingly infinite sea, contemplating their fates, hoping for the best, and preparing for the worst.

This story follows the actions of *Tate* and its crew as part of Transport Squadron 17, which carried the troops of the 77th Infantry Division during the Okinawa campaign. Including the story of the troops fighting ashore and the operations to keep them supplied with combat cargo provides an understanding of the vital role of combat logistics in amphibious warfare. The combination of these two stories provides a rare depiction of World War II amphibious warfare.

It was not until 1943 that attack cargo shipbuilding efforts began in earnest. A product of the lessons learned from earlier attack cargo ships converted from a variety of prewar designs, the AKAs that were built in the last half of the war were state-of-the-art cargo-carrying combatants. Their enhanced efficiency was a critical factor in sustaining the island-hopping campaigns across the vast expanses of the Pacific. Created by a fully mobilized war economy that was overwhelming the Axis nations, *Tate* faced an enemy that was resorting to the most desperate of tactics. On April 2, 1945, Transport Squadron 17, packed with assault troops, endured a savage sunset attack by a swarm of kamikazes off

Photo 1. The ship's comic logo and nickname, the Hot Tater, painted on its smokestack. Courtesy Howard C. Colley.

the coast of Okinawa. Often thought of as quickly trained pilots flying alone in single-engine aircraft, these kamikazes were mostly twin-engine bombers manned by their aircrews and flown by obviously experienced pilots who executed their mission with stealth and precision. Described in detail, this suicide attack on a transport squadron is representative of the Japanese strategy to sink the amphibious transports that were supporting the forces already ashore and engaged in battle.

As part of the Western Islands Attack Group, Transport Squadron 17 participated in amphibious landings on the islands surrounding Okinawa. The last of these landings—on Ie Shima—was one of the final, large-scale, amphibious assaults of the Pacific War. Taking place under ideal conditions, the invasion of Ie Shima successfully used the lessons of amphibious warfare learned from preceding campaigns. Overshadowed by the fighting on the nearby island of Okinawa, Ie Shima was a short-lived, but intense, battle. At Ie Shima, *Tate* fulfilled its primary mission as an attack cargo ship that landed combat-loaded cargo ashore in direct support of an ongoing amphibious operation.

Pulitzer Prize–winning war correspondent Ernie Pyle briefly visited *Tate* at Ie Shima. One of *Tate*'s landing craft then took Pyle ashore the day before his death in combat. The story of Pyle's final days while embedded with the 77th Infantry Division includes unpublished accounts of men who spoke to him shortly before he was killed. His brief appearance in the lives of those who met him just before his death left a lasting emotional imprint, much as President Roosevelt's passing had done the week before. Pyle was striving to bring recognition to the citizen soldiers and sailors who were struggling anonymously in the Pacific, just as he had done so effectively in Europe and North Africa. Ironically, most of the recognition the conquerors of Ie Shima received came from their proximity to Pyle's death and not from his writings.

The central character of this story is Rupert Estey Lyon, the second of *Tate*'s three commanding officers and the ship's skipper for all of its wartime service. Following the awkward, sudden removal of the first captain during the ship's trials, Lyon took over a ship that was manned predominantly by "ninety-day wonder" reserve officers and green recruit sailors. His large physical presence, charismatic communication skills, and confident, fatherly style were an effective leadership formula. A master mariner, Lyon gave his inexperienced officers the room to develop, while keeping a watchful eye on vital ship operations. He then quietly used his few experienced officers and chief petty officers to hold the ship together as he cultivated new leaders. Not a by-the-book commander, the colorful Lyon strove to maintain a happy ship. Although by nature a rule bender, he was abrupt and combative toward dereliction and incompetence. Anyone who threatened his ship's mission or took advantage of his easygoing nature felt his wrath. Lyon's legacy is one of wartime devotion to duty under the umbrella of wisdom and human understanding.

This story also describes the application of meteorology and oceanography in the planning and execution of amphibious operations. By mid-1944, the amphibious planning cycle had evolved to include hydrographic data, oceanography, airborne observations, and underwater demolition team reconnaissance reports. Using these multiple sources of information, amphibious planning staffs produced detailed landing charts in the field for distribution to the boat crews who would be making the assaults. The success of this integrated approach to understanding the ocean environment was essential not only for landing assault troops but also for supplying the combat-loaded cargo that was needed to sustain the battle.

The actions of Transport Squadron 17 following *Tate*'s combat experience yield an insightful picture of the postwar period. During those long, anxious months spent awaiting discharge, *Tate* and its squadron demonstrated an elevated operational efficiency honed by the brutality of war. Utilizing these skills, Transport Squadron 17 played a key role in countering the Communists' advances into Korea and Manchuria. During this significant, yet obscure, historical event, U.S. amphibious transports landed more than 50,000 U.S. Marines and 500,000 Nationalist Chinese troops in northeastern China in an effort to stabilize a region torn by postwar military and political chaos.

To date, no comprehensive ship history exists for any of the 108 AKA class ships commissioned during World War II. Thomas Heggen's 1946 novel, *Mister Roberts*, which is loosely based on his service on the attack cargo ship *Virgo* (AKA-20), is the only book even remotely related to an attack cargo ship. Converted to a successful stage play and a major motion picture, *Mister Roberts* focuses on the human relationships on board the cargo ship *Reluctant*, while paying only minimal attention to the ship's role in the Pacific War. Although the account is fictional, Heggen still provides one of the most poignant stories of service at sea in World War II.

Kenneth H. Goldman's 2004 narrative, *USS Charles Carroll, APA 28: An Amphibious History of World War II*, and Kenneth Dodson's 1954 novel, *Away All Boats*, are the only published accounts of the 236 APA class ships commissioned in World War II. While the more glamorous battleships, aircraft carriers, and destroyers dominate World War II naval literature, the frontline naval combatants of the amphibious campaigns—the AKA and APA transports—have waited nearly sixty years for their first comprehensive history.

This story started out as an effort to locate my father's World War II shipmates. Every step forward beckoned the pursuit of a story that was quickly fading from existence. The first man I located, John Borneski, started organizing a *Tate* reunion in the late 1980s, but his wife's terminal illness and his own ongoing bout with cancer compromised his efforts. Without prompting, John told me a riveting story of his brush with death from a kamikaze. He ended by saying, "I have never told that story to anyone, and I do not know why I just told it to you. Will you help me find my shipmates?" The initial motivation for this book resulted from that emotional conversation. Sadly, John did not live to see the realization of his dream, but unlike millions of other veterans, he knew the story of his World War II service was being preserved.

Alvin Joslyn was the second man I located. A schoolteacher who left his classroom and family to go to war, Joslyn faithfully wrote home, amassing hundreds of pages of correspondence. These evocative perspectives of the war first led me to believe that sufficient material existed for a book. Besides Joslyn's considerable primary source material, his persistent encouragement kept this project going through its early phases until a third veteran, Uel Smith, took the helm. Working tirelessly in tracking down his shipmates, Smith made hundreds of Internet searches and phones calls. By checking *Tate*'s roster against the Social Security death records, we managed to find all of the ship's surviving officers and more than eighty percent of its enlisted men. Smith's efforts in helping to locate more than fifty veterans were essential in elevating this project from a historical curiosity to a comprehensive story told through a chorus of voices.

The veterans' voices form the fabric of this story and represent the more than 50,000 crewmen who served on World War II attack cargo ships. Their experiences on the decks and in the boats of *Tate* are representative of any cargo attack ship. During the four years it took to complete this project, we lost many of these contributing veterans. Through contacts with other World War II ship organizations, it is apparent this project was blessed by its ability to locate so many veterans from a single ship so long after the war. It now seems unlikely that so many original voices will ever represent another World War II amphibious transport.

The long-term memory process of combat veterans is worthy of serious study in its own right. After nearly sixty years, many physiological and psychological processes can impair the recollection process. Yet, most of the veterans' stories had an unquestionable air of truth and were supported by other first-person accounts, secondary sources, and the official records. Where necessary, I have clarified or excluded conflicting information using the best assessment based on all appropriate sources. While the credibility of most of the operational accounts was easily verified, it was impossible to confirm some of the human-interest stories that provided such an important emotional perspective to this narrative. To help assess the overall accuracy of each interview, I pursued a line of questioning directed at each man's standard duties and his battle station. Having previously established many of the facts, I was able to determine any propensities for error. Then, if warranted, follow-up interviews were conducted with men who shared similar experiences. After nearly sixty interviews, I am confident that I made every logical effort to protect the credibility of the veterans' memories. The bibliography contains a listing of all of the interviews from which material was used. In order to acknowledge all of the contributing veterans, I must also thank M. Fidelis Blunk, Leroy Carter, Anthony J. Caproni, Otis Jones, and Paul Waletzko, whose interviews are not cited.

While the veterans provided the foundation for this project, it would not have been successful without the efforts of Gibson Bell Smith, Barry Zerby, Annette Williams, and Patrick Osborn. These archivists at the National Archives and Records Administration, Branch Depository for Modern Military Records, College Park, Maryland, tracked down the official war diaries, deck logs, and action reports that are so critical to this story. Others who also contributed in a variety of ways are Chris Robinson, Maury York, Terry Sanders, Russ Padden, Mark Slover, and Charles C. Bates. A number of my colleagues at the Naval Oceanographic Office added their talents to this endeavor: Bonnie Martino, Kerry Legendre, Ray Sawyer, Clay Hull, Tom Cuff, Peter Washburn, Capt. Philip Renaud, USN, and the staff of the Matthew Fontaine Maury Oceanographic Library. During the course of this project I frequently sought the advice of my historical mentor, Mark W. Johnson, whose numerous recommendations proved essential to the research for and the writing of this book. An army officer, author, and established academic historian, Mark provided positive guidance that, along with his considerable assistance with my maps, contributed substantially to the quality and impact of this story.

All of the best things in life spring from the family. Thankfully, this project did as well, with my family contributing in many ways both large and small. Charles, Nancy, Caroline, and Melissa Crew, with assistance from Brian and Cathy Rorai, hosted the first *Tate* reunion, which yielded a wealth of new information and insights. Carlie Welch helped iron out some of the early wrinkles with her editing before my sister, Cathy Rorai, an English teacher, wielded her red pen, providing on-target compositional recommendations that significantly increased the impact of the narrative.

The people who deserve the most credit are my beautiful wife, Brenda, and sons Jason, Nicholas, and Benjamin. They watched with curiosity as this project grew and then reached fruition. I hope the intangible effect this book will have on the legacy of so many World War II amphibious veterans and their descendants will compensate for the long hours I have spent on the computer. For my sons, I hope this book becomes a legacy to their American heritage and the debt we all owe those who defended the United States.

I owe my biggest debt of gratitude to my parents, Lewis and Alice Crew. Their consistent nurturing, support, and encouragement provided me with the education and confidence to undertake this project. This story is my tribute to my parents and all they have done for me. They are the Greatest Parents of the Greatest Generation.

Thomas E. Crew
Long Beach, Mississippi

Chapter 1

MOBILIZATION

Awaken a Sleeping Giant

ILLUMINATED ONLY BY STARLIGHT, the attack cargo ship *Tate* steamed across an uncommonly calm sea during the early hours of April 16, 1945. The clear, moonless night sky sparkled with the constellations *Tate's* captain knew so well. After two world wars, Lt. Cdr. Rupert E. Lyon, an expert navigator and decorated warrior, viewed the stars as friendly lighthouses in the sky. Yet, on this sleepless night, he would need no celestial bodies to guide his ship. Loaded with assault troops and combat cargo, *Tate* and the rest of Transport Squadron 17 were sailing up the west coast of Okinawa toward a gathering storm. The amphibious transports aimed their bows at the flashes of light on the horizon as the thunder of a naval bombardment raced across the peaceful sea toward the blacked-out ships. Peering through his binoculars, Lyon could just make out the dark outline of an island to the north as his squadron eased into the assembly area for the invasion of Ie Shima.

It had already been a long war in many ways for Machinist's Mate 2nd Class Milton J. Buswell, as he stood ready at his 40-mm gun mount. Not yet five months old, the battle-tested *Tate* was Buswell's third ship of the war. His previous two ships were now shattered hulks rusting on the seafloor half a world away. Buswell had joined the armed guard in 1941 and was training when the United States entered the war. His first ship, *Ballot,* a confiscated Italian merchantman, broke down during a convoy across the North Atlantic before limping into Iceland. The convoy sailed on but lost 11 of its 22 ships to submarines. Later, on a run to Murmansk, *Ballot* ran hard aground when the convoy scattered in heavy fog during a German attack. Buswell soon found himself again in the Barents Sea on the freighter *Greylock* as part of an 11-ship convoy. Spotting two torpedoes jumping out of the sides of the waves and heading for his ship, he sounded the general alarm in time to avoid one of them. Buswell then watched helplessly as the second torpedo slammed into his ship, scoring a fatal hit. Minutes later, he was in a lifeboat bobbing about the frigid Arctic Ocean. Rescued by the British corvette *Oxlip* (K-123), he returned to the

United States, where his next assignment was at the armed guard center in Brooklyn, New York, repairing laundry equipment, safe from the sea and the war. After transferring to Virginia in 1944, he was sent to gunnery school and then to *Tate*. A typical Midwesterner of average stature, Milton Buswell was hardly extraordinary except for his good fortune. What would end first, his luck or the war, would be determined on board *Tate*.[1]

With the eastern horizon beginning to glow just before sunrise, the heavy cruiser *Tuscaloosa* (CA-37) lowered her 8-inch gun barrels and began firing low-trajectory broadsides into Red Beach T-1 on the island of Ie Shima. For Buswell and those of his shipmates with a view of the action, the muzzle flashes from the big guns exposed the silhouettes of the assembled ships and boats of the invasion force in the predawn darkness. Each violent flash burned a glimpse of the future into the eyes of those searching for a hint of what would unfold.

For two and a half hours, the combined naval bombardment was relentless. Screaming shells passed directly over the heads of the men of the 77th Infantry Division embarked on the assault craft circling offshore. With the bombardment reaching its climax, the waiting U.S. assault forces did not have to check their watches to know their time of reckoning was at hand. The amphibious command ship issued the classic order "land the landing force," and the wave guide officers in their leading and flanking boats led the assault waves forward, keeping them on course and schedule.[2]

Carrying fuel and ammunition to help sustain the invasion once it moved inland, *Tate* waited offshore. A product of a mobilized war economy, in less than nine months the ship went from the drawing board into battle. Now it would carry out its primary mission: landing combat cargo in support of an ongoing amphibious invasion. Only a few hours before, *Tate*'s twenty-four landing craft, which were now taking part in the attack, had hung from the davits or been lashed down to the decks. The members of the crew that were not in the assault or below decks anxiously watched from their battle stations. Buswell was an ammunition loader on a 40-mm mount. His perspective of the war was limited at present to what he could see by looking over a pair of 40-mm gun barrels pointed toward an island that he had never known existed until now. With every gun the navy had within range firing at the island, explosions ripped apart the tree line, and volleys of rockets arched through the sky. As the assault forces approached the shore, they spotted a white horse standing chest deep in the water near the beach. Fleeing the island, the frightened animal had waded into the sea to escape the shelling.[3]

By 1945 U.S. forces had stormed the beaches of four continents under a wide variety of conditions, and amphibious assault planners had learned many costly lessons. Improvements in ships, boats, weapons, and assault vehicles had

Photo 1.1. Milton J. Buswell of Elyria, Ohio, lost two ships before joining Tate. *Courtesy Milton J. Buswell.*

facilitated the refinement of amphibious tactics. After three years of war, the planning cycle for amphibious operations had matured and taken on a mathematical character. As a result, the logistical chaos of the war's early amphibious campaigns had largely been resolved.[4]

From a tactical perspective, the planning for the invasion of Ie Shima was geometric. The battle space consisted of sectors neatly drawn on maps and charts as circles, squares, and other shapes. Assault forces and their supporting ships maneuvered and fired within assigned sectors in accordance with predetermined timetables. Similar to a gigantic chess game, forces moved ahead and were supported by those behind them. Amphibious ships launched their landing craft and assault vehicles, which then positioned themselves in their preassigned front-row squares. There they waited like pawns to move forward and engage the enemy. Behind the assault forces, the back-row pieces of destroyers, cruisers, and battleships pounded the island. Each ship fired a specified number and size of shells into an assigned sector during a predetermined interval and then moved its fire to a new sector to serve up yet another menu of destruction. With the landing of the infantry, the battle entered a phase in which its neat geometry was replaced by the chaos of ground combat.

To support the troops now ashore clashing with an enemy determined to fight to the death, *Tate* and the rest of the transport squadron moved to within a half mile of the island. From Milton Buswell's perspective, the appearance of the frightened white horse off the invasion beach symbolized the vulnerability of the innocent victims of war.[5]

Adm. Isoroku Yamamoto, commander of the Imperial Japanese Navy's combined fleet on December 7, 1941, and the reluctant architect of the devastating surprise attack on Pearl Harbor, believed the outcome of a war with the United States was predetermined. In his now famous response to his exuberant staff following the successful attack, Yamamoto said prophetically, "I fear that all we have done is to awaken a sleeping giant and fill it with a desire for vengeance." Yamamoto clearly foresaw the endgame: Checkmate was inevitable, but, unlike the white horse, he was neither innocent nor able to flee.[6]

By 1943 Yamamoto was dead and his prophecy fulfilled. The American giant was indeed fully awake. Gone were the holding actions and the come-as-you-are warfare of the dark days of 1942. The tide had turned in the skies and waters north of Midway and on the beaches and jungles of the Solomon Islands. Americans at home struggled to keep up with the influx of obscure geographical names such as Guadalcanal and Tarawa, which were now taking on a solemn and heroic significance. As the newspapers spoke of the geography of global war, they also carried frequent stories and advertisements of the mobilized industrial might of a democracy aroused and a giant fully awakened.

One such story was unfolding at the North Carolina Shipbuilding Company on the east bank of the Cape Fear River in Wilmington, North Carolina. Here on July 22, 1944, in a muddy shipyard, a routine keel-laying ceremony took place for U.S. Maritime Commission hull 1396. Destined to be named after an obscure rural county in the delta region of northwest Mississippi, the USS *Tate* (AKA-70) was conceived. The Wilmington shipyard would build 243 ships for the war effort. Of these, 32, including *Tate*, were based on the C2-S-AJ3 design and completed as *Tolland* (AKA-64) class attack cargo ships. The 459-foot *Tate* with a beam width of 63 feet had a draft of nearly 26 feet when fully loaded. Her single screw was driven by a 6,000-horsepower reduction-geared steam turbine capable of producing a maximum speed of 15.5 knots. *Tate*'s five cargo holds (three forward and two aft) had a total capacity of 380,000 cubic feet.[7]

As the giant stirred and flexed its muscles, the raw materials extracted from the mines of Minnesota and Michigan were fed into the steel mills of Indiana and Pennsylvania for processing into the currency of war. Transported by ship, rail, and truck to factories and workshops, skilled American hands transformed the currency of war into the implements of war. These implements then fed the assembly lines and shipyards of a thriving war industry to create the machines of war. A small fraction of this intricate system fed the Wilmington shipyard, which received its allocation of steel plate, steam turbines, and the specialized components needed for the construction of *Tate*.

The first attack cargo ships were converted from a variety of prewar designs and proved early on the necessity for a class of ships that could feed combat cargo directly into an amphibious battle. The United States began a concentrated ship-building effort for attack cargo ships in 1943. In itself another expression of military mass production, 108 attack cargo ships were in service by the end of World War II. Yet, by the time of the famed D-Day invasion at Normandy on June 6, 1944, only 24 of these ships were in commission. AKA ship production finally reached its full capacity in time to support the major Pacific War campaigns of 1944 and 1945.

On September 26, 1944, Mrs. C. E. Cox, of Wilmington, North Carolina, the wife of a shipyard foreman, proudly proclaimed, "I name thee *Tate!*" as she broke a bottle of champagne across the ship's bow. The shattering bottle and a spray of champagne sent the ship, now christened, sliding into the dark waters of the Cape Fear River just sixty-six days after construction began.[8]

On November 3, 1944, just forty-one days after launching, the navy accepted *Tate* for trials. The next morning the ship made the short trip to the Charleston Navy Yard under the command of Cdr. Elias M. Doar Jr. and manned by an auxiliary vessel ferry crew, who routinely sailed newly constructed ships from the builder to naval bases. Completion of the ship's outfitting took place in Charleston, South Carolina, and included the installation of

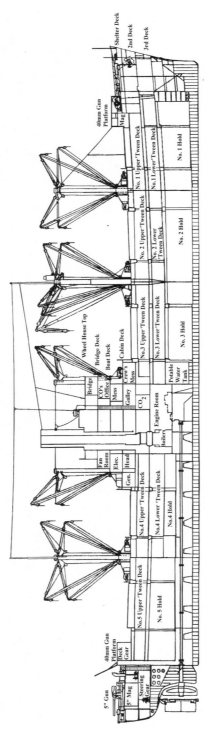

Figure 1.1. General profile of Tolland *(AKA) class C2-S-AJ3-type attack cargo ship built by North Carolina Shipbuilding Company in Wilmington, North Carolina. Courtesy Smithsonian Institution.*

Photo 1.2. Early photo of Tate *painted in camouflage and without most of its boats. Courtesy Naval Institute.*

its communications equipment, radar, and armament. All that was lacking was a trained crew.[9]

While shipbuilders toiled around the clock creating *Tate,* its crew mobilized. A notorious instrument in this process was the mail carrier. Only days after becoming eligible for the draft on their eighteenth birthdays, John F. Borenski and Howard C. Colley found in their mailboxes an order to report for induction. Allowed to finish high school, the young men went directly from the classroom to basic training. James K. Baker's high school in Mount Pleasant, Iowa, held its graduation three days early since all but five of the school's graduating males were scheduled to report immediately for induction into the military. Baker's situation was common as he "graduated Wednesday and was inducted Friday."[10]

Being drafted into the military was not a new experience for Israel Kampel. In 1935 he had joined the Polish Army for three years of mandatory service. Sensing the ominous prospect of being a Jew in Europe during the foreboding rise of German militarism, Kampel immigrated alone to New York City in 1938. The family he left behind in Poland stayed in touch through a series of increasingly depressing letters. Even the Nazi censors in their Jewish ghetto could not hide the heartbreaking truth of their impending fate. By 1944 the letters from his family stamped with swastikas had stopped arriving, and in their place he found a draft notice. Kampel's humble pursuit of the American Dream would have to wait. He left his wife, one-year-old son, and his job as a toolmaker to fight for his adopted country. One thing Kampel took with him as he entered the U.S. Navy was a nagging uncertainty of the fate of his family and friends in Europe.[11]

Many others chose not to wait for the inevitable draft notice, preferring to get into the fight as soon as possible. By enlisting, they were able to choose

Photo 1.3. *Drafted immediately after his eighteenth birthday, Howard C. Colley of Memphis, Tennessee, was allowed to finish high school. Courtesy Howard C. Colley.*

Photo 1.4. Israel Kampel immigrated alone to New York City after his compulsory service in the Polish army ended in 1938. Courtesy Lewis J. Kampel.

Photo 1.5. Israel Kampel as a member of the shore patrol after his second drafting. Courtesy Lewis J. Kampel

Photo 1.6. Charles H. Gries of Chicago, Illinois, enlisted the day after Pearl Harbor. Courtesy Charles H. Gries.

their branch of service. Those who were only seventeen needed to obtain the signature of a parent or guardian. Sixteen-year-old Leroy W. Kemske persuaded his father to alter his birth certificate. Teenagers from all regions of the country rapidly trained to make up the majority of *Tate*'s crew.[12]

Gerald W. Munro of Michigan's remote Upper Peninsula was exempt from the draft due to his employment on a Great Lakes iron ore freighter. Realizing that his seafaring skills were a valuable commodity and feeling compelled by his desire to fight, Munro joined the navy. A few men heading for *Tate,* such as Charles H. Gries, had already been to war. Gries, who had risen to the rank of Radioman 1st Class, was one of the few men with senior enlisted ratings who helped round out *Tate*'s predominantly green crew. Having presented himself at a navy recruiting station, where he enlisted the day after the attack on Pearl Harbor, Gries had already fought against the Germans. Now he would get a chance to finish the war against the Japanese.[13]

When Clinton E. Alexander felt the first tug of the train taking him from Charlotte, North Carolina, to war, his thoughts raced to his family. Just days before his enlistment in the navy, his mother had received the infamous War Department telegram. Her son, S.Sgt. Lewis Alexander, a U.S. Army Ranger, had been killed in Italy. Of her nine children, Clinton was now her only surviving son. As the oldest male, Clinton had taken over the duties of running the family's cotton farm at the age of twelve, three years after his father had died. Now replacing the harsh realities of subsistence farming were the harsh realities of war. At the completion of his training, he went home for a brief visit. Alexander was leaving his young wife and baby to go to war. When the train started to move, he felt a need to leave something behind in case he should die in combat like his brother. Removing his white sailor's hat, he quickly scrawled out a message on a piece of paper: "Whoever gets this hat please see that Mrs. C. E. Alexander 70 Cemetery St. gets it." He shoved the message

Table 1.1. Landing Craft General Specifications

Boat	Length	Power	Speed	Capacity	Armament	Troops	Crew
LCM	50 ft.	2 × 225 hp	9½ knots	60,000 lbs	.50-cal	100	5
LCVP	36 ft.	225 hp	9 knots	8,100 lbs	2 × .30-cal	36	4
LCP-L	36 ft.	225 hp	10 knots	8,100 lbs	2 × .30-cal	36	4

into his hat and threw it out the train window, where a stranger found it and delivered it to his wife.[14]

Tate's crew of sixty-two officers and 333 enlisted men rapidly began preparing for war. On the same day *Tate*'s construction began, the first member of the ship's precommissioning detail reported to the Naval Training Station at Newport, Rhode Island. The facility trained thousands of personnel to meet their ships when construction was completed. Much of the housing was in metal Quonset huts, which were difficult to keep heated in cold weather and like ovens in the summer. Yet, despite the hardships, many of the men joined the navy to escape the field conditions of army service. Having heard the stories of life in the trenches of World War I, Ens. David M. Waller felt he "would rather go down with the sharks than carry a pack and a rifle in the mud."[15]

The members of *Tate*'s landing division were conducting their specialized training at the Amphibious Training Base in Fort Pierce, Florida, where they were put through the paces of a recently developed curriculum: learning how to operate, maintain, land, and recover landing craft. Depending on circumstances, *Tate* would carry varying numbers of three types of landing craft. The optimum complement was six steel-hulled landing craft mechanized (LCMs), seventeen plywood (landing craft, vehicle and personnel) LCVPs, and one plywood landing craft personnel (LCP-L). The Higgins Boat Manufacturing Company of New Orleans, Louisiana, designed all of *Tate*'s boats, which were essential to executing the navy's doctrine for amphibious operations.[16]

Fort Pierce's obscure location on South Hutchinson Island, with its uninhabited sandy beaches, allowed for unrestricted practice landings by amphibious units. One future *Tate* officer who was making the best of the situation by demonstrating his leadership potential was Lt. (j.g.) Joseph E. Neblett. A Louisiana lawyer with a smooth, easygoing countenance, Neblett projected a capable confidence, quickly winning the attention and respect of those around him.[17]

On October 21, *Tate*'s landing division left Fort Pierce. Arriving at Naval Training Station in Newport two days later, they joined the rest of the ship's complement and conducted additional training. On November 13, three days before departing from Newport for Charleston to meet his ship, Steward's Mate 1st Class George V. Marshall wrote home to his wife in Piedmont, South

Carolina. An African American steward, Marshall wanted to reassure his family since he feared he would be unable to visit them during his short time in his home state. "It [is] no use for you to worry as I am OK. So keep your chin up and ask God to help you." Marshall was correct; after arriving in Charleston, he would not have much spare time as *Tate*'s crew scrambled to prepare for their ship's commissioning. Many of Marshall's shipmates also turned their thoughts toward home as they experienced the inevitable anxiety kindled by thoughts of sailing upon the oceans of a world at war.[18]

On November 23, the men assigned to *Tate* enjoyed a Thanksgiving dinner. Some of the crew who were just arriving had already eaten their Thanksgiving meal on the train. Enjoying a second repast seemed appropriate since there was no telling where they would spend their next Thanksgiving or whether they would even be alive. Milton Buswell was one of the men opting for a second Thanksgiving feast. As he prepared to enjoy the most traditional of American celebrations, Buswell prayed that *Tate* would be more fortunate than his first two ships.[19]

A web of fateful threads held *Tate*'s crew together on Thanksgiving Day of 1944: a forged birth certificate, parental permissions, voluntary enlistments, draft notices, sunken ships, an African American going to war from a segregated society, a Jew fleeing from the Nazi threat in Poland, and a man seeking retribution for a brother killed in combat. Regardless of the paths that had brought these citizen sailors of diverse perspectives together, their fates and those of their nearly 400 shipmates would be determined on the decks of *Tate*.

ACROSS THE PACIFIC

Gold Bars on Your Shoulders

ON NOVEMBER 25, 1944, Capt. R. N. S. Baker, aide to the commandant of the Sixth Naval District, placed the USS *Tate* into commission at Charleston, South Carolina. In their dress blue uniforms,
Tate's crew stood in formation for the brief but impressive ceremony, as
Lt. Cdr. William Jordan became the ship's first commanding officer. Family
and friends of the crew who were able to attend the ceremony toured the ship,
with the exception of the command and control spaces, which contained the
top-secret radar equipment.[1]

After the commissioning, Mary Boland, the wife of *Tate*'s executive officer,
Lt. Kells M. Boland, chatted with Jordan's wife. Mrs. Jordan was concerned
about her husband's mental state, commenting that "he really had a hard time
on his last cruise." She was clearly worried that he was close to his breaking
point. Jordan certainly did not lack experience as a mariner. Born in British
Guiana, South America, he had served throughout World War I on merchant
ships under the control of the British Admiralty. After the war, he joined the
U.S. Merchant Marine Reserve, obtaining his third mate's license. For the
next ten years he worked his way up, serving on tankers before earning his
master's license in 1929. Jordan then operated his own shipping business until
returning to the merchant fleet as chief mate on a bulk carrier shortly after the
war began. Called to active duty early in 1943, he received a reserve officer's
commission before joining the tanker *Niobrara* (AO-72). In November 1943,
Jordan took command of the transport *De Grasse* (AP-164) at its commissioning in California. *De Grasse* spent the next few months transporting troops to
the Central Pacific before taking part in the Marianas campaign and landing
assault troops on Saipan. After returning to Pearl Harbor, he received orders to
take command of a ship under construction.[2]

On December 1, *Tate* got under way to conduct trials and be degaussed
(a process that reduced its magnetic field) before returning the same day to
Charleston. On December 6 the ship sailed to Hampton Roads, Virginia,

Photo 2.1. The USS Tate*'s crew members salute the colors as they are raised over their ship for the first time during commissioning on November 25, 1944, at Charleston, South Carolina. Courtesy Alvin L. Joslyn.*

carrying out general drills en route. After a brief stay, *Tate* began a series of exercises in Chesapeake Bay as part of its shakedown cruise. From December 9 to December 15 civilian contractors tested the performance of many of the ship's systems. The exercises included full-power trials, maneuvering, and gunnery practice on canvas targets towed behind aircraft.[3]

Tate's single stern-mounted 5"/38 was its biggest weapon. The term *5"/38* refers to the fact that the barrel length of the gun was thirty-eight times the five-inch diameter of the shells. Its semifixed ammunition consisted of a fifty-five-pound explosive projectile with a variable-time delay fuse and a separate propellant charge in a brass casing. The gun's rate of fire was dependent on the proficiency of its crew of eleven. With a maximum range of ten miles, the powerful gun was best suited for long-range gunnery.[4]

Second in size and stopping power to the five-inch gun was the water-cooled, twin 40-mm Bofors. *Tate* had four sets of twin forties mounted in pairs of gun tubs on the bow and just forward of the five-inch mount. An automatic cannon with a range of more than six miles and accurate up to two miles, the hard-hitting 40-mm was the best close-in antiaircraft weapon of the war. From a pedestal behind each mount, a gun director used a handlebar device to aim an Mk-14 optical gun sight. After tracking a target, an Mk-51 gun director was fed gyroscopic corrections, creating a firing solution that automatically aimed the weapons via electric motors. As the guns fired, a battery officer, located in the director mount, called out corrections to the operator based on the tracks of the tracers. Two sets of manual traversing cranks also allowed each 40-mm to operate locally without its director. A twin mount could fire as many as 160 rounds a minute with a minimum crew of five, consisting of two loaders per barrel and a gun captain. The loaders handled four-round clips, dropping them into the top of the gun. Each clip contained one tracer that produced a reddish-orange vapor trail.[5]

The final weapons in *Tate's* arsenal were sixteen 20-mm Oerlikon anti-aircraft cannons. Mounted around the periphery of the ship and on top of the deckhouse, each 20-mm was operated by a crew of three and had a reputation as a reliable antiaircraft weapon with a rapid rate of fire of 450 rounds per minute. Sixty-round drums of 20-mm explosive-tipped shells contained white tracers to determine whether each gun's Mk-14 optical gun sight was working accurately or whether the gunner needed to rely on simple hand–eye coordination. The 20-mm's air-cooled gun barrels required changing after prolonged firing.[6]

The gunnery officer on the signal bridge controlled the ship's weaponry via sound-powered phone circuits that converted voices into electrical impulses, allowing vital communications to continue if the ship lost electrical power. Providing the overall tactical picture was the combat information center, located behind the bridge. All of the relevant data from radar signals, ship movements, and radio communications were marked on a transparent plotting board that defined the ship's combat situation at a glance. At the other end of the fire control system were the talkers, one on each gun mount with an oversized helmet containing headphones and a sound-powered microphone. The gunnery officer received radar contact reports from the combat information center. After identifying threatening targets, he used the sound-powered circuits to concentrate the guns on the most dangerous targets.

As the ship and crew worked themselves into shape, the skipper began exhibiting some unsettling behavior. Considered by his officers as nothing more than eccentric, Jordan remained beyond questioning in his position of ultimate authority. On December 10, after less than a week at sea, he ordered the enlisted men secured below decks and all officers who were not on watch to assemble in the wardroom, where they were surprised to find armed guards posted at the hatches. Jordon told his officers that, since sailing, he had become certain there was a German spy on board, and now he knew who it was, pointing at Ens. David M. Waller. Jordan stated that Waller had been in his stateroom rifling through his papers. Jordan then produced an enlisted man as a witness. When asked whether he had seen Waller in the captain's room, the sailor answered, "Yes." Jordon ordered the shocked Waller placed under arrest and taken to the brig. On the way to the brig, another officer told Waller, "Not to worry. The skipper has blown a fuse."[7]

The executive officer, Lieutenant Boland, knew that Waller was innocent and that Jordan himself had sent Waller to his quarters to retrieve papers that were needed on the bridge. Concerned for Waller's safety, Boland sent the ensign ashore without Jordan's knowledge. The officer of the deck now reported to Boland that he had seen Jordan point his pistol at a sailor. A few moments later he heard gunfire from inside the captain's cabin. A graduate of the Massachusetts Maritime Academy with four years in the navy, Boland knew he had to act. When he went to Jordan's cabin to discuss the matter, he found his skipper seated, looking down the passageway, holding a .45-cal. automatic pistol, and mumbling, "Someone is going to try and kill me."[8]

Boland and the ship's medical officer, Lt. Fredrick C. Heinan, an obstetrics doctor from Wisconsin, devised a plan to send Jordan ashore for medical treatment. A dummy naval message was created, stating that Jordan was to go on shore and meet an admiral concerning new orders for the ship. After notifying the Port Authority of the situation, Boland spent a long night with Jordan, reassuring him that he was not in danger. In the morning, when Boland asked his captain whether he wanted to go ashore and get some help, Jordan said, "Yes." The men manning the boat to transfer Jordan were armed. As he prepared to leave the ship, Boland said, "Captain, you can see you have plenty of protection. Don't you think you should give me your pistol, sir?" Nodding, Jordan handed Boland the weapon. Boland immediately ejected the clip and the chambered round onto the deck. Jordan climbed down into the boat under the guard of Lt. (j.g.) John H. Mahler and was then joined by Lieutenant Heinan, who escorted him ashore for medical evaluation. *Tate* had suffered its first casualty of the war but in a far different manner from what anyone had anticipated. The ship resumed its shakedown trials under the temporary command of Lt. Kells Boland, who executed the developmental activities of a general program designed for attack transports and cargo ships.[9]

On the evening of December 15, *Tate* moored at the Norfolk Navy Yard for maintenance to address some minor deficiencies that had been discovered during its shakedown. The next day, Lt. Cdr. Rupert Estey Lyon, *Tate*'s new captain, came on board unannounced. Having extensive prewar experience as a merchant mariner, Lyon was extremely competent. Enlisting in the navy in World War I, he quickly rose to the rank of chief quartermaster. After the war Lyon remained in the reserves and in January 1941 received a reserve commission as a lieutenant (j.g.). He then returned to active duty as the loading officer on the cargo ship *Capella* (AK-13). Transferred to the ammunition ship *Shasta* (AE-6) in January 1942, Lyon served as a gunnery officer before becoming the executive officer of the cargo ship *Celeno* (AK-76) in November 1942. Lyon's actions on *Celeno* off Guadalcanal earned him a citation for valor and his skipper's recommendation for a command of his own. Serving briefly on the attack transport *Baxter* (APA-94), Lyon was present at the initial amphibious landings on Leyte. Following his service in the Philippines, Lyon traveled to Wilmington, North Carolina, to serve as the commanding officer of the attack cargo ship *Ottawa* (AKA-101), which was still under construction. Lyon's experience and availability resulted in his transfer to *Tate* on short notice following Jordan's sudden departure.[10]

Upon boarding *Tate,* the first thing Lyon found was that the officer of the deck, Ens. Paul R. Leahy, was not at his post. Leahy had gone for a quick cup of coffee at the worst of times. Lyon had him tracked down and brought to his stateroom, where he reprimanded Leahy for leaving his post on the quarterdeck. Lyon, a large man, was quite excited and grew red in the face as he berated the young officer. It was an unfortunate introduction for Leahy to his new skipper. Leahy's key position as navigator made the rough start even more inauspicious.[11]

Unlike their new skipper, few of *Tate*'s officers had any real experience, and the few with prior sea duty were performing the ship's most important jobs. They became role models for the flock of green naval reserve ensigns who constituted most of *Tate*'s officer corps. One such experienced man was Lt. Walter R. Hall of Swansea, Massachusetts. Hall, a graduate of Brown University, grew up in a part of the country known for its seafaring traditions. More importantly for *Tate,* he served for two years on the transport *Susan B. Anthony* (PA-72) and participated in the invasion of Sicily. Hall's ship sank off Utah Beach at Normandy on June 7, 1944, after setting off a pressure mine. Though *Susan B. Anthony* was loaded with troops, miraculously not a single man was lost. Men like Hall were the exception on board *Tate,* as most of the real experience came from the senior enlisted chief petty officers or the "mustangs" who had received their officer commissions after proving their leadership potential as enlisted men. Mustang promotions were common during the war, when experience counted as much as (or more than) the minimum of two years of college required for an officer's commission. One such mustang was Ens. Glenn S. Parker Jr., the only regular navy officer on *Tate*.[12]

Lieutenant Hall was keeping an eye out for leadership potential in the enlisted ranks. Hall liked what he saw in Gunner's Mate 1st Class Hubert J. Six. Six's obvious strength and confidence made him a logical choice for master at arms, the person in charge of the ship's security. When Hall asked Six to take the job, he turned him down. Six explained that he did not want to jeopardize his good relationship with the men by being the tough guy who woke them up every morning. Hall told Six that he would write him up for disobedience if he declined. Hall then offered to go with Six on the morning wake-up rounds for several days to eliminate any opposition. Six accepted, and the two men worked together for a few days as Hall's humility helped with Six's transition into his unwanted duties.[13]

Some of the officers were getting their first taste of censoring the enlisted men's mail, a chore they would come to loathe. Reading the private details of a sailor's life was painful enough without having to mark up some of the letters and send them back as "denied." With his girlfriend, Coxswain Morris ("Mike") Larsen devised a code in which the first letter of each paragraph spelled out his location. It made writing difficult, but the officers never caught on. The duty also had its humorous moments, such as when one man's letter home contained the lamentable details of his seasickness in Chesapeake Bay: "Dear Mother, I was throwing up so hard I could taste the hair on my ass."[14]

Tate sailed from Norfolk on December 21 for the Advance Base Depot in Davisville, Rhode Island. Immediately upon sailing, the ship ran into overcast skies and poor visibility, preventing astronomic shots for navigational fixes. The bad weather continued into the next day but improved just prior to the approach to Rhode Island. When Lyon asked his navigator for a position update, Ensign Leahy admitted, "I have no idea where we are, sir." Anticipating a landfall around Narragansett Bay, Leahy radioed a passing ship for a position and was embarrassed once more to have let his captain down.[15]

The crew was trying to guess their ship's destination based on the type of cargo they were loading. The consensus guess was the Pacific, because of the need for amphibious ships there, plus the loading of a large amount of anchor chain. The chain was an item that seemed more appropriate for the island-hopping anchorages of the world's largest ocean than the harbors of Europe.[16]

With the imminent departure of *Tate* to some distant theater, the captain granted two periods of leave of four days each to the crew, with the married men getting the first period, which included Christmas Day. For the men remaining with *Tate,* the holiday season consisted of loading cargo and embarking the remaining personnel needed to fill out the crew. One of these men was Gunner's Mate 3rd Class Uel Smith. After joining the navy in May 1943, Smith saw hard service on the transport *General G. O. Squier* (AP-130), including a stint in the South Pacific and action off France and Italy. In nineteen months, he had had only twelve days of leave. When Smith's ship arrived at Staten Island, New York, he applied for and got permission for an extended leave of thirty days, but the leave would require his changing ships. Smith sent for his wife, who was expecting their second child, to join him in New York City. Four days later, on December 22, he received orders to report to *Tate* in

Norfolk. Sending his wife home to Illinois, he told her he would be home for Christmas.

After arriving in Norfolk, Smith found out *Tate* was now in Rhode Island. He was offered an alternative transfer to the battleship *Texas* (BB-35), but he would get only two weeks of leave. Like any sailor desperate to spend more time with his family, Smith chose *Tate*. Already having missed Christmas with his family, Smith traveled by train with several other sailors bound for *Tate*, which was docked in Davisville, Rhode Island. Upon arrival at about 0200, they immediately reported to the ship. Smith presented his papers and asked to speak to the executive officer about his thirty days of leave. As Smith and his companions had obviously enjoyed a few adult beverages along the way, they were told to go below to sleep it off. When he awoke, the ship was under way, and he asked a sailor, "Are we changing piers?" "Yes, next stop, Panama Canal" was the reply.[17]

Adorned in a multishade geometric pattern of gray camouflage paint, *Tate* got under way with sealed orders early on December 30. Once at sea, Lyon opened his secret instructions. His ship was directed to proceed to Pearl Harbor, Territory of Hawaii, via the Panama Canal. As the new year of 1945 began, *Tate* was steaming south alone and heading for the Pacific in what everyone hoped would be the last year of the war.[18]

Before departing from Rhode Island, Ensign Leahy addressed the members of his navigation department: "We have to really pull ourselves together." Leahy, a graduate of the Maine Maritime Academy, knew navigation by the book, but he lacked practical experience. Needing to build a competent team the captain could trust, Leahy demanded a maximum effort. After diverting to avoid a reported U-boat sighting, the ship passed through the Windward Passage within sight of Cuba and into the Caribbean Sea. The whole time, the navigation team worked diligently to hone their skills. On the morning of January 4 Lyon confronted his navigator: "Mr. Leahy, when can we expect to sight the sea buoy for our approach to the canal?" "At 1541, sir," answered Leahy. At 1538 Lyon again approached Leahy and said, "Let's go look for your sea buoy." The two officers walked to the signal bridge, where Lyon began searching the horizon with a range finder. When he spotted the buoy, he glanced at his watch and smiled. Then, looking at his navigator, he exclaimed, "It's 1541! Well! Christopher Columbus!" Lyon's ability to forgive his navigator and then to colorfully recognize a job well done exemplified a leadership style that was well suited to motivating a crew of predominantly mobilized civilians who were quickly trained and sent off to war.[19]

The ship moored at Cristobal, Panama, that evening before sailing through the Panama Canal the next day. The transit across Panama was quite exciting to the crew, most of whom had never been outside the United States. Not only was Panama the first foreign land they had ever seen, but the sheer magnitude of the canal's engineering and operation was also beyond anything they had ever witnessed. They were also passing through a significant portal in their military experience. Just as they had gone through the doors of a recruitment station, into boot camp, and across the gangway onto *Tate,* the Panama Canal led to a new ocean, a new reality, and the war itself.[20]

The uneventful cruise to Hawaii provided numerous opportunities for additional training, general drills, and weapons firings. This included flag hoist training in preparation for convoy cruising and maneuvering. To be ready for potential emergencies, *Tate*'s captain ordered all of his officers to rotate through each of the ship's departments for at least a few days. This would instill at least some minimal knowledge of all of the ship's operations so that, if required, they could serve in any capacity.[21]

Gunner's Mate 1st Class Hubert Six did not let his duties as *Tate*'s master at arms stop him from keeping a secret diary even though such documents were forbidden because of security concerns. Six's early entries convey an image of a young man dealing with exhaustion, fear, and loneliness while coming to grips with the reality of being on a ship heading off to war. Calling his ship "doomed," Six lamented that *Tate* was "getting farther away from the U.S. every day, hour, minute, second."[22]

The long transit provided an opportunity to square away some deficiencies. When the captain noticed that few of his crew were skilled at tying knots, he decreed that any man hoping to go on liberty in Hawaii first must pass a test for tying twelve basic knots. For the next few days, fingers twisted away at pieces of rope all over the ship since no one wanted to miss a chance to explore a tropical paradise. Another problem crying out for attention cropped up in the medical department. Lieutenant Heinan discovered that his chief pharmacist's mate, an old navy salt, was not up to the task of organizing the sick bay. Heinan had asked the Atlantic Fleet detailer in Norfolk for an experienced pharmacist's mate. His request happened to be submitted almost immediately after Pharmacist's Mate 1st Class Earl W. Buss reported, asking for an assignment on something bigger than the 110-foot wooden minesweeper he had left in France. Buss was just returning from service in North Africa and Italy after the transfer of his ship to the Free French.

Buss's new orders required him to report immediately to *Tate* with nothing more than his seabag and records. There he found the "sick bay in a shambles" and Doc Heinan candid about the situation. Putting Buss in charge of the sick bay, Heinan told him, "If anyone gives you any problems, let me know." After a couple of weeks, Buss ran afoul of the old chief, who complained that Buss was "showing him no respect" and that there would be repercussions. Buss responded, "Do what you have to do, but stay out of my way." The chief's threat was a bluff, and he then claimed to be ill and incapable of performing his duties. When a medical examination revealed no infirmity, the salty old sailor was transferred off the ship.[23]

On the evening of January 17, 1945, *Tate* made radar contact with the mountain of Mauna Loa and began its approach to Pearl Harbor. Once pierside, *Tate*'s crew began unloading the ship's cargo before embarking twenty-one enlisted naval personnel for transport. Across the busy harbor, rusting portions of the battleship *Arizona* (BB-39) jutted above the surface of the sea, marking the spot where more than twice *Tate*'s total complement of men were entombed below the ship's decks.[24]

Gunner's Mate 3rd Class Smith, who had missed out on Christmas with his family and his promised leave, rode into Honolulu as a mail guard in a jeep with his captain and a driver. What Smith observed on the way helped soften the sting of the fate that had landed him on his new ship. *Tate*'s skipper was personable and warm, while at the same time projecting an image of competence and strength. His good-natured qualities bode well for the hard times ahead.[25]

Tate's captain was not the only one in need of a vehicle. After spotting an army jeep unattended in the port, several men went into action. The vehicle was driven to the ship, then quickly hoisted into a cargo hold, and painted navy gray. In wartime, there is a fine line between resourcefulness and theft. For men preparing to fight and perhaps die for their country, appropriating equipment and supplies through nonregulation means often seems justified. Although being caught meant brig time, such capers helped unite the crew in their common cause.[26]

The peaceful waters of Hawaii offered one last chance for *Tate*'s landing division to train in their boats before heading into action. Lt. (j.g.) Joseph Neblett, the boat group commander, called his officers together. "I'm expecting you guys to be officers," Neblett told them. "That's why they put gold bars on your shoulders." To Neblett's surprise, the executive officer cancelled the training exercise and told the landing division to stand down and assist the ship's company in cleaning the ship. When Lyon found out about the cancellation, he gave the executive officer a good chewing out within earshot of some of the other officers. Lyon pointed out that the ship's mission was to deliver troops and combat cargo onto enemy beaches. *Tate*'s landing division was the instrument that would execute this mission, and its preparedness was far more important than the cleanliness of the ship. It was now too late to conduct the boat training, but the captain had clearly and publicly defined his ship's mission.[27]

On January 28 *Tate* made the short trip to Port Allen on the island of Kauai in northwestern Hawaii. There the ship took on more cargo and embarked 200 enlisted men and fifteen officers from the Kauai amphibious landing craft unit. *Tate* was to transport the men and cargo to southern Samar, an is-

land in the eastern Philippines. There they would set up an amphibious boat
pool to meet the emerging needs for personnel and cargo transport around
Samar. While anchored off Kauai, *Tate*'s captain walked into the chief's mess,
more commonly referred to by its nautical nickname, the "goat locker." Lyon
ordered a jug of 180-proof alcohol from the medical stores. As each chief
received a shot mixed with grapefruit juice, Lyon toasted his senior enlisted
men. "You are the backbone of the ship," he said, "and I will rely on your experience until the new officers are proven to be fully trained through practical
experience." The event was never to occur again, but Lyon effectively built a
bridge to the most experienced members of his crew.[28]

After three days at Kauai, *Tate* headed west at sixteen knots without an
escort. On February 3, the ship crossed the International Date Line at the
180th meridian. Most of the crew, who were new to sea duty, took part in
their first line-crossing ceremony. Their induction into the Silent Mysteries
of the Far East made them official members of the Imperial Domain of the
Golden Dragon. It was not Chief Water Tender Henry C. Noga's first date line
crossing. Noga had been on the *President Adams* (AP-38) in a convoy of four
transports loaded with marines heading for the Solomon Islands in the summer
of 1942. When the ships crossed the international date line, they gained a day
and missed most of Sunday, thus receiving the colorful nickname "the Unholy
Four." For a veteran like Noga, as well as the rest of the crew, the line crossing
was a pleasant diversion from the increasing number of drills and practice firings as a new sense of urgency began seeping into the training routine.[29]

Steaming westward toward what most men feared was a violent destiny, *Tate*
carried veterans from most of the war's major campaigns. However, these men
were in the minority, as most of the crew had never been to sea before the ship's
trials. Some of them shared their war stories with their inexperienced shipmates, whereas others chose to keep their memories to themselves, either because of a sense of professionalism or out of the pain of remembrance. One
man holding on to his memories was the ship's captain. Rupert E. Lyon's years
of maritime experience, his ship-handling skills, and his stints as a cargo, gunnery, and executive officer were in themselves adequate qualifications for command. Yet, it was Lyon's leadership in combat on the cargo ship *Celeno* that led
to a command of his own.

Off Guadalcanal on June 16, 1943, Lyon watched from the signal bridge as
a swarm of Japanese dive-bombers descended on *Celeno*. The first three aircraft dropped bombs that missed, but a fourth plane scored a hit on the stern,
knocking out the five-inch gun and jamming the ship's rudder. A second direct
hit started a fire in two of the ship's cargo holds. A third bomb exploded in a
pile of gasoline and diesel fuel drums on the deck. With *Celeno* out of control
and engulfed in flames, Lieutenant Lyon went to the gunnery control station

Photo 2.2. Rupert Estey Lyon, Tate's wartime commanding officer.

to offer the hard-pressed gunnery officer assistance. Remaining in a highly exposed and vulnerable position while the ship was being strafed, Lyon concentrated the ship's remaining operable guns on closing aircraft, shooting down the last three attacking bombers. With the attackers beaten off, Lyon then contributed materially to bringing the rudderless ship safely to rest on the beach and extinguishing its fires. Lyon's citation for his actions that day notes his "heroic achievement . . . cool courage and professionalism" and his "exemplary performance in the face of the enemy." Having seen 15 of his shipmates killed and another 19 wounded, Lyon hoped a similar fate did not await *Tate*.[30]

Lieutenant Commander Lyon's favorite perches on *Tate* were the bridge wings on either side of the wheelhouse. From here, seated in his captain's chair, he had the best view of his ship and what lay ahead. As the movement of the ship kept a steady breeze in his face, the freshening sea air reinforced the solitude of command. Looking westward, Lyon was at every moment coming closer to the reality of war. Steaming across the Pacific in command of a new ship that was carrying hundreds of men into battle, his memory of the burning *Celeno* was a dark and silent companion.

Chapter 3

THE PHILIPPINES

This Is No Goddamned Drill!

ON FEBRUARY 7, 1945, *Tate* entered the enormous anchorage of the lagoon at Eniwetok Atoll in the Marshall Islands. Passing the partially submerged hulk of a Japanese ship reminded those on deck of their potential fate. As a forward staging area, the lagoon was cluttered with the silhouettes of almost every class of ship, including many transports. Here *Tate* joined Transport Squadron 17, which was composed of Transport Divisions 49, 50, and 51. Each transport division consisted of six or seven ships. *Tate* was in transport division 50. Many of the squadron's ships were still scattered over the western Pacific, and its final assembly would not be complete until they reached the Philippines.[1]

Tate fueled and embarked marine 2nd Lt. Dewey Maltsberger to assume the duties of transport quartermaster (TQM). The TQM's duties involved managing the loading and unloading of the ship in accordance with carefully considered plans that allowed the most critical cargo to be fed into combat as needed. Assisted by a single noncommissioned officer, TQMs were typically junior army or marine officers. Maltsberger was responsible for executing *Tate*'s primary mission of feeding combat cargo into battle in direct support of amphibious operations.[2]

In convoy for the first time, *Tate* sailed for Ulithi in the Caroline Islands on February 9, under the watchful eye of three destroyer escorts. During the transit, the convoy conducted intensive firing exercises against target sleeves towed by aircraft. While many of the gun crews were still learning on the job, *Tate*'s main battery, its single 5"/38, had a very capable officer in charge: Ens. Glenn Parker, who came to his new ship with considerable gunnery experience from his service on surface combatants. Receiving a commission after thirteen years of enlisted service, Parker was a valued source of information for the "ninety-day-wonder" reserve officers, who respected his navy savvy, as well as his seemingly fearless style. The green sailors in Parker's gun crew watched with curiosity as he sighted in the ship's main battery. During a firing exercise, Parker's

Table 3.1. Initial Composition of Transport Squadron 17

Transport Division 49	Transport Division 50	Transport Division 51
Chilton (APA-38)*	*Henrico* (APA-45)*	*Goodhue* (APA-107)*
LaGrange (APA-124)	*Samuel Chase* (APA-26)	*Eastland* (APA-163)
St. Mary's (APA-126)	*Drew* (APA-162)	*Telfair* (APA-210)
Tazewell (APA-209)	*Natrona* (APA-214)	*Montrose* (APA-212)
Oberon (AKA-14)	*Tate* (AKA-70)	*Mountrail* (APA-213)
Torrance (AKA-76)	*Rixey* (APH-3)	*Suffolk* (AKA-69)
		Wyandot (AKA-92)

*Transport division command

gun made a direct hit on a sleeve towed by an aircraft and cut it loose. Ordered to cease fire to give the other gun mounts a chance, Parker immediately had another round rammed into the gun. He then asked permission to unload through the barrel to prevent a possible detonation while removing the shell from a hot gun. It became a bit of a joke during the continuing drills that Parker always got in one last shot.[3]

The 5"/38 was certainly the loudest weapon most of the men on *Tate* had yet heard. Feeling the big gun blasting away, most of the crew were filled with a sense of awe and wonder, but not so for the men in the aft 40-mm tubs when the 5-incher was trained forward. If the gun was too close when fired, the shock wave and flash were enough to stun, if not disable, a 40-mm crew. Ensign Waller's 40-mm gun crew were victims of one such event. They responded by showering the gun crew on the fantail with epithets and threatening gestures as they speculated on whether they would ever hear again.[4]

Just after breakfast on February 12, *Tate's* general alarm sounded, and Rupert Lyon's voice blared over the intercom: "General quarters! Man your battle stations! This is no goddamned drill!" The radar was tracking an unidentified plane approaching at a range of thirty miles. The men hustled to their posts, and all stations reported in about two minutes. It was a dramatic improvement from the early days in Chesapeake Bay, when it took more than five minutes to man the battle stations. This time it was all for naught, however, as the aircraft reversed course and disappeared.[5]

The following day the convoy eased through Ulithi's Mugai Channel as a single line of ships and anchored. In October 1944 Ulithi's massive atoll, which was part of the Caroline Islands, became the major forward fleet anchorage and staging area for operations in the western Pacific. During the two-day stop at Ulithi, the ships topped off their fuel tanks and then departed on February 15 for Kossol Passage, Palau, in the Western Caroline Islands. Now joined by several more ships from Transport Squadron 17, they were under orders to zigzag due to the threat of submarines during the short transit. Again they anchored for two days before getting underway for the Philippines.[6]

The weather turned dark and rainy on the morning of February 21, as the convoy approached the entrance to Leyte Gulf, zigzagging through the waters where the largest naval battle in history had occurred just four months earlier. Here the Imperial Japanese Navy was decisively defeated in its attempt to destroy the U.S. invasion fleet off Leyte. The liberation of Leyte and Samar followed, and, with the conquest of Manila, the fighting on the main island of Luzon had passed its decisive phase. With the skipper on the bridge, *Tate* broke from formation and steamed at full speed for Tarraguna on the island of Leyte. Minus *Tate,* the convoy continued on to San Pedro Bay for the final assembly of Transport Squadron 17.

The waters east of Leyte were familiar to *Tate*'s skipper. It was here that he had helped land the 96th Infantry Division on October 20, 1944, during the initial assaults in the Philippines. While the convoy was joining the rest of the squadron, *Tate* anchored and awaited orders for the delivery of the passengers and cargo it had loaded at Kauai. The next day the ship got underway for southern Samar, a distance of about forty-five miles, where it halted off Manicani Island to await a pilot. When no pilot arrived, *Tate* proceeded at slow speed and anchored less than two miles off the southernmost tip of Botic Island. Immediately lowering all of its boats, *Tate* began transferring cargo to Samar. The cargo facilities on shore were poor, and *Tate* needed to deploy buoys to mark a navigable passage for its boats. As a result, the unloading was slow. The whole operation lasted ten days and was interrupted numerous times by enemy aircraft. The crew witnessed several actions in which enemy planes tangled with U.S. P-38 fighters, which shot down some of the snooping Japanese. Watching the Japanese aircraft spinning down in flames and crashing into the jungle was grimly entertaining. The crew was hoping their air cover would continue to be as effective as it was during this—their introduction to the shooting war.[7]

On March 3, *Tate* returned to Tarraguna and joined its squadron in the anchorage for the night. At dawn, the ship cruised to San Pedro Bay to fuel before returning to Tarraguna, where it received orders to deploy its paravanes to sweep for moored mines. The ship's training had not included the use of paravanes. A search for men with minesweeping experience revealed that Boatswain's Mate 1st Class W. F. Holm was the only crewmember who knew how to deploy the minesweeping gear. After some hurried on-the-job training, Holm and a few volunteers had *Tate*'s paravanes streaming from both sides of the ship.[8]

On March 5 *Tate* began using its boats to load 1,554 tons of gasoline, ammunition, and preloaded trucks. To ensure that the cargo was loaded in the right order on the correct ships, army TQMs staged and numbered the items

Photo 3.1. Underway with boats and equipment cluttering the main deck. Mine-sweeping paravanes are just forward of LCVP-13. Courtesy Alvin L. Joslyn.

on the beach. On March 9, the loading operations concluded, and *Tate* embarked fourteen officers and 225 soldiers of the 305th Regimental Combat Team (RCT), 77th Infantry Division. The army personnel were mostly combat engineers whom *Tate* would carry into battle in the Ryukyu Islands.[9]

The 77th Division, also known as the Liberty Division, had been resting and refitting following a successful campaign in Leyte's Ormoc Valley. The 77th's reputation was that of a fast-moving, hard-hitting outfit driven by a colorful Texan, Maj. Gen. D. Andrew Bruce. During the division's first campaign of the war on Guam, the marines, typically critical of the army during joint operations, nicknamed them the 77th Marine Division out of respect. The 77th Division's landing at Ormoc on December 7, 1944, was a turning point on Leyte. Within three weeks, organized Japanese resistance on the island ended.[10]

The core organic components of the 77th Division were the 305th, 306th, and 307th Infantry Regiments and the 304th, 305th, 306th, and 902nd Field Artillery Battalions. This basic artillery-infantry combination was supplemented by the 302nd Engineer Combat Battalion and the 302nd Medical Battalion and supported with headquarters, military police, quartermaster, reconnaissance, and signal companies. Additionally, many specialty units (for example, armor, intelligence, bomb disposal, antiaircraft, and amphibious tractor) were attached to the division based on the anticipated needs of the upcoming campaign.[11]

The Liberty Division's proud history began in World War I with one of the best-known stories of that war—that of the Lost Battalion. Cut off, surrounded, and besieged for five days, only 194 of the approximately 550 men emerged unwounded. For a generation the Lost Battalion exemplified the best of America's involvement in World War I. Until World War II pushed the Lost Battalion out of the national memory with its own scenes of horror and heroism, mere mention of the unit's name called to mind the qualities America admired the most in its soldiers: courage, persistence, and admirable performance under adversity.

In World War I, the men of the 77th came predominantly from the New York City area. As a representation of their geographical roots, they selected for their divisional emblem the Statue of Liberty. In World War II, the men of the 77th Division proudly displayed their unit's heritage by painting the blue and gold divisional emblem on both sides of their helmets. Like the torch held by the division's icon, their motto conveyed the unit's reverence of its country's ideals: "Ours to Hold It High."

Two days after embarking the troops, five of *Tate*'s officers temporarily transferred to landing ship tanks (LSTs) as wave-guide officers for the forthcoming Okinawa campaign. Gunner's Mate 3rd Class Arthur L. Norman and several other enlisted men from *Tate* also received orders for temporary transfers to LSTs as radio operators. After the personnel transfers were complete, *Tate* began exercising emergency drills.[12]

Having the soldiers from the 77th Infantry Division on board was quite an experience for *Tate*'s crew. Bloodied and saucy after a successful campaign, they spent two months refitting and looking for recreation, but the entertainment options on Leyte were sparse. As a result, some of the soldiers had adopted pets to allay their boredom. Two of them were brought on board *Tate:* a female monkey named Josephine and a rather obnoxious parrot. When combined with the ship's mascot, a dog named Penny, animal antics ensued. Upon embarking on *Tate,* the soldiers bought all of the Aqua Velva aftershave lotion from the ship's store to drink for the limited alcohol content. An even more peculiar pastime was shark fishing. The soldiers chummed the water with rotten goat meat. After catching a few sharks, they chopped them up with machetes and threw them back into the water as bait. The sea was eventually boiling with sharks, which the bored soldiers shot with rifles.[13]

The native Filipinos from Leyte tried to make the most of the navy's presence, selling trinkets and souvenirs on land and from dugout canoes. When one of these boats, containing a young girl of about fifteen dressed in flimsy native garb, approached *Tate*, the sailors started hooting and waving. One sailor threw a pair of panties and a brassiere from the rag locker down to her. After holding them up and examining them, she threw them back and said, "I don't need them," much to the great amusement of the howling men gathered along the rails.[14]

As his crew worked under the tropical sun, *Tate*'s captain looked down from his bridge and saw Gunner's Mate 1st Class Hubert Six wearing a nonregulation World War I helmet. Lyon liked the cut of the petty officer and called him up to the bridge. After being severely sunburned, Six had bought the broad-brimmed helmet on Samar and then gotten a permission slip from Doc Heinan to wear it. However, it was not Six's nonregulation headgear that the skipper was interested in. After a long conversation, Lyon confessed to Six that he had summoned him because he wanted the perspective of a senior enlisted man on how things were going. Six said that he was satisfied with the crew's performance. Lyon ended the conversation by mentioning that he would continue to keep a cautious eye on his junior officers, who still needed mentoring.[15]

On the morning of March 13, in compliance with the movement orders for Commander Task Group 51.1, *Tate* moved out in formation with various units of the group and its screen. The officer in tactical command, Rear Adm. Ingolf N. Kiland, was on board the amphibious command ship *Mount McKinley* (AGC-7). This movement was the beginning of an amphibious rehearsal in Hinunangan Bay in southern Leyte, resembling Kerama Retto, the first objective in the upcoming campaign. When *Tate* suffered a sudden engine failure, it looked as if both the ship and its embarked troops would miss the exercise. A burned-out bearing had frozen the propeller shaft, requiring a tricky repair.

Seaman 2nd Class J. C. Bostic, an experienced welder, quickly volunteered for the duty. A former shipyard worker who had left his job and draft exemption because of work-related health problems, Bostic was soon drafted and, to his surprise, passed the physical. This ironic set of circumstances put him in a position to use the specialized skills that for a time had kept him out of the war. Now, with a cutting torch in hand, he made the skillful repairs that put his ship back into action. As a result, Bostic happily found himself transferred from the deck force as a chipper and painter to the construction and repair division, where he quickly made Shipfitter 2nd Class. With *Tate* only briefly delayed, the ship's crew soon found their previous training insignificant compared to a full-scale dry run for a major invasion. The crew engaged in gunnery practice and drilled repeatedly on emergency turns, simulated air attacks, and damage control problems.[16]

Early on March 14, *Tate* lowered nine LCVPs in the transport staging area to embark troops for landing exercises from the coast guard–manned attack transport *Samuel Chase,* a veteran of the Normandy invasion. The APA attack transports were slightly bigger than AKA attack cargo ships. In place of some of an AKA's cargo capacity, attack transports had additional berthing areas filled from the deck to the overhead with stacked bunks for a full battalion of assault troops. An APA's boat complement and armament were similar to those of an AKA, although some attack transports had a second 5"/38 gun mounted forward of the deckhouse.[17]

At night, LCVPs patrolled the anchorage and made smoke to obscure the ships. Armed with rifles and machine guns, the boat crews also watched for Japanese swimmers. The landing drills were repeated over the next two days, and then Task Group 51.1 headed north in a single file behind the guide ship, *Samuel Chase*. *Tate*'s recently promoted navigator, Lt. (j.g.) Paul Leahy, was leaving nothing to chance. Taking repeated fixes on navigational aids and landmarks, Leahy suddenly concluded that the column was off course. Dashing into the wheelhouse, Leahy ordered the ship to maneuver hard to starboard and to increase to flank speed. The startled officer of the deck, Lt. (j.g) John F. Dalton, complied, and the helmsman spun the wheel as the engine room telegraph rang up "flank." As his ship lurched unexpectedly, the captain came in from the bridge wing, and Leahy explained the situation. By now, *Samuel Chase* was hard aground, with its screw stirring up mud. The rest of the ships followed *Tate*'s lead, steaming wide of the stranded ship. Lyon's early questions about his navigator's competence were now resolved, and the two men were building a relationship that would prove to be one of the most important on the ship.[18]

The attack transport *Pitt* (APA-223) joined the squadron to replace *Samuel Chase,* whose damaged hull required repairs in a stateside shipyard, but bad weather forced the cancellation of most of the second phase of the rehearsals for the capture of Ie Shima. Only the 77th Division's reserve unit, the 307th Infantry, got an opportunity to practice its landings on March 16. Over the next four days, additional cargo was loaded, while the remaining units of the task group formed up, including two tractor units of landing vehicles tracked (LVTs), embarked onto the LSTs. Despite the reduced training schedule, Major General Bruce, the 77th Division's commanding officer, was pleased with the results. He reported that "all elements scheduled for a specific mission [were] satisfactorily executed [in] a close approximation of their mission."[19]

Monsignor Thomas J. Donnelly, regimental chaplain of the 305th Infantry, wanted to give the men as much comfort and spiritual assistance as possible before the forthcoming campaign. Donnelly spent the days before departure hitching rides on small boats between the nine LSTs, three APAs, and the AKA on which his regiment was embarked. With the numerous ships continually shuttling about the bustling anchorage, the boat crews became confused when trying to find their way. On the afternoon of March 17 Donnelly paid *Tate* a visit, conducted mass, and stayed for dinner before boarding an LCVP run by two young ensigns. After departing at sunset, they had difficulties navigating in the crowded anchorage. According to Motor Machinist's Mate 2nd Class

x

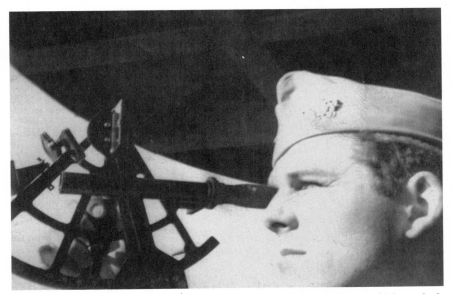

Photo 3.2. Through his performance and conduct, navigator Paul R. Leahy set a high standard of professionalism for his fellow officers. Courtesy Paul R. Leahy.

Ivo E. Cecil, a member of the boat's crew, the behavior of the frustrated chaplain was not helping the situation. Donnelly called the boat crew "boots" and became agitated with their plight. The night turned out to be a hectic one that Donnelly described in his memoirs:[20]

> Our boat started out, but when it arrived at the area where my ship should have been, it was discovered that it had left for some other part of the Gulf. A hurried search was made while it was still light but there were hundreds of ships there. It kept getting darker as approaches [were] made to this ship and that in an attempt to get information. It was decided to turn back to the cargo ship [*Tate*] and sleep for the night. It started to rain, and since there was no cover, everyone got soaked, whereupon it was learned that the crew had not taken a bearing on their own ship or the number of the anchorage. Now we did not know where either ship was. We sailed all over Leyte Gulf that night. It rained three times; ships riding at anchor loomed up out of the night but no one could give us any information, and we moved on searching everywhere. Once after moving for over an hour, it was noticed that no ship had been sighted for some time and the craft was hastily swung about before it would get lost in the Pacific Ocean. Finally, after dawn had broken, the cargo ship [*Tate*] was located, and

having changed to another landing craft, I returned to my own ship,
said Mass and went to bed. That was one night I was really mad at
the Navy.[21]

As *Tate* continued to prepare for its first major campaign, the skipper, who
normally ate alone, invited Ensigns Alvin L. Joslyn and Lewis A. Crew to
join him for dinner. The intent was not strictly social; their skipper informed
the two officers that they would be detached to serve as wave guides for the
upcoming invasion. So, on March 19, with little notice, the two officers transferred to LST 484 just before its departure with the tractor flotilla of eigh-
teen LSTs, eleven landing ships medium (LSMs), and more than forty landing
craft infantry (LCI) and patrol craft. As their LST headed for the open sea,
Ensigns Joslyn and Crew watched *Tate* grow smaller and then disappear. The
ship they had thought would carry them into their first battle remained resting
safely at anchor as they left Leyte Gulf. Two days later, *Tate*'s windlass began
hauling up the anchor chain with a foreboding, clattering noise that resounded
throughout the ship. Sailing two days behind the slower tractor flotilla, Transport Squadron 17, with all ships darkened, was heading northeast from the
Philippines, zigzagging at twelve knots and with air coverage from Support
Carrier Unit Four and screened by Destroyer Squadron 49. Emergency drills
and gunnery practice resumed with a new vigor as the Western Islands Attack
Group headed for a showdown in the Ryukyu Islands.[22]

Chapter 4

KERAMA RETTO

Ours to Hold It High

O N MARCH 23, 1945, the Western Islands Attack Group was zigzagging toward its destiny in the Ryukyu Islands. Only 350 miles southeast of Japan's main islands, the Ryukyus were considered part of Japan and not an occupied territory or colony. These islands would be the first part of the Japanese homeland to be invaded. Japanese resistance was expected to be desperate and even suicidal. This bold attempt to kick in the front door of the Japanese empire was code-named Operation Iceberg. The Fifth Fleet attack force under Admiral Spruance was the largest naval armada ever assembled. Vice Adm. Richmond Kelly Turner was in charge of Task Force 51, the Joint Expeditionary Force containing all of the amphibious forces, which were divided into six separate commands. Turner wanted the Western Islands Attack Group (Task Group 51.1) to open the operation with an assault on the Kerama Retto islands, twenty miles west of southern Okinawa. Seizing these islands would provide a forward staging and ship repair facility close to the main objective: Okinawa.

This idea met with a great deal of opposition from Turner's peers. The numerous islands and restricted waters of Kerama Retto were vulnerable to attacks that could be launched from airfields on nearby Okinawa and Ie Shima. Critics of the plan feared that land-based air attacks would hammer the troop-laden ships and produce losses that could jeopardize the entire Okinawa campaign. Turner was convinced of the necessity of securing the Keramas as a sheltered anchorage to support the main assault on Okinawa. Rear Admiral Kiland, in command of Task Group 51.1, recommended simultaneous landings on five of the six largest Kerama islands in a fast-moving operation that would allow little opportunity for organized resistance.[1]

Operation Iceberg would begin with the seizure of the Kerama Retto island group on Palm Sunday, March 26, a week before the invasion of Okinawa. The Keramas were a cluster of islands without roads and with steep rocky inclines that ran up to ridges 400–600 feet high. Intelligence estimated that

1,000–1,500 Japanese soldiers were on the islands. Although several narrow landing beaches existed, their approaches were treacherous.[2]

To deceive the Japanese with regard to the fleet's real intentions and to protect the 122 ships conducting mine-sweeping operations, eight battleships and twelve destroyers heavily bombarded the southeast coast of Okinawa three days before the scheduled landings. Passing through lanes that had been cleared of mines, Task Group 51.1 approached Kerama Retto from the southwest on March 25 and headed to three separate staging areas. The tractor flotilla of LSTs, LSMs, patrol craft, and numerous auxiliaries split into two groups. Four LSTs headed for a staging area northwest of Zamami Shima, while the other fourteen LSTs, eleven LSMs, and the bulk of the support ships headed for an area two miles southwest of Kuba Shima. The faster transport convoy, which consisted of the amphibious command ship *Mount McKinley,* nineteen large transports (APAs and AKAs), a screen of destroyers, two destroyer escorts carrying underwater demolition team (UDT) personnel, and two escort carriers, positioned itself just over the horizon west of Yakabi Shima. As *Tate* approached the transport area, an escort detonated a mine with gunfire three miles off its starboard quarter, providing a hint of things to come.[3]

At dusk on March 25, a single Japanese scout aircraft approached *Tate*'s convoy. It came as close as eight miles before retiring without drawing fire. Before dawn, a single-engine floatplane flew down *Tate*'s starboard side about 150 feet above the water and close enough for the crew to see sparks blowing from its exhaust. Flying between two columns of transports, it passed by before the ships could react. The plane's appearance was a complete surprise, and it was gone as quickly as it had come. Obviously on a reconnaissance mission, the Japanese aircraft had located the blacked-out convoy.[4]

At daybreak on March 26, approximately ten aircraft attacked the transport area. In an action that lasted approximately thirty minutes, *Tate* did not have an opportunity to fire. Three suicide planes crashed harmlessly into the sea, one splashing 3,500 yards astern of *Tate* and narrowly missing a cruiser. The result of these suicidal efforts was nothing more than a few patches of flaming gasoline on the surface of the sea. Then a suicidal Val dive-bomber, maneuvering wildly by changing both its speed and direction, attacked the destroyer *Kimberly* (DD-521) from astern. Trailing smoke and fire, the plane tumbled into the destroyer, striking it between its two aft five-inch mounts. A huge ball of orange flame blossomed over the destroyer's stern as the plane and its bomb exploded, killing four and wounding fifty-seven. The stern attack was obviously a tactic to avoid the majority of the destroyer's guns.

For the men on *Tate*'s decks, the sky around them was filled with tracers, a scene that would eventually be repeated all too often. During the action, Quartermaster 2nd Class Donald L. Patrie was on the bridge wing drawing

Photo 4.1. Five of Tate's officers on the bridge: (left to right) Kells M. Boland, Walter R. Hall, Benjamin O. Propek, Albert H. H. Dorsey, and Glenn S. Parker Jr. Both Boland and Hall served as executive officer. Courtesy Alfred S. Coslett.

sketches of the enemy aircraft. Before entering the combat zone, one of Tate's junior officers asked that drawings be made of enemy aircraft to assist in their recognition. When the captain saw Patrie out in the open, he yelled, "Get in here, you dumb son of a bitch!" When things calmed down, Lieutenant Commander Lyon confronted Patrie, who explained he was acting as directed. He gave the young sailor a fatherly hug and said, "Those instructions were stupid," and "I don't want to see you killed." After the antiaircraft fire ended, the horizon to the east continued to flash with the spectacle of war as U.S. warships bombarded Kerama Retto.[5]

Rear Adm. C. Turner Joy embarked on San Francisco (CA-38), peeled off from Rear Admiral Deyo's Bombardment Group Four, navigated through the narrow passages of the Keramas, and, with the aid of radar, began pounding five separate landing areas. Joy had fired the first salvos of Operation Iceberg the day before, giving the whole area a good shellacking from the World War I vintage battleship Arkansas (BB-33) and the heavy cruisers Minneapolis (CA-36) and San Francisco. Now the cruisers, plus four destroyers and forty-two smaller gunboats, resumed the assault in preparation for the scheduled morning landings. The postwar cruise book of the attack transport Mountrail offers the following description: "The LCI rocket boats moved in and we could see the patterns of their projectiles hissing through the air. Destroyers began firing their five-inch guns at point blank range. Then group after group of our dive-bombers added the screaming crescendo of their deadly loads to this symphony of amphibious war."[6]

Implemented after the heavy losses at Tarawa, the UDTs scouted the landing zones and blasted away obstacles. More commonly called frogmen, the UDTs usually went into action on high-speed destroyer transports (APD). These ships were either converted destroyer escorts or World War I flush-deck, four-stack destroyers with two boilers (stacks) removed to make room for boat davits and additional berthing. These fast-moving, shallow draft ships carried four landing craft each. Their speed and armament also allowed them to serve in a screening role and provide close-in fire support for landings.

On March 25 UDTs 12, 13, and 19 conducted seven beach reconnaissance patrols. Naval historian Samuel Eliot Morison described their tactics:

> Following standard doctrine, each team proceeded to a point about
> 500 yards off its assigned beach in an LCVP. The landing craft then
> turned parallel to the reef, casting off a swimmer about every 50 yards.
> Each man, clad only in trunks, goggles and rubber feet, was festooned
> with the gear of his trade. He carried a reel of marked line knotted ev-
> ery 25 yards, the bitter end of which he secured to the edge of the reef.
> He then turned toward the beach, uncoiling the line as he swam, halt-
> ing every time he felt a knot to take soundings with a small lead line;
> or if the depth were one fathom or less, with his own body, which was
> conveniently painted with black rings at 12-inch intervals. The swim-
> mer recorded his soundings with a stylus on a sheet of sandpapered
> Plexiglas wrapped around his left forearm. After an hour or more of
> reconnaissance, depending on the width of the reef, each swimmer
> was picked up by his LCVP, which in the meantime had been planting
> little colored buoys on dangerous coral heads. The method of recover-
> ing swimmers was simple and effective. A sailor held out a stiff rope to
> the swimmer, who grasped the "monkey fist" at the rope's end, while
> the boat was making three or four knots, and was hauled on board.
> Landing craft then returned to the APDs, where the swimmers' data
> were correlated and entered on a chart. All of this went on under
> gunfire support from destroyers and gunboats and "really beautiful air
> support" . . . from escort carrier planes. This kept the enemy so busy
> ashore that he never even fired on the underwater demolition teams.[7]

The UDT swimmers found the approaches clear of man-made obstacles but studded with reefs and numerous coral heads that were barely submerged even at high tide. The use of landing craft was deemed impractical. The tracked LVTs (Landing Vehicle Tracked) would make the amphibious assault.

Unknown to those preparing to hit the beaches of Kerama Retto, a single Avenger torpedo bomber from the escort carrier *Wake Island* (CVE-53) was flying over each of the landing areas in Kerama Retto. On board the aircraft was Lt. (j.g.) Warren C. Thompson, one of only three trained hydrographic and special beach observers in the navy. His job was to make preinvasion aerial observations of weather, sea, and surf conditions for the landing beaches. This surveillance was critical to determining the effects of the sea on amphibious craft and vehicles. Since they were first employed at Peleliu, these airborne oceanographers provided a critical, final go or no-go decision check for every invasion in the Pacific. Like the UDT concept, the use of beach observers was another technique born of the lessons learned at Tarawa, where the dearth of environmental knowledge was costly. So valuable were the three observers that they were generally not together on board the same ship.

However, as Thompson wrote after the war, "as fate would have it," all three of them were on the escort carrier *Bismarck Sea* (CVE-95) off Iwo Jima when it was struck twice by kamikazes and sunk the night of February 21, 1945. Pulled from the sea, the three observers found themselves quickly back in action. Now, a little more than a month later, Thompson was flying over hostile shores, applying scientific techniques formulated in the minds of academic oceanographers for the requirements of amphibious warfare. He reported that the seas were calm at Kerama Retto since the beaches and their approaches were sheltered from the effects of the wind by the islands' high cliffs and mountains. The conditions were favorable for the assaults to proceed as planned.[8]

Although *Tate* had a ticket to the big show, it was the ship's seven officers, who were serving as wave guides on the LSTs, who had the front-row seats. One of these men, Ens. Alvin Joslyn, would lead a wave of LVTs to the island of Zamami Shima. Attending a preinvasion briefing on LST 484, Joslyn listened as an army officer asked his colonel whether he wanted his troops to take prisoners. The answer was a terse "no," followed by the qualification that "one or two prisoners would be useful for interrogation purposes."[9]

Each LST carried sixteen LVTs enclosed on a tank deck roughly level with the waterline. As the LVT engines started on the crowded tank deck inside the ship's belly, engine fumes, ship motion, and precombat nerves stretched the time as the infantrymen waited for the iron, jawlike bow doors to open. Then, as a rush of fresh air filled the soldiers' lungs, the tracked vehicles clanked forward up and over the bulge in the bow of the metal tank deck and splashed into the sea, where the guide boats waited to lead them to their assembly area. Zamami Shima had only two possible landing zones, and the one selected appeared to be a death trap.

Photo 4.2. Tate *loaded with most of its twenty-four landing craft. Courtesy Hubert J. Six Sr.*

The main harbor was flanked by high ground on both sides of the approach. It would offer the defenders a chance to catch the landing craft in a cross fire as they made a tricky dogleg approach. The LVTs, led by the LCVP guides, navigated through a narrow channel requiring an initial forty-five-degree turn followed by a ninety-degree turn between Zamami Shima and two small reef-ringed islets before making the final half-mile run to the beach.[10] Two months later Joslyn described the action in a letter home to his wife, Erma:

We have at last been authorized to tell something of our part in the Kerama Retto . . . campaign. I will try to give you an all over picture and tell as much as I can at the present time. I was transferred to LST 484 the 18th of March to act as a wave guide officer . . . to hit the island of Zamami Shima in the Kerama Retto Group. Our job was to land assault troops of the 77th division, which were aboard the LST. [Ens. Lewis] Crew from our ship was also assigned to the same LST. We got underway the morning of the 19th. Our trip was uneventful except that we had bad weather and our LST rolls like nothing I have ever been on before. On the evening of the 25th a Jap observation plane spotted us and kept us under surveillance for a while then flew away. L Day for Kerama Retto was 26 March. We arose early the morning of the 26th and by 3 o'clock in the morning I had had my breakfast. I put on my helmet and jacket and went up on the bridge. The sky was cloudless and the air was cold. By 0430 we could hear the

sound of heavy guns and see the flash of shell bursts on the islands. Two
Jap planes came in over our LSTs to strafe us but were driven away by
A.A. fire. By 0545 the first strokes of dawn crept into the sky, and we
could see the outline of the islands. They were rather small and clus-
tered together. By 0630 the ships were in their assigned anchorage for
disembarkation of the troops. My boat was lowered into the water and
we proceeded to the bow of the ship to pick up our wave of LVTs (Buf-
faloes). By this time our air power had moved in and started bombing, strafing and shooting rockets at the islands. The first waves were
formed up and we started to move in. Our objective was the town of
Zamami on the island of the same name. As we started to move in a
pill box . . . started to open fire on our right as did a mortar on our
left. Fortunately for us their shots were falling short and we went down
through a path which was clear of bursts about 250 yards wide. As we
were striking this island other islands of the same group were being hit.
As we moved in toward the rock the Japs must have had some machine
guns set up which were battering our boats and troops. As I arrived by
the rock . . . about 3 of our planes tried to clear the Japs off the rock. I
moved in as close to the rock as possible because they (the planes) were
coming in from the other side. Some of their rockets and machine gun
bullets passed over us and landed about 50 feet away in the water. In
the mean time our rocket boats started to finish where the air force had
left off. We started to move into the town. The boats were only able to
go in to about 100 yards of the beach because of the coral. It was there
that we left the tracked vehicles.[11]

Tate's boat group commander, Lt. (j.g.) Joseph Neblett, was tasked with direct-
ing the assault on Aka Shima. Early on March 26, Neblett visited Ens. Albert
H. H. Dorsey, who was temporarily assigned to a coast guard LST. Neblett
handed Dorsey four letters from his wife and informed him he was leading the
assault on Aka Shima. Dorsey's boat lined up on the left flank of the front wave
of amphibious tanks, with Ens. Owen ("Frank") Conwell of Iowa from *Tate*
guiding the right flank. As they approached Aka Shima, Dorsey's boat began
taking long-range machine-gun fire. He ordered his men to lie on the deck
and his guide flag hauled down. Conwell, seeing Dorsey was in trouble, continued to ramrod the wave forward. Told that there were no friendly aircraft
in the area, Dorsey was delighted to see a lone F6F Hellcat slam two rockets
into the Japanese machine-gun position, ending any direct opposition to the
landings.[12]

 According to *The Complete History of World War II*, published just after the
war in 1945, "The first man to set foot on Japanese soil was Sergeant Fred A.
Myers, of Maybrook, New York, who jumped ashore on the islet of Aka at

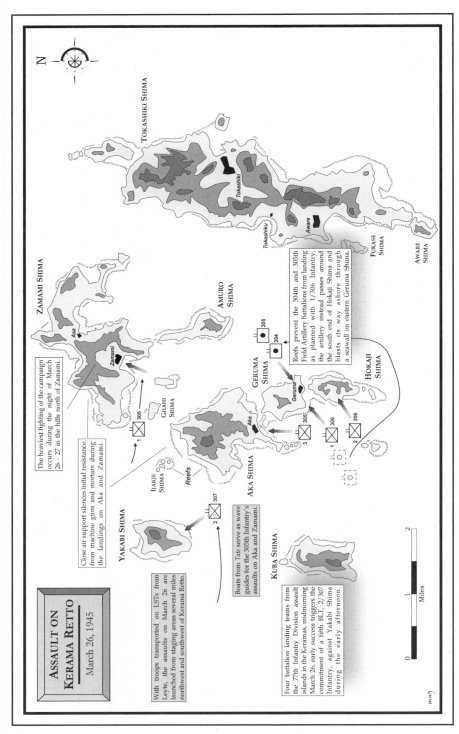

ASSAULT ON KERAMA RETTO
March 26, 1945

With troops transported on LSTs from Leyte, the assaults on March 26 are launched from staging areas several miles northwest and southwest of Kerama Retto.

The heaviest fighting of the campaign occurs during the night of March 26 – 27 in the hills north of Zamami.

Close air support silences initial resistance from machine guns and mortars during the landings on Aka and Zamami.

Boats from *Tate* serve as wave guides for the 305th Infantry's assaults on Aka and Zamami.

Four battalion landing teams from the 77th Infantry Division assault islands in the Keramas, midmorning March 26; early success triggers the commitment of a fifth BLT, 2/307 Infantry, against Yakabi Shima during the early afternoon.

Reefs prevent the 304th and 305th Field Artillery Battalions from landing as planned with 1/306 Infantry; the artillery instead passes around the south end of Hokaji Shima and blasts its way ashore through a seawall on eastern Geruma Shima.

TOKASHIKI SHIMA

Tokashiki

Aware

Tokashiku

FUKASE SHIMA

AWARE SHIMA

ZAMAMI SHIMA

Asa

Zamami

AMURO SHIMA

GHAHI SHIMA

305
1

GERUMA SHIMA

Geruma

305
3

306
1

306
2

304

305

HOKAJI SHIMA

IJAKJE SHIMA

Reefs

AKA SHIMA

Aka

YAKABI SHIMA

307
2

KUBA SHIMA

N

0   1   2
Miles

mwj

Map 4.1. Assault on Kerama Retto, March 26, 1945. Courtesy Mark W. Johnson.

8:04 A.M., beating by a step Lieutenant Robert Berr, of Decatur, Illinois, commanding Company K of the Third Battalion 305th Infantry Regiment." Certainly, a publication quickly compiled in the immediate postwar period cannot be considered authoritative. However, the men going ashore in the Keramas knew the significance of the landings. Myers was in Conwell's guide boat and hit the beach just ahead of the first wave of amphibious tanks. Before the landing ramp dropped, *Tate*'s Boatswain's Mate 1st Class Holm jumped over the side into the shallow water. Holm, a longtime navy veteran who liked to twirl his mustache while making colorful remarks, enjoyed being under fire. At Aka Shima, he wanted to claim for himself the title of being the first American to land on Japanese soil. What nobody considered were the UDT swimmers who had secretly scouted the landing areas, prowling about in the shallow water just off the beach. While the first landings in Kerama Retto occurred on Aka Shima, if anyone had a right to the claim of being the first invading American to have the Japanese homeland under his feet, it would have been a UDT frogman.[13]

The kickoff of Operation Iceberg was an unqualified success. Aided by the UDTs and airborne hydrographic reconnaissance, the operation went off, as described in the 77th Infantry Division's official history, "with a smoothness born of practice and experience; five battalion landing teams hit five separate islands almost simultaneously." The resistance to the landings was sporadic, and, though fierce in places, it was ultimately ineffective. The combined use of shellfire, rockets, and close air support proved a successful combination.

One of the innovative ideas tested during the Kerama Retto assaults was the assignment of intelligence specialists to each battalion landing team. These personnel were responsible for collecting information relevant to the upcoming landings on Okinawa. Preinvasion intelligence had overestimated the number of combatants on the islands, many of whom turned out to be Korean laborers of negligible military value. It also missed one other important item. The islands contained numerous shoreline caves with rail tracks leading to the water's edge. These caves hid a heretofore unknown menace: suicide boats configured to carry stern-mounted depth charges or bow-mounted explosives. Depending on their configuration, the boats would ram into the waterline of a ship or drop their explosives next to it. The Japanese had mapped out the probable assembly areas of the transports off Okinawa and prepared attack plans using the suicide boats. Before ever going into action, U.S. forces destroyed 359 of these boats in Kerama Retto, completely frustrating the Japanese plans. Most of the Japanese boat personnel were members of the 1st Sea Raiding Regiment stationed on Zamami Shima. Promised posthumous promotions to lieutenant for conducting a suicide attack, most of the boat crews were only sixteen or seventeen years old.[14]

While *Tate* refueled the high-speed destroyer transports *Hopping* (APD-51) and *Barr* (APD-39), most of its boats worked as part of a pool for moving reinforcements, cargo, and casualties. Two of *Tate*'s LCVPs aided in the evacuation of the wounded from the damaged destroyer *Kimberly* to the evacuation transport *Rixey* (APH-3). Although armed and painted as a warship, *Rixey* was a hybrid hospital ship that carried troops into battle and casualties out. Two other LCVPs served as ambulance boats for transporting casualties from the beachheads to medical facilities afloat. Motor Machinist's Mate 2nd Class Ivo Cecil was on one of these vessels. Cecil's boat first delivered a load of artillery shells to a barge off Zamami Shima and then went ashore to embark wounded. Just as they finished unloading, Japanese machine-gun fire started kicking up the water around them. With a line still attached to the sternpost, the LCVP pulled back abruptly, carrying the post away and damaging the boat.[15]

Cecil's boat then went ashore and began loading wounded infantrymen. An army sergeant who was hit in the shoulder handed him his .45-cal. Thompson machine gun, saying, "Take my weapon. My war is over." Later that day, in rough seas, one of the LCVP's .30-cal. machine guns broke loose from its mount and started firing. Gunner's Mate 3rd Class F. W. Haywood threw himself at the runaway weapon, swinging it up and securing it before anyone was hurt. After delivering the wounded to *Rixey,* the boat returned to Zamami Shima, where the beach master ordered Cecil's crew to evacuate two Japanese women who had been wounded by mortar fire. One had lost an arm. Upon arriving at *Rixey,* the crew were told the ship could not take civilians and to return the women to the beach. The situation worsened when the boat crew noticed the transports getting under way for their night retirement. Fearing that they would be stranded in a damaged boat in a combat zone, one man suggested throwing the two women over the side. The rest of the crew objected to that idea, and they returned to the beach, where they discovered that the woman who had lost an arm was now dead.[16]

Things went well on Geruma Shima and Hokaji Shima, as both islands fell by noon. After Maj. William D. Caveness, commander of the 2/306, planted Old Glory on a Hokaji Shima hilltop at 0920, the Liberty Division could once again rightfully boast that it had lived up to its motto: "Ours to Hold It High."[17]

After securing Geruma Shima, the 1/306 was followed ashore by the 304th and 305th Field Artillery with their 105-mm howitzers. Roughly at the center of Kerama Retto, Geruma Shima offered the artillery a position from which to support U.S. troops on the rest of the islands. Using amphibious trucks (DUKWs), the artillery landings ran afoul of coral heads and potholes in the reef surface, which made it impossible to land where the 1/306 had gone ashore. This forced the DUKWs to circle completely around Hokaji Shima and land on Geruma Shima's eastern beaches. They again ran into trouble crossing the reef front before finally getting ashore, only to sink up to their axles in the soft beach sand. Every vehicle required winching and towing across the beach before it could pass through an opening in the seawall created with a 105-mm gun at point-blank range.

Despite the hardships, the guns were in place and registered by early afternoon. The operation is a good example of the difficulty and danger of landing artillery as part of an amphibious assault. The cumbersome guns and their large amounts of ammunition prevented their presence on a congested and possibly contested beach. By 1945, the initial placement of artillery on nearby islands that were either undefended or only lightly held had become standard procedure for amphibious assaults. By nightfall, Yakabi Shima had fallen to the 2/307, and Aka Shima to the 3/305. On Zamami Shima, the 1/305 met the most resistance of any of the landings. Miraculously, not a single landing craft was lost in any of the assaults.[18]

Greeting the first wave on Zamami Shima was a seawall that hindered the use of its LVTs. Bordered by stone walls, the town's narrow lanes were not wide enough for the passage of even the smallest armored vehicles. With the exception of sporadic sniping and mortar fire, the naturally fortified town was undefended. Ensign Joslyn spent the day ferrying wounded soldiers to ships with medical facilities under the sporadic sniper fire. By the end of the day, the 1/305 had cleared the ruins of Zamami town, and as the sunlight faded, they began digging in on the terraces of the steep hills above the town.[19]

At 1800 a night retirement began to the southwest, with Transport Squadron 17 zigzagging out to sea down a prearranged retirement track swept free of mines. The four LCVPs assigned as ambulance boats remained behind for the night with their crews, including Carpenter's Mate 3rd Class James W. Anthony. Anthony's boat had evacuated casualties from Kimberly. Seeing the burned, broken, and dismembered bodies off-loaded from the destroyer, he became physically ill and remained sick off and on for three days.[20]

The hardest fighting in the Keramas occurred that first night on Zamami Shima. As the soldiers peered into the darkness, trying to determine whether the rustling sounds they heard were the wind or the enemy, PFC Bob B. Merrill lamented, "This is a helluva place for a perimeter." Just as the rustling became louder and more foreboding, shadows appeared about fifteen yards in front of the men in the forward foxholes. The soldiers opened fire as the Japanese charged out of the underbrush, yelling "Banzai!" Using carbines, rifles, and pistols, the soldiers fought at short range and often ended up fighting hand to hand in foxholes against Japanese wielding sabers and pistols. Due to the darkness and the proximity of the enemy, only two machine guns were able to fire. The fighting ended abruptly, only to resume after the Japanese regrouped. The scenario repeated itself eight times before morning.[21]

Daylight revealed sixty dead Japanese lying in and around the U.S. positions. The enemy on Zamami Shima had wasted themselves in the night attacks, and only negligible resistance remained. The 1/305 spent the day patrolling the island and securing the village of Asa. While sweeping the rugged western end of the island, a patrol encountered a small group of civilians on the edge of a cliff about thirty feet away. The terrified civilians consisted of two women, one holding a baby and another with a small child. Behind them was a man in uniform brandishing a grenade. Not wanting to shoot down the women and children to protect themselves from the Japanese soldier, the U.S. infantrymen motioned for the women to approach. The Japanese then all jumped over the precipice, bouncing off the cliff face on the way down.[22]

The 1/305 returned to Zamami town that evening and was relieved by the 2/305. The following day, the 2/305 eliminated the last organized Japanese positions, consisting of a few caves and entrenchments. Widespread patrolling continued, and any suspicious caves were sealed with satchel charges.[23]

After watching the action through field glasses on LST 484, Ensign Joslyn returned to Zamami town:

> It had been pretty well leveled, however the goats which were kept by the inhabitants were eating in their stalls. On a terrace above the town I saw the bodies of some 80 or 90 Japs who were killed in a banzai raid. . . . I was asked if I wanted to see a cave where the Okinawans had hung their children, because of the fear of what American troops would do to them, inspired by the Jap soldiers. I didn't feel equal to this so returned to the beach. I picked up a few souvenirs. On the beach was a Jap suicide boat. Several of us were going to examine it but decided not to. It was lucky for us for upon our return to the ship we learned that two army officers and an enlisted man had been killed during the examination of one on another island.

Joslyn ventured close enough to the suicide boat to discover that, ironically, it had a Chevrolet gasoline engine made in his home state of Michigan.[24]

On the morning of March 27, under the support of the artillery on Geruma Shima, the 306th Infantry's three battalions landed on Tokashiki Jima, the largest of the Kerama islands. Sweeping across the island from two separate landing beaches, the infantry encountered only sporadic light resistance. Fearing that the rapidly approaching Americans would ravish the island's women and children and torture the men, more than 250 civilians killed each other with knives, rocks, and grenades or by strangulation. Upon discovering this grim scene, American medics began caring for the wounded civilians and promptly came under fire from Japanese troops. The ensuing combat was a wrenching revelation to the civilians who were awaiting medical attention. The Americans were fighting Japanese soldiers to save Japanese civilians. The bitterest of realities confronted the survivors of these suicide attempts as they realized they had slaughtered their friends and families because of a sadistic and perverted delusion.[25]

For some, viewing the bodies of children who had been killed by their own families fueled their motivation to destroy the Japanese soldiers. For others, like Joslyn, the image of dead children was not something he wanted to carry through life. For such men, war itself was as much an enemy as the Japanese. They were fighting to end the war and all that it represented and to return home with a minimum of emotional baggage.[26]

Tate returned to the inner transport area on the morning of March 27 to fuel and provision smaller ships with food and ammunition. The ship came close enough to the shore to view a group of natives emerging from under cover on a hillside near a knocked-out gun emplacement. In less than two days, Kerama Retto was already providing a vital enclosed anchorage, with its main entrances netted to prevent submarine access.[27]

Daybreak on March 28 found *Tate* anchored again in the transport area off Kuba Shima after returning from a night retirement to resume fueling and supplying other ships. While ashore delivering cargo, Seaman 1st Class J. W. Worthington was shocked to see two Japanese soldiers come out of some nearby bushes with their hands up. Except for the machine guns mounted on their nearby LCM, the boat crew was unarmed. One of the Japanese was bigger than any of the startled sailors, but, fortunately, he wanted only to surrender. The sailors quickly herded the two prisoners onto their LCM for transport to *Tate*. Worthington observed that the tall heavyset man was a Japanese Imperial Army officer, and the other prisoner was a small, very insecure-looking enlisted man. After placing the prisoners in *Tate*'s brig, the Japanese officer complained to an army interpreter about his confinement with an enlisted man. Asking to speak to the commanding officer, the prisoner was escorted to the bridge, where he made his complaint to *Tate*'s captain. Rupert Lyon replied brusquely, "You have no choice, and if it were up to me, I would put you over the side."[28]

After returning to the brig, the Japanese officer asked (through the interpreter) Gunner's Mate 1st Class Hubert Six for his pistol to commit suicide since he was disgraced and could never go home. Many of *Tate*'s crew got their first close look at the enemy when they went to the brig to view the prisoners. Included in the curious observers were several of the African American stewards,

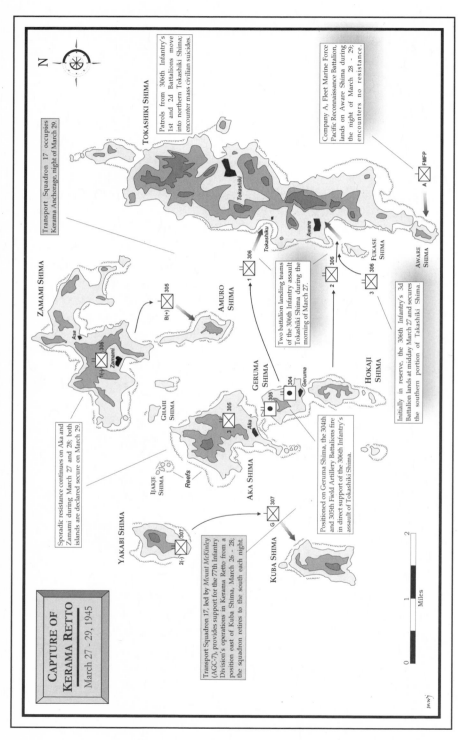

CAPTURE OF
KERAMA RETTO
March 27 - 29, 1945

Transport Squadron 17, led by *Mount McKinley* (AGC-7), provides support for the 77th Infantry Division's operations in Kerama Retto from a position east of Kuba Shima, March 26 - 28; the squadron retires to the south each night.

Sporadic resistance continues on Aka and Zamami during March 27 and 28; both islands are declared secure on March 29.

Transport Squadron 17 occupies Kerama Anchorage, night of March 29.

Patrols from 306th Infantry's 1st and 2d Battalions move into northern Tokashiki Shima; encounter mass civilian suicides.

Company A, Fleet Marine Force Pacific Reconnaissance Battalion, lands on Aware Shima during the night of March 28 - 29; encounters no resistance.

Initially in reserve, the 306th Infantry's 3d Battalion lands at midday March 27 and secures the southern portion of Takashiki Shima.

Two battalion landing teams of the 306th Infantry assault Tokashiki Shima during the morning of March 27.

Positioned on Geruma Shima, the 304th and 305th Field Artillery Battalions fire in direct support of the 306th Infantry's assault of Tokashiki Shima.

YAKABI SHIMA

ZAMAMI SHIMA

TOKASHIKI SHIMA

AMURO SHIMA

GHAHI SHIMA

GERUMA SHIMA

AKA SHIMA

IJAKTE SHIMA

KUBA SHIMA

HOKAJI SHIMA

FUKASE SHIMA

AWARE SHIMA

N

0   1   2
Miles

Map 4.2. Capture of Kerama Retto, March 26–29, 1945. Courtesy Mark W. Johnson.

the sight of whom frightened the Japanese, who had never seen men of African descent. It was all quite amusing to the guards, who were enjoying the prisoners' emotional distress. Fearing their imminent interrogation, the next morning, when they were due to be transferred to the amphibious command ship *Mount McKinley,* the prisoners asked to remain on *Tate.* Sent along with the prisoners was a small valise and canvas bag full of documents and personal effects of possible intelligence value. That night Transport Squadron 17 retired to sea, going to general quarters twice without incident.[29]

At 0400 on March 29, during the return to the transport area, a Japanese Val dive-bomber, probably following *Tate's* fluorescent wake, approached its stern at low altitude with its engine silently throttled back. With *Tate* suddenly appearing out of the dark just in front of him, the obviously surprised pilot gunned his engine to gain altitude. The aircraft passed so close to *Tate* that a gust of wind from its revving engine knocked Hubert Six from his perch atop the ammunition hoist and into a 40-mm gun tub. Rebounding from the surprise, *Tate* got its first opportunity to use its guns in anger and fired 32 rounds of 40-mm and 240 rounds of 20-mm at the low-flying aircraft. The Val quickly found another target—the attack cargo ship *Wyandot*—and dropped two bombs. One exploded harmlessly in the water off its stern. "The second bomb plunged into the water near the attack cargo ship's starboard side and scored an underwater hit, opening two large cracks in her hull."[30]

With its two forward cargo holds and magazine flooding, *Wyandot* broke formation and headed directly for Kerama Retto, listing to starboard and down at the bow. Army Sgt. Birdell B. Dunham of the 233rd Engineer Combat Battalion immediately went below into the flooding number two cargo hold, which had a fire trailer on the top deck. Dunham and his fellow engineers quickly put the fire pumps into action to counter the flooding. Fourteen hours later, the ship limped into the Kerama anchorage, which was now cynically referred to as "Davy Jones Auxiliary Locker." The fire pumps, the counter-flooding, and the removal of cargo from the damaged compartments helped save the ship. *Wyandot's* crew hoisted twenty-three trucks and seventeen trailers from its flooded cargo holds. *Tate's* boats assisted in transporting *Wyandot's* submerged vehicles ashore to Zamami Shima, along with tools and spare parts for reconditioning and salvage. In eight days, a detachment of thirty-one men from the 777th Ordnance Light Maintenance Company, along with the truck drivers, completely rebuilt the vehicles, making them ready for use in the next operation. Salvage experts at Kerama Retto pumped out and patched up *Wyandot.* Temporary repairs quickly put the ship back in service, and it rejoined the squadron.[31]

As the fighting died down in the Keramas, cargo operations continued, with *Tate* providing medical supplies and fuel. The fast-moving invasions met only sporadic resistance and did not call for the large amounts of combat cargo *Tate* was carrying. Additional landings and sweeps by the infantry met little resistance. *Tate* retired to sea that evening, leaving behind Zamami Shima, which was now declared secure. Logistical, communications, meteorological, and antiaircraft elements began landing to garrison the island. During the retirement, enemy planes attacked the transport convoy. As heavy firing and bombs exploded around the escort ships, *Tate* executed several emergency turns in the dark. Although *Rixey*—directly in front of *Tate*—opened fire, *Tate*'s guns remained silent since its radar showed the aircraft were out of range. Gunner's Mate 1st Class Hubert Six recorded the day's air attack in his dairy as if it were a baseball line score: "No runs, no hits, no errors. Glad." [32]

The Kerama campaign came to a quick and decisive conclusion due to its complete surprise, the precise execution of the landings, and the effectiveness of the fast-moving infantry. The Japanese had no plan for a coordinated defense of Kerama Retto, and their commanders had no authority to react except locally. The Japanese goal to use the Keramas as a base to launch suicide boat attacks against shipping off Okinawa was shattered. Japanese casualties consisted of 530 dead, 121 prisoners of war, and 1,195 civilians in custody. U.S. losses were 78 dead and 177 wounded. [33]

Kerama Retto became the Pearl Harbor of the Western Pacific. Its entrances were secure against submarines, and a ring of land-based antiaircraft positions surrounded its natural anchorage. The U.S. Navy would use Kerama Retto to furnish supplies to the beaches of Okinawa and as a haven for damaged ships. Seaplanes based there patrolled the East China Sea and the vulnerable approaches from mainland Asia. Vice Admiral Turner's bold and controversial plan for seizing Kerama Retto proved remarkably visionary and yielded profound strategic benefits.

Arriving at Kerama Retto from Guam via Ulithi Atoll on March 29, the hydrographic survey ship *Bowditch* began checking the Japanese charts, installing aids to navigation, and conducting tide and current investigations. Within a week, new hydrographic field charts of the anchorage constructed from data collected by *Bowditch*'s sounding boats and printed on board the survey ship were ready for distribution. Every ship and boat using the newly won anchorage was soon navigating by these charts, which had been produced under trying field conditions. [34]

Tate spent the next two nights anchored in the relative security of the newly won Kerama anchorage, as the 77th Division began reembarking onto the transports. On March 31, two of *Tate*'s LCMs, loaded with artillery ammunition, followed several other LCMs towing pontoons through an approach that UDT swimmers had cleared to the island of Kiese Shima, just west of Naha, Okinawa. After deploying the pontoons for use as a near-shore causeway, the

531st and 532nd Field Artillery Battalions landed their twenty-four pieces of artillery from several LSTs and LSMs. The 155-mm guns, commonly called "Long Toms," were to support the landings scheduled for Okinawa the next day. Unlike the artillery landings on Geruma Shima five days earlier, this operation went smoothly. Nevertheless, nightfall came before all of the ammunition was unloaded, requiring some of the boats to remain for the night.[35]

Gunner's Mate 3rd Class Mark I. Johnson was on one of *Tate*'s LCMs that spent the night anchored behind the small sandy island. While Johnson stood night watch, the Japanese artillery on Okinawa opened fire on Kiese Shima. Shrapnel whizzed overhead and occasionally rattled off the bulkheads. When the boat's coxswain awoke after a close call, he asked, "Why didn't you wake me?" "If anything hit this load of 155-mm ammo, nothing would have mattered," replied Johnson.[36]

On March 31, Major General Bruce received a message from Adm. Chester Nimitz: "My congratulations on the speedy and effective manner in which you accomplished assigned tasks in Kerama Retto. The present readiness of the 77th Division to go again is characteristic of its fighting spirit and comes up to the expectations I have learned to have for that fighting organization." The 77th Division's wait to "go again" would be a short one since *Tate* and the other ships of Transport Squadron 17 were beginning to prepare for the assault on the beaches of Ie Shima.[37]

Chapter 5

OKINAWA

For Those in Peril on the Sea!

THE INTERNATIONAL DATE LINE runs north to south roughly through the middle of the sparsely inhabited Central Pacific Ocean. By convention, each new day is born at midnight in remote darkness along this line. As the first rays of sunlight crossed the line on April 1, 1945, they gave birth to the holiest of Christian holidays, Easter Sunday, a date set by celestial events. U.S. military planners also chose this date for the start of the largest operation of the Pacific War: the invasion of Okinawa. The event, designated L–Day, was more commonly referred to by its radio call sign, Love Day. Oddly, the climactic battle of the Pacific War began on the same day on which Christianity remembered the sacrificial death of Jesus Christ, who preached universal love for both friend and foe. The men in the largest U.S. naval force ever assembled, which was preparing to throw four divisions ashore at Okinawa in a single day, could not miss the irony of these two events falling on April Fool's Day.

The amphibious landings at Okinawa were a masterpiece of logistics and planning. At the start of the assault, the United States employed more than half a million men, including 182,000 assault troops, 60,000 of whom landed on Love Day. Of the 1,213 ships assembled, 318 directly supported the landings. This massive projection of sea power required movement across the vast expanse of the Pacific Ocean. The Normandy D–Day invasion, although heavily contested from the onset, originated from just over the horizon in England. The 156,000 men who landed in Normandy on D–Day were within reach of land-based airfields and the thousands of ships and support craft operating from British ports. The Okinawa campaign relied on vulnerable aircraft carriers for air support and maritime supply lines thousands of miles long.[1]

Strangely, the landings of two army and two marine divisions on Love Day met little resistance. Unlike Normandy on mainland Europe, the invaders did not have to worry about yielding the element of tactical surprise with a prolonged bombardment. On an island such as Okinawa, the navy could indulge in as much preparatory and diversionary shelling as needed without fear of enemy reinforcement. This meant that the landing zones were pulverized by a well-coordinated naval bombardment that was supplemented with air strikes.

The Japanese answer to this dilemma was to wait in the island's interior behind a well-prepared series of defensive lines. While the Americans attacked their fortified positions in what would surely be a long and expensive campaign, the Japanese planned to sink the navy's support ships, cutting off the U.S. Tenth Army's supplies and escape. This plan, code named Operation Ten-Go, primarily called for the destruction of the amphibious transports.

Love Day ended with the Americans' consolidation of their successful opening moves. At home, many families and friends of the servicemen were attending Easter worship services, unaware of the unfolding events at Okinawa. A common hymn selection was "Eternal Father, Strong to Save," also known as the "Navy Hymn" and sung regularly as part of church services during the war:

> Verse 1
> Eternal Father, strong to save,
> Whose arm hath bound the restless wave,
> Who bidd'st the mighty ocean deep
> Its own appointed limits keep;
> Oh, hear us when we cry to Thee,
> For those in peril on the sea!

While most of those on the home front remained blissfully ignorant of the events that were developing at Okinawa, forty-five Japanese pilots at the Kanoya airbase on Kyushu, the southernmost of Japan's four main islands, were readying themselves for what would be, for many, a final mission. From the Japanese perspective, an aircrew had little or no chance of surviving the war. The ever-increasing U.S. air superiority had severely reduced Japan's air power. The chances of surviving even a routine mission were becoming unlikely. Japanese pilots came to accept their deaths as a logical outcome of the conflict.

Many of these pilots were now resolving to die as kamikazes, after inflicting the greatest possible loss on the Americans. Kamikaze philosophy defined a successful suicide mission as killing ten or more of the enemy and causing significant damage to a ship. Kamikaze pilots trained to aim for the vital sections of ships, depending on their type. Striking an aircraft carrier in an elevator would likely knock the ship out of action and perhaps ignite a fire in the enclosed hangar deck, with disastrous results for the carrier. Hitting a destroyer amidships, behind the bridge and above its thinly armored engineering spaces at the juncture of many critical systems, could cause fatal damage. Striking a transport in the bridge would likely produce a tactical kill—that is, probably not sinking a ship but requiring its removal from combat and making subsequent attacks on it more effective.[2]

Although Japanese air power was a fraction of what it had been during its first battles with the United States, it still had more than 4,000 aircraft and sufficient volunteers for suicide missions during Operation Ten-Go. Many of the pilots were experienced aviators who had fought in Mainland China and other regions under Japanese control. Most of these special attack missions originated from the islands of Kyushu and Formosa.[3]

Twice during the early morning hours of April 2, *Tate*'s squadron repelled attacks from enemy planes. At 0336 Gunner's Mate 2nd Class Alvin F. Maw was looking into the inky darkness from his battle station at one of *Tate*'s forward 40-mm guns, when several ships in front of him opened fire. No aircraft was visible from *Tate* as the tracers from neighboring ships reached upward into the night sky. When the firing stopped, Maw heard an aircraft approaching, but he could still see nothing. Then, directly in front of *Tate*'s bow, a cockpit light came on in a single-engine plane. The pilot was clearly visible to Maw for a brief moment before the aviator slumped over and crashed into the water just as *Tate* opened fire.[4]

Again, at 0608, in the early morning light, *Tate* opened fire on a Sonia-class aircraft closing from the east. At a range of more than 2,000 yards, *Tate* pounded away for two minutes with two of its 40-mm mounts, nine 20-mm guns, and, for the first time in combat, its five-incher. The aircraft sustained several hits before dropping a bomb that just missed the attack transport *Eastland*. *Eastland*'s aim was better, and it splashed the Sonia with 20-mm fire.[5]

On the morning of April 2 Transport Squadron 17 visited Kerama Retto for the last time to finish embarking the 77th Infantry Division. The attack transports *Drew* and *Pitt* remained behind. *Drew* became a receiving ship for the survivors of kamikaze attacks, while *Pitt* continued to support the troops of the 2/305, which was garrisoning Zamami Shima. That evening, fully laden with troops, the ships conducted a night retirement to the south, utilizing the same route as on the two previous nights. The squadron of sixteen transports (eleven APAs, four AKAs, and an APH) from three transport divisions formed into three columns 1,000 yards apart, with 600 yards separating each row of ships. Its escort consisted of two high-speed destroyer transports and the destroyer minelayer *Harry F. Bauer* (DM-26). The destroyer minelayer *Thomas E. Fraser* (DM-24) was also to join the convoy but was still several miles behind. With sunset approaching, *Dickerson* (APD-21) passed close along *Tate*'s port side, the men waving and cheering on the way to a screening position in front of the convoy's port column.[6]

The squadron flagship—attack transport *Chilton*—was in the center of the front row. Embarked on *Chilton* was the officer in tactical command responsible for coordinating the squadron's movements and defense. To *Chilton's* starboard was the attack transport *Goodhue,* and to its port was *Tate's* divisional flagship, the attack transport *Henrico,* carrying the regimental headquarters of the 307th and 305th Infantry respectively. *Tate* was the fourth ship in the port column behind *Rixey* and in front of the attack cargo ship *Suffolk.* The convoy formed with the attack cargo ships outboard of the more important attack transports carrying the bulk of the 77th Infantry Division.

The skies were partly cloudy, and a dark haze was hanging above the water, limiting visibility to approximately eight miles. Although the weather had improved throughout the day, the seas remained rough with nine-foot swells. At 1823 the convoy was proceeding at twelve knots in a 45-degree zigzag east of its 180-degree base course when the first sign of trouble came via the TBS, a short-range, very-high-frequency radio used for tactical communications. The officer in tactical command declared a "flash blue, control yellow," indicating that an attack was possible and that the gun captains could open fire on their own initiative if a threatening target came within range. With the gun crews already alerted and the unidentified planes still forty miles to the southwest, general quarters did not sound.

Although the short-range SG surface search radar was a reliable tool, the long-range SK air search radar was not as dependable. Commonly affected by significant interference, the SK radar screen was often hard to interpret. Differentiating between radar contacts with a friendly "identification friend or foe" (IFF) recognition signal and those without was difficult even under ideal conditions. Radar was a new technology, and the inefficiency of the air search sets was partly due to the low-frequency bandwidth of its "bedspring antenna."[7]

Those of *Tate's* personnel who had been detached to the LSTs had returned to their ship that morning and begun sharing stories about their experiences in the Keramas. Glad to be off the hard-rolling LST and back on his own ship, Ens. Alvin Joslyn went to view the sunset from the signal bridge, where the ready 20-mm guns were manned. Sitting on an ammunition locker, he saw an escort carrier to the east, recovering combat air patrol (CAP) planes for the night. Some of the carrier aircraft waiting to land began circling toward the convoy.

Below, on the main deck of *Tate,* several chief petty officers were gathering just forward of the deckhouse on the starboard side to enjoy an after-dinner smoke or dessert carried outside while watching the setting sun. Chief Pharmacist's Mate Earl Buss looked to the west, saw four aircraft emerge from the clouds, and remarked, "Looks like we have friendly cover." "Sure glad those planes are ours," replied Chief Storekeeper William G. Newton. The four twin-engine aircraft then dived abruptly. Any peace the men hoped to find watching the sunset ended at 1841, when firing began at the front of the convoy. A call to general quarters immediately followed, and the voice of *Tate's* skipper urged his gunners: "For God's sake, don't forget to lead!" Enemy planes in proximity to the returning carrier aircraft, sending friendly recognition signals, had muddled the tactical picture, allowing the Japanese to approach out of the setting sun without detection.[8]

When ready gunners on *Chilton* reported unknown aircraft approaching the convoy, the bridge reassured them the planes were friendly. Knowing the restriction that prohibited friendly aircraft from flying over convoys, the gunners were confused. When a rapidly closing plane began strafing *Chilton,* the matter was no longer in doubt. Three Wildcat F4F fighters were now in pursuit of three enemy planes, and a fourth Wildcat had just shot down a Japanese aircraft southwest of the convoy. One of the carrier pilots put it all on the line, closing in on a twin-engine bomber diving at *Chilton*'s bridge from the starboard side. The U.S. pilot wagged his wings to show he was friendly, and, with Japanese bullets striking *Chilton*'s decks, the plunging Wildcat poured fire into the suicidal aircraft at close range.

PFC Max Drucker, 306th Infantry, became the most popular man on the nearby attack transport *LaGrange* when he manned a 20-mm during the surprise attack, firing into the diving plane before any other of the ship's guns were brought into action. Signalman 2nd Class Nicholas Cologeli was standing a signal watch on the *Chilton* when he picked up some binoculars just before the gunfire began. Looking at the approaching aircraft, he saw the distinctive Japanese "meatball" wing markings. He ran to the squawk box to notify the pilot-house to sound general quarters and then manned a 20-mm. He recalled, "The loader failed to put the magazine in right, and the first shell jammed. As I unstrapped myself from the gun, I looked up and saw the pilot's face as his wingtip struck the radio antenna and smokestack just before he exploded into a million pieces alongside the number three hatch." The Wildcat's bullets had either hit the Japanese pilot or disabled his aircraft, deflecting its path at the last moment. A bomb released by the plane fell harmlessly 200–300 yards off the starboard beam and exploded in the water. Only grazed by the kamikaze, *Chilton* was lucky. Just one 20-mm had gotten into action and fired only fifty-two rounds. The ship lost a signal halyard, an antenna, and a port-side davit, while its decks were strewn with aircraft metal, a Japanese machine gun, a great deal of aviation gasoline that miraculously did not catch fire, and a Japanese airman's leg.[9]

A third plane appeared to be diving directly at *Tate* just as its crew began responding to the call for general quarters. There was no time to ponder the fate that brought them to this crisis. Men from diverse lifestyles scrambled through hatches and on ladders, pulling on life vests and helmets as they ran. Among them were a hardware storeowner from Kansas, a schoolteacher from Michigan, and a kid right out of high school from Cleveland. They were a representation of a democracy at war, fighting on a ship that had been mass-

Photo 5.1. Tate had sixteen 20-mm guns mounted around the periphery of the ship. This is the 20-mm Oerlikon in action. Courtesy George N. Larsen.

produced by a mobilized war economy. Hurriedly trained on a foundation of navy traditions and a rapidly evolved doctrine, they now faced a daunting task as a Mitsubishi twin-engine bomber, loaded with explosives and flown by a suicidal pilot, dived on their ship at nearly 300 mph.

Any of the crew's postwar dreams or aspirations quickly gave way to the mechanics of a no-quarter air-sea battle. Gun crews fed ammunition into their guns, eyes searched the sky, and hands felt for the devices that had become familiar through repeated training. Electric motors whirred, springs compressed and released, and propellants ignited, as orange and white tracers etched out a cruel geometry from the angry ship.

Tate's crew manned their guns in less than a minute, but it was too late to make a difference, as only the ready guns were able to open fire on the diving bomber. Through binoculars from *Tate's* bridge wing, the pilot's face was clearly visible, looking back and forth for a good target. The bomber then winged over hard, heading for *Henrico* at the front of the squadron. The angle at which the plane approached hindered *Henrico's* gunners. Only a single starboard-side 20-mm got off 10 rounds, and a portable 40-mm set up and manned by the army starboard of the forward cargo hatch fired 25 rounds in a desperate attempt to destroy the suicidal bomber. At the last instant before impact, the pilot released two armor-piercing bombs that penetrated *Henrico*'s superstructure and exploded near its main deck level. The explosions ruptured a fire main and some sanitary lines, causing seawater to pour into the engine room and flood the main and auxiliary generators. Severed control cables to the fuel interlocks required shutting off the engines—but not before the ship went out of control.[10]

It was a perfectly executed attack by an obviously experienced pilot who, in his last seconds of life, knew he was fulfilling his mission and sacrificing himself at great cost to the enemy. In the brief moment between the release of his bombs and the awareness that he would strike the ship's bridge, the pilot's thoughts are unknown. Did he feel complete resignation to duty or the ecstatic rapture of ultimate success? What is known is that the kamikaze struck the starboard side of *Henrico*'s bridge near the commodore's cabin, killing 49 men and wounding another 125. Among the dead were the commander of Transport Division 50, Captain E. Kiehl; the ship's commanding officer, Capt. W. C. France; the commanding officer of the 305th Infantry Regiment, Col. Vincent J. Tanzola; and the executive officer of the 305th Infantry Regiment, Lt. Col. Lyman O. Williams. Upon impact, one of the plane's burning engines broke off and careened down a corridor into a wardroom, where it also caused considerable loss among the officers gathered there. Among the injured was army Major Winthrop Rockefeller, a future governor of Arkansas.[11]

The crew of *Tate* witnessed the fatal flash from *Henrico* off its starboard bow. Debris blew out of the far side of the stricken ship opposite the impact, followed by the sound of the explosion and the involuntary shrieking of *Henrico*'s steam whistle. *Henrico*, a veteran of D-Day in Normandy, was dead in the water with its superstructure aflame. It was a sight *Tate*'s crew would never forget.[12]

The fourth plane passed down the convoy's port side in a strafing run before turning east and circling back. In the confusion, *Rixey* and the attack transport *Natrona* fired on a pursuing Wildcat as it flew an "irregular course off the port bow [of *Rixey*] in a maze of antiaircraft gunfire." The enemy plane was now in the open and under fire from every gun on the port side of the convoy, including the escort *Harry F. Bauer*, with its dual 5"/38 mounts. This aircraft seemed to have singled out *Tate*, a thought probably shared by every gunner on every other ship as they poured out a sheet of fire in its direction.[13]

From his casualty treatment station on the port side on the main deck, Chief Buss had an unobstructed view of the attacking Japanese aircraft. The plane was now weaving back and forth and diving at an angle of 30–40 degrees. Buss could only watch and yell, "Hit him! Hit him! Hit him!" like a spectator at a football game. The combined fire finally knocked out both of the bomber's engines, and the plane continued gliding downward. From *Tate*'s fantail, Shipfitter 2nd Class William M. Polikowski was momentarily stunned as he clearly

Photo 5.2. 40-mm Bofors antiaircraft cannon in action. Tate *had four 40-mm guns mounted in pairs fore and aft. Courtesy Alvin L. Joslyn.*

saw the pilot's face while he fought to gain control of his plummeting aircraft, which splashed just off *Tate*'s port side, showering seawater on the men cheering the narrow escape.[14]

While the convoy continued in its southeasterly zigzag, a new wave of three twin-engine Japanese aircraft approached from the west. The attack transports *Montrose, Mountrail,* and *Eastland* were in the best position to engage them. As the first plane attacked perpendicular to the convoy's course, it came under heavy fire. A direct hit by a 5"/38 tore its tail off, sending it into the sea just off *Eastland*'s port bow. The second plane headed straight at the attack transport *Telfair* from astern. Hit hard by 20-mm and 40-mm fire, the aircraft burst into flames directly over *Telfair* and passed down the length of the ship. Its port wing sheared off the SG radar antenna, causing the aircraft to slew to the left before ricocheting between the port and starboard king posts like a "billiard ball from hell." The tumbling plane struck the ship's port bow with a glancing blow before landing in the water, killing one man and wounding sixteen others. Almost immediately, the third plane approaching *Telfair* took a direct hit from a 5"/38. The severely damaged Betty bomber began smoking heavily, with debris falling from its starboard engine, before crashing astern of *Telfair*. Like *Chilton, Telfair* narrowly missed a catastrophic hit.[15]

At 1855 the convoy came under attack from a low-flying plane coming from the east. *Chilton*'s good fortune continued, as its forward 5"/38 got off eleven rounds and exploded the attacker into a fireball with a direct hit.[16]

When the attack began, the high-speed destroyer transports *Dickerson* and *Herbert* (APD-22), both converted World War I–era destroyers, could do little from their forward screening positions. With *Henrico* on fire directly behind it, *Dickerson* was attacked by another twin-engine bomber. Approaching *Dickerson*'s starboard side from an altitude of about 600 feet, the plane strafed the ship before missing it with three bombs. The plane then approached an escort carrier several miles to the east, drawing heavy fire from its escorts, including the high-speed destroyer transport *Bunch* (APD-79) before circling back toward Transport Squadron 17. Passing high over *Tate*'s port bow, the aircraft drew considerable fire from the transports. *Tate* scored some hits before the plane changed course and made a low-angle stern attack on the *Dickerson,* whose guns set the plane's port engine on fire just before the aircraft sheared through the ship's smokestacks, toppling the mainmast and striking the bridge from the rear. *Dickerson* continued on, wavering to port and starboard, before disappearing in a tremendous explosion. From *Tate*'s decks three miles away, it appeared that the Japanese pilot had flown right down the ship's smokestack. Then, after a few painful seconds, the escort disappeared in a column of smoke and fire. From that distance, it was unimaginable that anyone could have survived.[17]

After the squadron changed its course to due south, a single Betty bomber came straight at *Goodhue* head-on, five degrees above the horizon. *Goodhue* was able to engage the attacking aircraft only with its forward guns, and the plane flew right through the limited antiaircraft fire and struck one of the ship's cargo booms before crashing into its aft gun tubs, starting a large fire, and then careening into the sea. With the damage confined to the main deck, the ship was able to maintain its position in the formation. *Goodhue* lost 24 men killed and 119 wounded, many of whom were army personnel crowded together on the main deck.[18]

For the soldiers below decks on the transports, the situation was depressing. With few exceptions, they were supposed to report to their berthing areas during an attack. As they worked their way down into the bowels of the ships, they made way for the navy personnel hustling to their battle stations. Crowded into their quarters, they lay in their bunks looking for ways to divert their nervous energy. During attacks, ships were required to secure hatches and shut off ventilation systems to prevent the spread of fires and to conserve electricity for the gun mounts. The veterans of prolonged jungle fighting on Guam and in the Philippines could think of no fate worse than being trapped in a steel box, breathing stale air and trying to interpret the sounds of a ship in battle. Interservice rivalry faded as the soldiers hoped that their navy comrades' nerves were cool and their aim true. Topside, the guns banged away—the five-inchers crashing, the forties thumping, and the twenties rattling urgently—as the targets drew closer. Muffled explosions moved through the water and into their

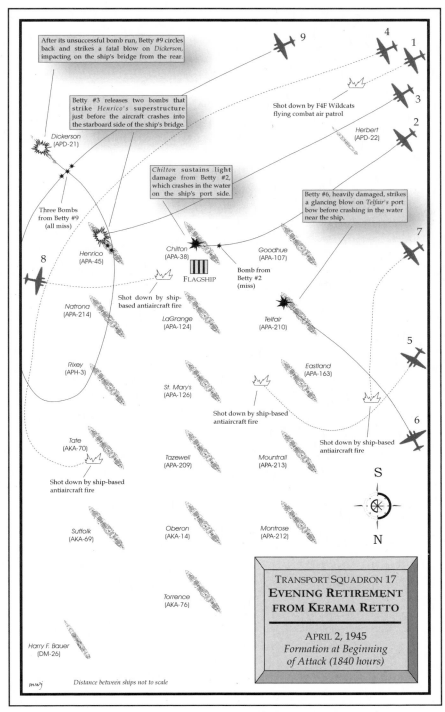

After its unsuccessful bomb run, Betty #9 circles back and strikes a fatal blow on *Dickerson*, impacting on the ship's bridge from the rear.

Betty #3 releases two bombs that strike *Henrico's* superstructure just before the aircraft crashes into the starboard side of the ship's bridge.

Shot down by F4F Wildcats flying combat air patrol

Herbert (APD-22)

Chilton sustains light damage from Betty #2, which crashes in the water on the ship's port side.

Betty #6, heavily damaged, strikes a glancing blow on *Telfair's* port bow before crashing in the water near the ship.

Dickerson (APD-21)

Three Bombs from Betty #9 (all miss)

Henrico (APA-45)

Chilton (APA-38)

FLAGSHIP

Goodhue (APA-107)

Bomb from Betty #2 (miss)

Shot down by ship-based antiaircraft fire

Natrona (APA-214)

LaGrange (APA-124)

Telfair (APA-210)

Rixey (APH-3)

St. Mary's (APA-126)

Eastland (APA-163)

Shot down by ship-based antiaircraft fire

Tate (AKA-70)

Tazewell (APA-209)

Mountrail (APA-213)

Shot down by ship-based antiaircraft fire

Shot down by ship-based antiaircraft fire

Suffolk (AKA-69)

Oberon (AKA-14)

Montrose (APA-212)

Torrence (AKA-76)

S

N

TRANSPORT SQUADRON 17
EVENING RETIREMENT FROM KERAMA RETTO

APRIL 2, 1945
Formation at Beginning of Attack (1840 hours)

Harry F. Bauer (DM-26)

mwj   Distance between ships not to scale

Map 5.1. Transport Squadron 17, Evening Retirement from Kerama Retto, April 2, 1945 (1840 hours). Courtesy Mark W. Johnson.

spaces. In some instances, the men below decks felt the sudden shudder and heard the unmistakable noise of a direct hit on their ship. In the case of *Henrico*, those below decks found themselves thrust into darkness as the stricken ship lost power.

At 1900 radar detected five more enemy planes approaching from the northwest and southeast. The convoy began executing emergency turns to allow the maximum number of guns to fire. A single-engine Val dive-bomber with fixed landing gear was heading at the convoy's port side, coming in low, jinking back and forth just above the waves. Every available gun, including five .50-cal. machine guns mounted on *Tate*'s LCMs, was firing at it. A seemingly murderous cone of fire converged on the plane. The twin forties were steadily hammering away, and 20-mm tracers passing through the aircraft were deflecting obliquely as they exited. Pieces of the Val's wings were chipping off, as if it were flying into a giant milling machine. Yet the plane kept coming.

From *Tate*'s port bridge wing, the ship's captain, Rupert Lyon, realized the plane was heading for his ship and that his 5"/38 main battery had not yet fired. Lyon turned to his bridge talker, Seaman 1st Class Ray A. McCaffrey, who was tethered to the sound-power phones in an oversized helmet. "Why hasn't Parker fired?" Lyon barked. "Sir, Ensign Parker is holding fire for a single shot," McCaffrey responded with a steady voice, "as he will not have time to reload." Satisfied with the answer and realizing there was nothing else to do, Lyon could only watch as the plane rapidly closed on his ship. He also hoped his selection of Parker, his only regular navy officer, for one of the ship's toughest jobs, was the right choice.

From Parker's perspective on the fantail, the aircraft approaching on a flat trajectory presented a simplified two-dimensional gunnery problem. McCaffrey listened and repeated what he heard, as Parker's gun talker echoed his commands: "Hold it, hold it, hold it." The gun table turned slowly as the gun trainer tracked the closing aircraft. At around 100 yards Parker finally yelled, "Fire!" Machinist's Mate 2nd Class Milton Buswell, who was dropping a clip of ammunition into the aft port-side 40-mm, glanced up as the 5"/38 discharged. Its five-inch shell struck the plane's starboard wing root without exploding. The force of the shell's impact seemed to cause the plane to hesitate before the damaged wing started folding up. The twisted wing caused the kamikaze to climb involuntarily as it approached *Tate*. Buswell, who had already lost two ships, believed his luck was finally running out. His gun crew hit the deck behind the splinter shields of their 40-mm mount. The roaring plane passed directly over Buswell, who was close enough to reach out and touch its landing gear. As the plane, with a bomb visible on its fuselage, crossed over the *Tate*'s stern, Motor Machinist's Mate 2nd Class John Borenski could see the pilot's eyes, flying helmet, and white scarf. The aircraft continued to climb be-

Photo 5.3. Tate's 5"/38 stern-mounted main battery saved her from a catastrophic kamikaze hit. Courtesy George N. Larsen.

fore breaking apart, snap-rolling into the sea, and exploding less than 100 feet away on the starboard side.[19]

Making no aggressive movements, another intrepid Japanese pilot in a single-engine plane was apparently scouting. Flying between the columns of ships, the plane was so low that the guns could not fire at it without endangering adjacent vessels. As the plane passed along *Tate's* starboard side, Lt. (j.g.) Paul Leahy on the bridge wing was close enough to make eye contact with the pilot, who saluted the young navigator. The obviously damaged aircraft continued toward the head of the convoy, passing out of sight while still under fire.[20]

At the rear of the starboard column, *Montrose, Mountrail,* and *Eastland* opened up at 3,500 yards on two twin-engine bombers diving out of a cloud-bank to the northwest, twenty seconds apart. Another direct hit from a 5"/38 destroyed the first aircraft, while tracers hit the second one repeatedly. At 1,500 yards, the plane turned abruptly to the right with both engines smoking. Its tail then fell away, and it cartwheeled into the sea.[21]

A single-engine Kate, with a bomb attached to its underside, circled off to the east of the convoy before approaching *Tate* from the stern and drawing considerable fire. Ens. Albert Dorsey, *Tate's* 40-mm captain for the gun mount on the starboard bow, sized up the situation. Frustrated by the inability of the

Mk 51 gun directors to track aircraft at close range, Dorsey pointed his guns vertically. The aircraft then passed directly overhead, diving at *Rixey* in front of *Tate*. Dorsey's mount opened fire and got off only four rounds, but they "put it straight on him," hitting the aircraft twice in the fuselage and "lighting him up like a torch." The plane struck the water thirty-five yards astern of *Rixey,* exploding and showering the men on *Rixey*'s fantail with seawater. A few moments later *Tate* steamed directly over the spot where the aircraft had splashed, leaving the remnants of its victory in its wake.[22]

The remaining enemy aircraft disappeared to the south and did not return. East of the convoy, some final nervous fire was aimed at some friendly F4U Corsair fighters, which quickly disappeared into the fading light and the haze. The fighting was over. The TBS radio crackled with a reprimand from the nearby escort carrier, complaining that tracer fire from the transports had passed just fifteen feet over its flight deck. Still, the escort carrier was far luckier than the five ships that had been hit by kamikazes during the battle.[23]

Even though it was hard to know who had hit what in the melee, *Tate* officially shared in the credit for the destruction of two planes. During the battle, all twenty-one of *Tate*'s gun mounts fired. Shipfitter 2nd Class J. C. Bostic, a 20-mm gunner, needed to have his overheated gun barrel replaced three times during the furious action, which lasted barely more than twenty minutes.[24]

The port column of the convoy, including *Tate,* maneuvered around the burning *Henrico* while the battle was still under way. The escort *Harry F. Bauer,* dashing to the burning ship's assistance, passed down *Tate*'s port side at more than thirty knots, then held within ten feet of *Henrico*'s starboard side to assist in fighting the fires. The escort then remained alongside, coordinating the efforts to save the burning ship. The other troop-laden transports continued south on their night retirement, leaving the forlorn *Henrico* behind.[25]

The situation was far worse on *Dickerson,* whose demolished bridge was a mass of flames. A hole 20–25 feet wide and 12–15 feet long had been torn in the main deck where the three-inch gun had been. The ready ammunition lockers in the forward areas were still exploding. Almost no one in that part of the ship remained alive, and the unchecked fires threatened to detonate the forward magazine. Many men were already in the water before *Dickerson* was able to launch an LCVP to pick them up. Now, with only a lieutenant (j.g.) in command, *Dickerson*'s crew began to abandon ship.

Bunch, which was screening the escort carrier to the east, came to assist and was soon joined by *Herbert.* Together the two ships began fire-fighting and rescue operations and by 1930 had the fires under control. After flames broke out again, the *Bunch* passed over three fire hoses and a towline. The rescue parties also succeeded in getting portable gasoline-powered pumps into action to pour water onto the fires before cutting away the two remaining LCVPs on

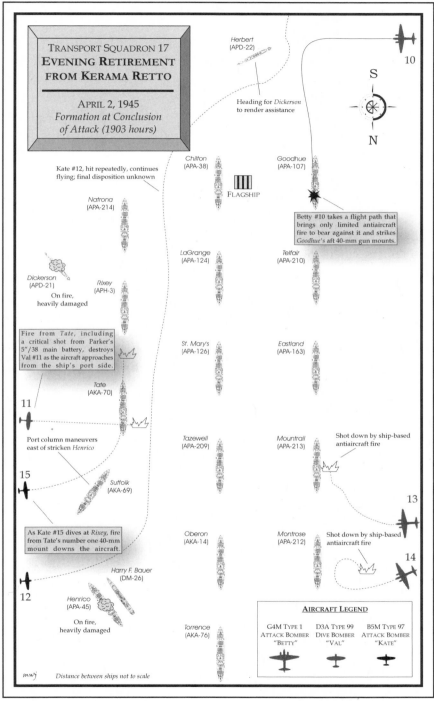

TRANSPORT SQUADRON 17
EVENING RETIREMENT
FROM KERAMA RETTO

APRIL 2, 1945
*Formation at Conclusion
of Attack (1903 hours)*

Herbert
(APD-22)

Heading for *Dickerson*
to render assistance

S

N

10

Kate #12, hit repeatedly, continues
flying; final disposition unknown

Chilton
(APA-38)

Goodhue
(APA-107)

FLAGSHIP

Natrona
(APA-214)

Betty #10 takes a flight path that
brings only limited antiaircraft
fire to bear against it and strikes
Goodhue's aft 40-mm gun mounts.

Dickerson
(APD-21)

On fire,
heavily damaged

Rixey
(APH-3)

LaGrange
(APA-124)

Telfair
(APA-210)

Fire from *Tate*, including
a critical shot from Parker's
5"/38 main battery, destroys
Val #11 as the aircraft approaches
from the ship's port side.

St. Mary's
(APA-126)

Eastland
(APA-163)

Tate
(AKA-70)

11

Port column maneuvers
east of stricken *Henrico*

Tazewell
(APA-209)

Mountrail
(APA-213)

Shot down by ship-based
antiaircraft fire

15

Suffolk
(AKA-69)

13

As Kate #15 dives at *Rixey*, fire
from *Tate's* number one 40-mm
mount downs the aircraft.

Oberon
(AKA-14)

Montrose
(APA-212)

Shot down by ship-based
antiaircraft fire

14

Harry F. Bauer
(DM-26)

12

Henrico
(APA-45)

On fire,
heavily damaged

Torrence
(AKA-76)

AIRCRAFT LEGEND

G4M TYPE 1 ATTACK BOMBER "BETTY"	D3A TYPE 99 DIVE BOMBER "VAL"	B5M TYPE 97 ATTACK BOMBER "KATE"

mwj   *Distance between ships not to scale*

*Map 5.2. Transport Squadron 17, Evening Retirement from Kerama Retto, April 2, 1945
(1903 hours). Courtesy Mark W. Johnson.*

Dickerson's port side to reduce its list. After the towline and fire hoses parted due to rough seas, the fire regained strength and began spreading. The tug *Arikara* (ATF-98) joined the effort, helping to finally put out the fire and then taking the ship under tow. *Bunch* recovered its fire crew at 0320 on April 3, after more than eight hours on board the now burned-out hulk. *Dickerson's* losses were 54 officers and men killed, including the commanding officer, and 23 wounded.[26]

A horizon punctuated with burning ships was a scene that was to become common in the battle for Okinawa. A prolonged and desperate conflict lasting three months, it would see casualties of the supporting forces at sea keep pace with the bloodiest land campaign of the Pacific War.

The remaining ships of Transport Squadron 17 continued their night re-tirement to the relative safety of the open sea. *Suffolk,* which had launched an LCVP to rescue a soldier blown overboard from *Henrico,* remained behind and offered its assistance. As *Suffolk's* crew rigged their ship to tow *Henrico* back to Kerama Retto, a bright moon began rising, illuminating the stricken ships and those who had come to their aid. Two columns of smoke ascended into the night sky above the ships "burning like candles," as moonlight and prayers spread across the water.[27]

Chapter 6

IN FLOATING RESERVE

We Slept at Our Guns

THE MORNING OF APRIL 3, 1945, brought a new and tragic awareness
to the crew of *Tate*. They wore a somber communal expression that
only a fellow combat veteran could appreciate. As one of the ship's
veterans recalled, "There was a lot of activity in the ship's laundry that day."
The question on everyone's mind was surely "Why were we spared?" Was it
luck, fate, or divine intervention? The arbitrary manner in which war selects its
victims has always been a mystery to those who escape unharmed.

The men who were below and missed the action listened to their shipmates' descriptions of their narrow escapes and the destruction of neighboring
ships. Decades after the war, Ens. Lewis Crew summed up the near miss of the
plane passing over *Tate*'s stern: "It was so close, I could have hit him with a
potato."[1]

Seaman 1st Class Fortunate ("Forty") Salerno was the hot shell catcher on
the 5"/38. His job was to knock down the hot five-inch brass shell casings with
asbestos mitts as they ejected, then kick them out of the way of the men serving the gun. During the previous day's attack, he had remained focused on the
gun's breech, never looking up while waiting for an ejecting shell. Concerned
only with his job, Forty saw none of the action around him. This was exactly
the type of behavior the navy expected of its men.[2]

Gunner's Mate 1st Class Hubert Six was now over his pessimistic foreboding that *Tate* was a doomed ship. In his last diary entry prior to the major air
attack, he boasted that he believed his ship was "Ready for anything." Then,
after the attack he wrote these words: "Fired at Jap Betty, got hits [as it] made
[a] run on *Tate*, but my 40mm was throwing too much lead for him to stand.
This ship must have a 4-leaf clover in her keel. We got 6 Jap Bettys. They got
five of our ships. We sure lost on that raid, but we will get the damned devils.
My gun ran two away from the ship. Boy, I love that baby."[3]

This was the first experience in a major air attack for most of the men on
Tate, just as it was for the majority of those in Transport Squadron 17. *Telfair*'s

Photo 6.1. Fortunate ("Forty") Salerno, hot-shell catcher for the 5"/38. Courtesy Fortunate G. Salerno.

captain noted that 30 of the 51 officers and "377 of the 488 enlisted men were serving their first sea duty." In their captain's eyes, *Telfair's* crew performed admirably despite their lack of experience. He reported that the forward 40-mm mount continued firing despite the impact of a kamikaze six feet away. "Fire and damage control parties were on scene almost immediately and extinguished the fire caused by burning oil so that absolutely no damage was caused from the fire. The stretcher bearers and First Aid people handled casualties expeditiously and personnel were quickly transferred to dressing stations. Some personnel refused to leave their stations and were not treated until after the action ceased."[4]

Four survivors of *Dickerson* spent the night in the water clutching an oil drum. Their fate took an auspicious turn when the destroyer escort *Abercrombie* (DE-343), returning from a night retirement, nearly ran over them. Spotting the screaming survivors bobbing in *Abercrombie's* wake in the moonlight, the ship stopped. Rescued from the heavy seas by a rubber boat, one man was burned and a second was barely conscious, but they were still more fortunate than many of their shipmates.[5]

After being towed to Kerama Retto, *Henrico's* embarked troops transferred to the attack transport *Sarasota* (APA-204), which assumed its operational role in Transport Squadron 17. The hospital ship *Solace* (AH-5), a veteran of Pearl Harbor, received *Henrico's* wounded. Over the next several days, the ship underwent emergency repairs to restore its engines and electrical power, but the ship needed to return to a stateside shipyard for extensive repairs. The war was over for *Henrico*.[6]

Under tow, *Dickerson* arrived at Kerama Retto during the night. The next day some of its officers returned with a salvage inspection party. Finding the ship fatally damaged, they recovered as many of the ship's records as possible. The removal of the dead from the burned-out forward section of the ship followed. *Dickerson* was towed out to sea on April 4, where a blast of friendly gunfire sent the ship to its grave south of Kerama Retto.[7]

Goodhue departed Transport Squadron 17 several hours after the battle. The destroyer escort *Richard W. Suesans* (DE-342) led the ship back to Kerama Retto for repairs and the removal of casualties. The dead from *Goodhue, Henrico,* and *Dickerson* were interred on Zamami Shima in a U.S. cemetery created there just days before by the 77th Infantry Division. An anonymous crewmember of *Goodhue* described the sad affair in his ship's postwar cruise book. Zamami Shima, "with its half moon of pebble strand enclosing a blue lagoon and backed by a little village, and its tiny green valley encircled by terraced hills—that is the scene of idyllic beauty in which we laid our dead to rest. . . . And when the services were over the bugle notes of taps echoed through the drowsy hills, until at last the air seemed filled with loneliness and peace."[8]

Natrona took over *Henrico*'s guide position at the head of the port column in what continued to be a busy night for Transport Squadron 17. The ships went to general quarters twice, opening fire both times on approaching aircraft. The second occurrence took place in the first light of morning, with several ships firing for two minutes at four aircraft passing in formation over the convoy and a fifth aircraft flying at extreme altitude. Several 5"/38 shells burst well beneath the high flyer, which turned out to be a B-29 bomber. Boatswain's Mate 2nd Class Harold Russell was a 20-mm gunner on *Tate*'s signal bridge. Recognizing the four aircraft in formation as friendly, gull-winged F4U Corsairs, he held fire. Yelled at for not shooting, Russell was vindicated when the order came to cease firing. The perceptive gunner was not the only one who was reprimanded, as *Tate*'s captain was chewing out anyone he could find with a role in the mistake. His "language was terrible" and in stark contrast to the calm professionalism he had portrayed during the hard fighting the night before.

Lyon believed that stoically accepting one's fate in battle was commendable, whereas shooting at friendly forces was condemnable in the harshest terms. The gun crews had spent a long and stressful night at their battle stations. As during the previous evening, the radar had been tracking both enemy and friendly planes in the area. This similarity to the preceding day's successful attacks nearly caused casualties from friendly fire. No damage was done, but the carrier pilots learned that flying over friendly ships was not only against regulations but also dangerous.[9]

Of the 45 Japanese aircraft that flew from the Kanoya air base on Kyushu on April 2, 31 returned. Those that attacked Transport Squadron 17 were predominantly twin-engine Betty bombers, which typically carried a crew of seven to ten. Their actions that day demonstrated that their bombardiers and machine gunners were on board. Therefore, it seems unlikely that the aircraft were under specific orders to fly special attack missions. The pilots probably acted on orders allowing them to use their own initiative to make suicide attacks, and a transport squadron protected by a minimal screening force was a suitable target.

Tate's good fortune may have been due in part to its cargo booms and king posts looming in the way of aircraft approaching from the bow or stern. Perhaps deterred by these cargo-handling structures, two of the three planes shot down near *Tate* exposed themselves to as much fire as possible by attacking the ship's beam. The third plane, which splashed behind *Rixey,* took a more favorable approach and passed directly overhead, aiming for the hospital ship, which was uncluttered with vertical structures. The attacks on *Goodhue* and *Telfair* also support this conjecture. Aircraft attacking from the bow and stern, respectively, struck cargo structures, mitigating much of the damage to these ships.

While *Tate*'s cargo booms and king posts may have discouraged attacking planes, the ship's vertical structures did not intimidate its own gunners. Although the guns were cammed to miss the ship's superstructure, they could not always avoid hitting the movable booms and cargo gear. *Tate*'s cargo masts thus suffered a number of hits from its own antiaircraft fire. In the heat of battle, a 20-mm cut loose a cable attached to one of the aft booms between the number four and five cargo holds. The cable and its attached pulley fell crashing to the deck just as the kamikaze hit by *Tate*'s 5"/38 passed over its stern. Seaman 1st Class Wilmer J. Bosarge, struck by the falling cable, hit the deck face first simultaneously with the nearby explosion of the kamikaze and its bomb. Not only was Bosarge's face bleeding from the fall, but a pencil-sized piece of shrapnel was protruding from his leg. Bosarge and several other men with minor wounds made their way to the sick bay. Quickly treated for their wounds, they all returned to their battle stations.

A piece of shrapnel also found Motor Machinist's Mate 2nd Class Colley's helmet, which was now sporting a fashionable dent. *Tate* also had a dent of its own to show off. The shock of the nearby explosion, which wounded several of *Tate*'s crew, also opened up a seam on the starboard side of the number five cargo hold and cracked some of the structural supports. The damage was relatively minor, but since the cargo hold was filled with ammunition and gasoline, the ship's escape from serious harm seemed providential.[10]

The determination and skill exhibited by the Japanese kamikazes took a toll on morale. Knowing that your enemy aspired to die in battle and take you with him was a concept completely alien to those who were schooled in the Western practices of warfare. The kamikazes held a death wish for which there was only one obvious remedy. For navy gun crews serving off Okinawa, the continual knowledge that you were part of this remedy and waiting for the next call to general quarters created a growing emotional burden. After seeing badly damaged planes, often on fire, continuing to press home their attacks, it seemed as if the battle was a fight of men against meteors. In the words of author and Pacific War veteran Kenneth Dodson, "only by God's grace and the full fury of every gun in the fleet" would anyone "have a chance of living to tell the tale of it."[11]

Although the navy anticipated the use of kamikazes in the Ryukyus, it had underestimated the scope of the threat. Nonetheless, the defenses designed to stop them were considerable and consisted of four formidable, nested layers. The first, the combat air patrol, operated from aircraft carriers. Guided by the second defensive layer of radar picket ships, the CAP would ideally intercept any enemy aircraft before it reached the pickets. Stationed at intervals around Okinawa's perimeter, the pickets consisted mostly of destroyers or similar ships. Aircraft that made it through the picket next faced the five-inch guns of the screening ships, which often used proximity-fused munitions. The final layer consisted of the numerous 20-mm and 40-mm mounts of mutually supporting ships.[12]

Fifteen radar picket stations were arranged in a rough circle around Okinawa. For a ship, the average life span before being hit at picket station number one, the closest to Japan, was an incredibly short six hours. An unanticipated side effect of the picket ships was that Japanese planes, once attacked by the CAP, would then often attack the picket ships rather than try to penetrate the screen. Although unfortunate for the pickets, this turn of events helped contribute to the success of their mission: protecting the transports.[13]

For the next ten days Transport Squadron 17 cruised within predefined sectors approximately 200 miles south of Okinawa to avoid air attacks. With the 77th Infantry Division embarked, Transport Squadron 17 was in floating reserve, awaiting orders to assault Ie Shima. Those orders were contingent upon the progress of the fighting on Okinawa. Advances on the northern half of Okinawa were rapid since the marines were encountering less resistance than expected. The army was running into well-prepared positions in the rugged southern half of the island. The fighting for every parcel of land was brutal, and marines from the northern part of the island began moving south to fight alongside the army. At the rate the fighting was wearing down units on Okinawa, it seemed likely the 77th Infantry Division was headed there, too.[14]

Operation Ten-Go, whose objective was to destroy the shipping off Okinawa and cut off the U.S. forces fighting on the island, started in full force at dusk on April 6. A massive attack by 355 kamikazes cost the United States 6 ships sunk, with major damage to 10 others, and minor damage to 12 more. Most of the ships hit were destroyers. It was the first of 10 mass kamikaze raids intermixed with intermittent small-scale suicide attacks. In the skies around Okinawa, the navy was facing its worst threat of the war.[15]

On April 7 Tate's convoy and its screen moved even farther to the southeast, putting extra distance between them and a Japanese task force that had been sighted off Kyushu. The task force contained the largest ship in the Japanese navy, the battleship Yamato, carrying eighteen-inch guns, the largest naval weapons in the world. Yamato, without air cover, was heading for Okinawa in a desperate attempt to break up the U.S. naval forces massed there. In a ninety-six-minute span, nine torpedoes and five 1,000-pound bombs struck the battleship before it capsized, blew up, and sank.[16]

While waiting in floating reserve, the soldiers of the 77th Infantry Division took part in abandon-ship drills, calisthenics, training classes, and briefings on potential operations. Life belts became part of the uniform of the day, as the fear of submarine attacks had the infantrymen ordered topside on the blacked-out transports during the most vulnerable times—dawn and dusk.[17]

The troops also spent a great deal of time in the slow-moving chow lines. Navy fare was certainly better than the grub they got when ashore in action. The memories of scratching out a few spoonfuls of cold, greasy, canned rations while under fire in a muddy hole helped ease the experience of waiting for meals. As the soldiers inched closer to the mess decks, they could smell the aroma of the hot food gradually overcoming the musty, salty, oily ship odors.

Despite the relatively easy life on board ship, the troops were anxious to get ashore. "Maybe it would be tough on the beach with sand and grit in your teeth, eyes and hair, but when a Japanese Kamikaze plane started at you . . . you could at least dig in, and that's more than you could do on these steel decks. It's always that way with a land soldier when trouble comes at sea; he is lost and doesn't know what to do; there is no place to dig on deck."[18]

Anticipating Tate's return to Okinawa, Gunner's Mate 1st Class Hubert Six recorded his thoughts in his diary: "Still running in circles, hope we unload soon and get away from here. Hope we don't have as hot a time this time. I hate those suicide dives (Nuts) those Japs."[19]

The Japanese attempts to use submarines against the U.S. ships off Okinawa were unsuccessful. The submarines had a difficult time operating in the shallow waters west of Okinawa, where the bulk of the U.S. ships were working. In April 1945 the restricted waters and the large number of screening ships resulted in the sinking of four Japanese submarines around Okinawa. U.S.

forces also destroyed another six midget submarines in their pens on Okinawa's Motobu Peninsula. During this time, the screening ships in *Tate*'s convoy used their sonar to explore several potential subsurface contacts that never materialized into a threat.[20]

On the night of April 9 boats like those discovered in Kerama Retto assaulted the attack cargo ship *Starr* (AKA-67) and the destroyer *Charles J. Badger* (DD-657). A wooden boat carrying explosives struck some of the landing craft tied up alongside *Starr*, which suffered minimal damage but lost several of its boats. Hit by a depth charge from a suicide boat, *Charles J. Badger* lost power and was heavily flooded, necessitating a tow to the Kerama anchorage for repairs. These events, along with a successful suicide swimmer attack on an LST off Zamami Shima, demonstrated that constant vigilance was required among the anchored ships.[21]

On April 13 the men in *Tate*'s radio room were shocked by the news of the sudden death of Pres. Franklin D. Roosevelt. As the captain made the announcement over the public address system, many of the men were hard pressed to name the vice president, who would take over their country's war effort. *Tate*'s skipper followed the announcement with a remarkably colorful and effective impromptu speech. His sentiments were so touching that the men who were listening froze in their tracks. An American icon, Roosevelt had been president since most of the crew were young boys. It was difficult enough trying to imagine a new leader after more than twelve years, but Roosevelt's unexpected death, combined with the stress of combat, only added to the drama and sorrow of the situation. For eighteen-year-old Storekeeper 2nd Class Norman M. Nisen, the news was "earth shattering," and he nearly broke down wondering what was to become of everyone at home.[22]

Tate headed back to Okinawa, arriving on April 14 at the Hagushi anchorage, near the Love Day landing beaches. Hagushi was a gigantic parking lot packed full of transports and support ships, protected to the east by newly conquered land and to the west by a screen of surface ships. The anchored ships generated smoke as needed to obscure the entire anchorage from view. Boats containing a lookout armed with a rifle patrolled around the ships on flycatcher duty, searching for Japanese swimmers, suicide boats, and floating mines. Some LCVPs were equipped with obscurant smoke generators that fed a mixture of diesel fuel and oil into the engine exhausts to help conceal their mother ships. Serving on a smoke boat was miserable duty because it consisted of patrolling around the congested anchorage and sucking down smoke, while the artillery boomed and flashed on the main island. On one occasion, a smoke generator caught fire on an LCVP alongside the blacked-out *Tate*, but the boat crew extinguished the flames even before the *Tate*'s fire lines could be manned.[23]

Photo 6.2. Clinton E. Alexander of Charlotte, North Carolina, enlisted less than a month after his brother was killed in Italy. Courtesy Timothy S. Alexander.

When two lights were spotted coming out of the smoke toward *Tate,* a warning was issued over the ship's loudspeaker: "Halt or be fired upon!" The object turned out to be an amphibious truck (DUKW) full of lost marines, looking for directions and not wanting to land behind Japanese lines. Given a navigational fix, the marines headed for the beach, feeling their way through the smoke.[24]

Not everyone was so tolerant of unknown objects approaching in the dark. While patrolling *Tate*'s decks during a night watch, Seaman 1st Class Clinton Alexander saw something out of the ordinary in the water next to his ship. Toting a .45-cal. Thompson machine gun, Alexander opened fire. After pouring an entire clip into the object, a shipmate jokingly pointed out that he had just killed a large piece of floating canvas. Hearing the gunfire, the officer of the deck sounded the general alarm. With his shipmates roused and now ribbing him, Alexander saw no humor in the incident as the war had already claimed his only brother.[25]

Tate's boats were frequently running about the Hagushi anchorage on a variety of assignments and occasionally going to Okinawa. Motor Machinist's Mate 2nd Class Ivo Cecil asked Lt. Walter Hall for permission to go ashore to visit his brother Sam, who was a staff officer at the Tenth Army Headquarters. Hall responded, "Absolutely not! Do you know what's happening there?" He was not about to approve a sailor's visit ashore where a major land battle was raging. Undeterred, Cecil ignored the officer and jumped into a boat heading for Okinawa. Walking right into army headquarters, he asked for his brother. Cecil was technically over the hill, but he believed the chance of sharing a few brief minutes with his sibling was worth the risk. Having lost another brother, Henry, when a German Stuka dive-bombed the destroyer *Shubrick* (DD-639) off Sicily, he was determined to see Sam. The uncertainty of war did not often provide second chances to connect with loved ones. For these two brothers, the war stopped for a few brief, happy moments under the canvas of Tenth Army Headquarters.[26]

On April 14 the seven wave-guide officers detached to the LSTs for the Kerama Retto campaign again transferred to the same LSTs for the upcoming assault on Ie Shima. The attack transport *Natrona* replaced *Drew* as a casualty-receiving ship at Kerama Retto. The *Drew,* along with its vital cargo of armored vehicles and ammunition, then rejoined Transport Squadron 17. General Buckner, commander of the Tenth Army, ordered the date for the Ie Shima landings moved up, based on favorable progress in northern Okinawa. Buckner's authority to make major campaign decisions did not sit well with Admiral Spruance, who felt the army had trumped him. It was Admiral Nimitz who gave Buckner his authority. Nimitz then ignored complaints by Spruance, commander of the Expeditionary Force, a title that traditionally carried the overall command responsibilities. Nimitz felt the primary goal at Okinawa was the conquest of territory, and the commander of the ground forces needed to make the major tactical decisions. The navy provided the following rationale for the new command structure:

> The operations which involve the establishment of the forces of the
> Pacific Ocean Areas in the Ryukyus differ from previous operations
> in the Central Pacific campaign, in that although initially they will be
> amphibious in nature, they will involve the use of a Field Army in one
> or more large islands for a considerable period. Also the positions to be
> occupied are so close to major enemy bases that active combat condi-
> tions will continue for an extended period.[27]

The command structure for Operation Iceberg's invasion of the Ryukyu Islands was a test for the anticipated invasion and conquest of the main Japanese islands. It was crucial to establish and refine the command relationships prior to the largest battle yet of the Pacific War.

After sunset on April 14 *Tate* went to general quarters and made smoke, but no enemy planes appeared. The same thing happened the following morning and then again that evening. This time three aircraft approached from over Okinawa, and shore batteries shot two of them down. At 1920 *Tate* took a Betty bomber under fire as it passed over at 2,000 feet but scored no hits. An hour later, under cover of yet another choking smoke screen, six explosions thought to be bombs dropped by an aircraft detonated near *Tate*'s berth. For the next several hours the shore batteries and ships to the north continued to direct heavy antiaircraft fire into well-defined areas.[28]

An air attack under smoke concealment often provided only hints of the action. Hearing an approaching Japanese aircraft, gun crews would sometimes get just a glimpse of the enemy plane. Only ships equipped with five-inch guns capable of firing radio-proximity-fused ammunition could effectively engage the aircraft through the heavy smoke. While at general quarters under smoke, a single gun fired from a nearby ship. Looking up through a hole in the smoke screen, Electrician's Mate 2nd Class Byron W. Larsen saw the shell explode directly beneath a Japanese plane. The enemy aircraft then disappeared, tumbling through the smoke and presumably into the sea.[29]

For more than two weeks the crew maintained a heightened level of battle readiness. Condition 1, or general quarters, with all guns manned, was occurring several times a day. When not at general quarters, the crew spent most of their time at Condition 2, with half of the guns manned in four-hour shifts. Condition 3, with only a third of the guns manned, was set when no apparent threats existed. Men whose battle stations were below decks served some of the gun watches, allowing the gun crews to rest.

Ens. Alvin Joslyn wrote home that, during the time they operated near Okinawa, he tried to keep count of the number of planes he saw shot down. He counted nine downed in a single raid, but after twenty-seven he lost track. The "Japs were in dead earnest about bombing us out. We slept at our guns when they were not being used."[30]

For the U.S. servicemen fighting on or around Okinawa, the last few weeks had revealed their fragile mortality. Yet, the sight of such an overwhelming naval force reinforced the notion that, although you yourself might not survive, the Japanese would undoubtedly be defeated. The strangely beautiful fluorescent walls of antiaircraft fire that were thrown up each night into the dark skies off Okinawa reinforced the concept of ultimate victory.

Chapter 7

COMBAT LOADED

The Entire Beach Seemed to Be on Fire

E MERGING FROM A PROTECTIVE BLANKET OF SMOKE, *Tate* and
the rest of Transport Squadron 17 steamed from the Hagushi anchorage at 0440 on April 16, 1945. Finally free of the smothering layer of
smoke, the ships formed into three columns before heading up the west coast
of Okinawa. Under the control of the squadron flagship, *Chilton,* the ships
steamed north at fifteen knots, with all their guns manned. The flashes of light
to the north provided an eerie navigational landmark as their destination, the
island of Ie Shima, underwent an intense naval bombardment. Arriving at 0530
in the staging area for the invasion, the men on the ships whose battle stations
were above decks watched the systematic shelling as the first rays of daylight
revealed their objective. Ie Shima's distinctive single mountain jutted above the
smoke from the numerous fires started by the shelling. Whole sections of the
island remained obscured under the fog of battle as the landing craft prepared
for the assault.[1]

   Tate was still carrying the troops and most of the cargo loaded at Leyte. In
the Keramas the ship provided ammunition, miscellaneous supplies, and fuel
to smaller ships while supporting troop landings with its boats and personnel.
At Ie Shima *Tate* would finally fulfill its primary mission as an attack cargo
ship: landing combat cargo ashore in direct support of an ongoing amphibious
operation. The brunt of the fighting at Ie Shima would fall on the fundamental
fighting element of war—infantry. Without ground troops, territory cannot
be conquered and held. Logically, in amphibious operations, U.S air and naval
power were primarily support mechanisms for the soldiers and marines. To
sustain these operations on shore, the infantry needed a continuous supply of
equipment, ammunition, food, and vehicles. This was the mission for which
the AKA class ships were designed: amphibious attack cargo operations.

   Operations against Japan had required the United States to develop an amphibious capability in addition to competence in large-scale ground operations. Anticipating the Japanese threat as early as the 1920s, the U.S. Marine

Table 7.1. Composition of Transport Squadron 17 at Ie Shima

Transport Division 49	Transport Division 50	Transport Division 51
Chilton (APA-38)*	*Sarasota* (APA-204)*	*Goodhue* (APA-107)*
LaGrange (APA-124)	*Drew* (APA-162)	*Eastland* (APA-163)
St. Mary's (APA-126)	*Tate* (AKA-70)	*Telfair* (APA-210)
Tazewell (APA-209)	*Rixey* (APH-3)	*Montrose* (APA-212)
Oberon (AKA-14)		*Mountrail* (APA-213)
Torrance (AKA-76)		*Suffolk* (AKA-69)
		Wyandot (AKA-92)

*Transport division command

Corps began exploring tactics to support a potential island war against the Japanese. The development of amphibious weapons, procedures, doctrine, logistics, and force structure followed in the 1930s. The early amphibious operations of World War II had revealed many weaknesses in prewar planning. By 1945 these issues had been largely resolved, and the process of planning joint amphibious operations had matured.

One of the lessons learned was that troops that landed in enemy territory needed to be as self-sufficient as possible until secure lines of communication were established. To help meet this requirement, infantry regiments had been reorganized into regimental combat teams (RCTs). Essentially organized like a small infantry division, each RCT had as its core three battalion landing teams (BLTs) of approximately sixteen hundred men. Each BLT consisted of three rifle companies, one heavy weapons company, and a headquarters unit. An RCT contained a mix of specialists based on the requirements for a specific operation or campaign. Typically these included combat engineers, a medical company, armor, antiaircraft, chemical warfare personnel, and boat operators for the LVTs. The artillery remained a divisional asset, with each of the three 105-mm howitzer battalions dedicated to support an RCT, who provided their own forward observers. A longer-range heavy 155-mm battalion supplied general artillery support to the entire division.

Before 1945 each RCT with its considerable equipment and supplies embarked on a single transport division of three or four attack transports and a single attack cargo ship. Three transport divisions were combined to form a transport squadron, which could carry an entire division of three RCTs. During the early preparation for Okinawa and Iwo Jima, the amphibious planners determined that the now larger marine and infantry divisions required increasing the transport divisions to five attack transports and two attack cargo ships. For Okinawa, the transport squadrons usually contained fifteen attack transports, six attack cargo ships, and one hospital evacuation transport.[2]

Each tactical unit embarked on a single ship with its equipment and supplies. The loading of these ships for Okinawa was "conducted according to the transport doctrine of the Amphibious Forces Pacific Fleet and the logistical directives published by Tenth Army." Specialized quartermaster teams assisted in loading troops and equipment. Cardboard cutouts made to scale of cargo items were jigsawed together using ship blueprints and characteristics to determine loading patterns. Large items such as artillery, trucks, and armor required special attention since some cargo hatches were too small for them to pass through. The army and marine quartermasters and the navy transport division staff jointly worked out the cargo manifests. "All loading plans and operations were subject to the approval of the captain of each ship as well as of the transport squadron commander concerned."[3]

Early amphibious operations in the Pacific war demonstrated a critical need for supplies and equipment to be loaded in a logical and systematic manner. Cargo was to be stowed in inverse order to its anticipated tactical use. High-priority material such as ammunition, fuel, and vehicles needed to be near the top and center of ships' cargo holds. Low-priority materials were loaded near the bottom and on the outside of the cargo spaces. When more than sixty percent of a ship's available cargo space was utilized in this manner, it was classified as "combat loaded."[4]

Tate's transport quartermaster, marine 2nd Lt. Dewey Maltsberger, was responsible for executing the ship's combat loading plan. The large items, mostly trucks and vehicles taken on back at Leyte, went into the holds with the largest hatches. The vehicles themselves and their trailers were preloaded with supplies. After landing, they would drive directly into battle and deliver their equipment. Most of the remaining cargo space was filed with gasoline drums and mortar ammunition. Being sandwiched between tons of gasoline and high explosives became a source of dark humor for the men working below decks in the engineering spaces. Lieutenant Commander Lyon's experience with a burning cargo of gasoline on the *Celeno* off Guadalcanal had him anxiously awaiting the orders to execute the combat unloading plan.[5]

On April 14 the 77th Infantry Division went on alert for the invasion of Ie Shima. The assault troops of the 305th and 306th RCTs were on the same LSTs they had boarded in Leyte, minus the 2/305, which was garrisoning Zamami Shima. The remainder of the 305th RCT was on board *Tate;* the rest of Transport Division 50, the 306th RCT, was on Transport Division 49, and the 307th RCT was on Transport Division 51. The 304th, 305th, and 902nd Field Artillery battalions were on board LSTs, and the 306th Field Artillery was on *Montrose.* The 77th Infantry Division's mission was to capture Ie Shima and establish air base facilities.[6]

Ie Shima, code named "Indispensable," is a potato-shaped island slightly less than five miles long from east to west and no more than two and half miles wide. Just three and a half miles west of Okinawa's Motobu Peninsula, both islands were in a position to support each other with artillery. A predominantly flat limestone plain approximately 130 feet above sea level, Ie Shima contained several large, strategically important airstrips. Dominating Ie Shima's geography is a rocky, conical mountain named Iegusugu Yama, which juts 607 feet above the island's eastern end, just north of Ie town. The island's northern coast contains rocky cliffs, whereas the remainder of the island has sand beaches.

The intermittent naval bombardment of Ie Shima began on March 26. On April 13 the shelling began in earnest, with the battleship *Texas* and six smaller ships firing at targets all over the island but concentrating predominantly on the eastern end. That night, six LSMs conducted a harassment with rockets, 40-mm shells, and illumination munitions. A similar bombardment continued the next day and then halted while the fire support ships prepared for an all-out bombardment on the morning of April 16. Navy aircraft also attacked strong points during the first ten days of April. The air strikes resumed with a greater intensity on April 13, after a two-day respite brought on by bad weather.[7]

On April 13 and 14 Underwater Demolition Teams 21 and 24 conducted the last major UDT operation in the Ryukyus, scouting, mapping, and marking the approaches to Ie Shima's beaches. They found no obstacles other than the reefs, similar to those in the Keramas, which required the use of the LVTs. The swimmers drew scattered rifle fire from the southwestern beaches but encountered no resistance on those near Ie town. Ordered not to go ashore, one of the intrepid UDT frogmen ignored the command and went on a personal adventure:

> As a pair of swimmers reached the shore, one of the men stayed in the surf while his buddy crawled inland between the enemy's sand dunes. On the nearest gunboat, Chief Loban, who had to keep track of the swimmers, marked the man's name down as lost, never expecting to see him alive again. But the man got back from the Jap-held-shore and reported back aboard with his beach information. Chief Loban bawled him out for exceeding orders (something Loban himself had done a little earlier near Naha!). The swimmer replied in a hurt tone: "I was perfectly safe, Chief. My buddy was covering me with his knife."[8]

The Fleet Marine Force reconnaissance battalion, which was attached to the 77th Infantry Division, landed on the small island of Minna Shima just before dawn on April 13 and quickly secured the area with no resistance from its thirty civilian inhabitants. Not much more than a large sandbar, the island provided an excellent position only 6,500 yards southeast of Ie Shima from which to utilize the 155-mm and 105-mm artillery in support of the upcoming invasion. On April 15 the 305th, 306th, and 902nd Field Artillery battalions landed on Minna Shima. In an operation similar to that on Kiese Shima the day before the Okinawa landings, the artillery was in place to support an amphibious assault without running the risk of landing guns and ammunition on a congested and perhaps contested beach.[9]

Reconnaissance flights in January 1945 led U.S. intelligence analysts to estimate the Japanese forces on Ie Shima as two infantry battalions and some airfield service troops. One Japanese battalion was organized for a linear defense of the southern and western beaches. The second was organized in depth between the airfield and Ie town. Subsequent photographic surveillance flights failed to show any troop activity. Between March 27 and April 15 low-flying planes continued buzzing the island at treetop level and sighted only five people. The excavations seen on and around the airstrips appeared to be attempts to prevent the Americans from using them. Yet, the guns previously spotted were now absent, and the island appeared to be undefended.[10]

Thinking the island was abandoned, the Tenth Army staff recommended that only two companies of infantry land for a daylight reconnaissance. Major General Bruce's intelligence staff disagreed, fearing the Japanese were preparing a trap, and they were correct.[11]

As on Okinawa, the Japanese on Ie Shima conducted an effective camouflaging operation while preparing for a defense in depth centered on the high ground away from the beaches. Under the command of Maj. Masashi Igawa, almost 7,000 defenders were in fact concealed on Ie Shima. Igawa's strongest asset was his veteran 930-man 1st Battalion, 2nd Infantry, which had fought in China. In addition to his regulars, Igawa had 350 men from the 50th Airfield Battalion, 120 men from the 118th Independent (aircraft) Maintenance Unit, and 580 Okinawan conscripts in the Gilbo Labor Battalion for airstrip construction. The Japanese commander also convinced more than 1,500 civilians to join in the fighting. "Iegusugu Yama boasted a maze of hidden firing positions, the village of Ie was a veritable fortress, and the intervening ground was honeycombed with caves, tunnels, bunkers and spider holes. The skill and industry of the Japanese in preparing this hidden defense system presaged a bitter fight for the 77th."[12]

The planners believed that the firing that the UDTs had encountered during their reconnaissance was a deception, making those beaches appear heavily defended, while the quiet beaches near Ie town were likely fortified. Major General Bruce's inclination for "landing where they ain't" became the premise for the initial landings. Bruce selected the southwestern beaches Green T-1, Red T-1, and Red T-2. However, these beaches had limited clearance over the fringing reefs even at high tide, thus hindering their use as supply points. Bruce was hoping a quick-moving attack would uncover the more favorable landing beaches to the east for use as a supply avenue.[13]

Bruce's plan had the entire 306th RCT landing on beach Green T-1, then advancing with two battalions abreast, and quickly overrunning the airfields. The 306th would then press toward Ie town and Iegusugu Yama. The 3/305 and 1/305 would land on beaches Red T-1 and T-2 respectively before swinging east to secure Red Beach T-3 and T-4, where supplies could be more easily landed. The 305th would then assist the 306th RCT in capturing Ie town and Iegusugu Yama. The 307th RCT would remain in floating reserve.[14]

Tate's boats would take part in the assaults on Red Beaches T-1 and T-2. From the assembly areas shoreward, the approaches to both beaches were clear of obstructions. Fringing reefs extended to 620 yards off Red T-1 and 396 yards off Red T-2. The reef fronts and surfaces were irregular with 70–80 yards of ragged live coral containing isolated coral heads. Inside the reef was a ring of smoother dead coral, interspersed with patches of sand and weeds. A small channel existed to each beach, but they were usable only by small boats under ideal conditions. Both gently sloping, sandy beaches were backed by an abrupt and heavily vegetated cliff 10–30 feet high. A single road leading from Red T-2, along with several drainage cuts in the cliff, would provide egress for troops pushing inland.[15]

The code name for the day set for the invasion of Ie Shima was William Day (W-Day), and the time for the landings as Sugar Hour (S-Hour). Less than an hour before dawn on W-Day, the Ie Shima Attack Group (Task Group 51.21), including *Tate,* rendezvoused with their covering force of cruisers and destroyers as they approached the transport area southwest of the island. The four tractor units carrying the assault troops that were embarked on LSTs arrived forty-five minutes later and immediately began launching their boats and LVTs under ideal weather conditions. As the process continued, the amphibians circled in their designated areas. To minimize confusion, troops boarded the same vehicles assigned to the same landing waves used at Kerama Retto.[16]

The tides at Ie Shima were not an issue. Tidal predictions utilized the established historical measurements from Naha, Okinawa, and only minor differences were expected. Okinawa's tides were diurnal in nature, with one high and one low per day and a maximum range of about seven feet. The invasion would take place during rising water at levels approximately two feet under the highest high water of the month. Timing an assault for high water was no longer a necessity since sufficient numbers of LVTs were available. Not only did the tracked vehicles increase the flexibility of scheduling landings, but they could also carry the fight to the enemy with their guns and light armor. Almost any period of rising water was adequate to help carry the LVTs shoreward and,

KA70-3

Photo 7.1. LCMs and LCVPs tied up alongside. Courtesy Alvin L. Joslyn.

if needed, float them off obstructions. Even though the Higgins boat landing craft were more than twice as fast, by 1945 the LVT, with its firepower, armor, and ability to cross coral reefs, was the preferred assault vehicle for an amphibious invasion in the Pacific theater of operations.[17]

On the morning of April 16 the battleships *West Virginia* (BB-48) and *Texas* (BB-35), heavy cruisers *Tuscaloosa* (CA-37) and *Portland* (CA-33), light cruisers *Birmingham* (CL-62) and *Mobile* (CL-63), seven destroyers, twenty-four mortar boats, and six gunboats bombarded the island by sectors in accordance with a gunfire support plan. "At 0725, the volume of fire was stepped up as missions in direct support of the landing attempt were fired." A thick layer of smoke and dust now obscured the island. "Puffs of white smoke against the gray pall over the island showed where the rocket and mortar ships were preparing the beaches."[18]

Some of *Tate*'s boats were again serving as guide boats for the LVTs. Lt. Joseph Neblett, the *Tate*'s boat group commander in an LCP-L, was the assistant control officer for Red Beach T-1. Neblett's boat was alone 500 yards in front of the center of the first wave. The first two waves consisted of LVT(A) amphibious tanks. Armed with turret-mounted 75-mm howitzers, they could blast their way off the beach if necessary, paving the way for the following LVTs armed with machine guns.[19]

Stationed between Red Beach T-1 and T-2 was PCC-1603 at the line of departure. The 173-foot patrol craft carried additional personnel and communications equipment for managing the ship-to-shore plan. The eyes of the control officers, wave guides, and boat coxswains watched PCC-1603's signal halyard. The appearance of the Peter flag signaled that the departure of the first wave of LVTs was five minutes away. SCC 1349 and SCC 1350 were on the outside lanes of the Red Beach assault waves. These 110-foot wooden-hulled converted submarine chasers served as beach control craft. Together the three patrol craft coordinated the boat traffic, utilizing both radio and visual signals. To assist in guiding the assault waves, each control craft carried one of the UDT frogmen who had scouted the beaches. The patrol craft could also provide or call for additional fire support.[20]

At forty-five minutes before the initial landings, with naval gunfire passing directly overhead, PCC-1603 lowered the Peter flag, signaling that it was time for Lieutenant Neblett to lead the attack on Red Beach T-1. The first wave of amphibious tanks roared across the line of departure to hit the beach just as the bombardment shifted inland from the landing zones. At the reef front, Neblett peeled off, leaving the LVTs to go it alone. As the first wave neared the island, sixteen Corsair F4Us swooped in low, dropping napalm and firing rockets behind the beaches. The second wave was only one minute behind, with the third wave landing only two minutes later, and five additional waves scheduled

Photo 7.2. Moored to the quarter boom, the LCP-L was used by the boat group commander as a wave-guide boat and doubled as the captain's gig. Courtesy Alvin L. Joslyn.

to land at intervals of five minutes. In all, sixty LVTs landed on each beach in less than thirty minutes.[21]

Tate's boat officers detached to the LSTs served as wave guides on the flanks of the LVTs. They were navigating off 22" × 17" beach landing charts that had been freshly printed on the amphibious command ship *Panamint* (AGC-13). These charts contained color-coded landing zones and approach routes drawn on top of hydrographic data and seafloor composition. Water-level sketches with significant landmarks were included to aid the wave guides in finding landing zones. The detailed terrain mapping showed elevation changes, land usage, roads, and enemy positions. The charts also contained tables listing tidal heights and solar-lunar illumination. The reverse side of the charts contained aerial photographs of the landing zones and beach egress routes. The beach landing charts, compiled from multiple sources of data in the field, were one of the critical innovations that had evolved during three years of amphibious warfare.

Again Ens. Alvin Joslyn found himself heading for an enemy beach with the 1/305, but with far more sound effects than at Zamami Shima:

As we moved up to the island there was a bombardment such as I have never seen before. Battleships, cruisers, destroyers, rocket ships, gunboats and planes were laying salvo after salvo of shells on the island

Table 7.2. Ie Shima Red Beach T-2 Landing Diagram

Left Flank Control
PC 1603: TD 50 from *Sarasota*

Lead Boat
LCP(L): BGC *Rixey*

Right Flank Control
SC 1349: BGC *Sarasota*

Wave	LVTs from LST	Wave guide officers from ship in LST #	Guide boat from	Int. in yards	Distance in yards/ minutes	BLT 1/305 in tractor unit one	Wave guide officers from ship in LST #	Guide boat from	Leave transport area	Arrive tractor area Able	Leave tractor area Able	Leave LOD	Land
1	796	One from *Sarasota* 796	LST 796	40	—	12 LVT(A)s	One from *Sarasota* 796	LST 796	—	Lower boats promptly	S-60	S-45	S
2	793 946	One from *Sarasota* 793	*Rixey*	50	300 2	8 LVTs	One from *Sarasota* 946	LST 946	—	Lower boats promptly	S-58	S-43	S+2

3	793 946	One from *Sarasota* 793	*Rixey*	50	750 5	8 LVTs	One from *Sarasota* 946	LST 946	—	Lower boats promptly	S-53	S-38	S+7
4	484	Joslyn *Tate* 484	LST 484	50	750 5	8 LVTs	Crew *Tate* 484	LST 484	—	Lower boats promptly	S-48	S-33	S+12
5	793 946	Bunch *Rixey* 793	*Rixey*	50	750 5	9 LVTs	Carter *Tate* 946	*Rixey*	S-105	S-80	S-43	S-28	S+17
6	793 484	Conner *Rixey* 484	*Rixey*	50	750 5	7 LVTs	Bloxom *Rixey* 793	*Rixey*	S-105	S-80	S-38	S-23	S+22
7	946 484	One from *Sarasota* 484	*Rixey*	50	750 5	8 LVTs	One from *Sarasota* 946	*Rixey*	S-105	S-80	S-33	S-18	S+27

Line of departure: 4,000 yards
Course to beach: 360 degrees
Line of transfer: as close to reef as possible

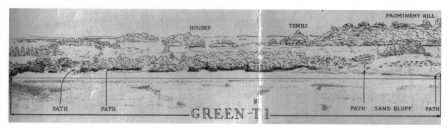

Photo 7.3. Combat landing chart panorama of Green Beach T-1, which was assaulted by all three battalions of the 306th RCT on April 16, 1945. Courtesy Alvin L. Joslyn.

Photo 7.4. Combat landing chart panorama of Red Beach T-1, which was assaulted by the 2/305th RCT on April 16, 1945. Courtesy Alvin L. Joslyn.

Photo 7.5. Combat landing chart panorama of Red Beach T-2, which was assaulted by the 1/305th RCT on April 16, 1945. The caves and tombs behind the beach provided the Japanese with ready-made defensive positions. Courtesy Alvin L. Joslyn.

and the beaches. Planes dove and dropped their loads of destruction and strafed the ground. As the first waves started to move the tempo of the firing increased until the entire beach seemed to be on fire. Black smoke rolled up making it almost impossible to see the landmarks. Planes dove over our heads spraying the beach with machine gun bullets. Salvoes of 6 inch shells whirred over our heads.[22]

Panamint became the 77th Division's command ship after a kamikaze damaged *Mount McKinley* on April 11. On board the *Panamint* was Rear Adm. Lawrence F. Reifsnider, who was in command of Amphibious Group Four and the Ie

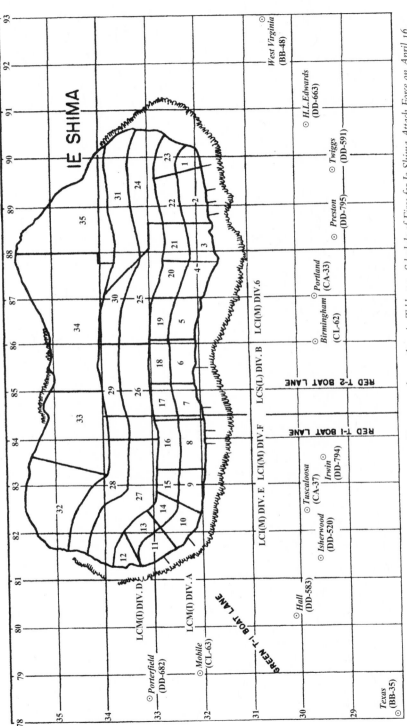

Map 7.1. Naval Gun Fire Map for Ie Shima, April 16, 1945. (Sectors correlate to those in Table 7.3, Schedule of Fires for Ie Shima Attack Force on April 16, 1945.)

Table 7.3. *Schedule of Fires for Ie Shima Attack Force on April 16, 1945*

Unit	Gun Cal.	(Expend) Sect. S-150 or Dawn to S-35	(Expend) Sect. S-35 to S-15	1st Wave 600 Yards from Beach	1st Wave 300 Yards from Beach	Sugar Hour S-000	S+10	S+30
Texas (BB-35)	14"	(40) 26, 28, 29, 32, 33	(70) 26, 28, 29, 32, 33 →				(25) 9,32,33	
	5"	(100) 26, 28, 29, 32	(200) 26, 28, 29, 32, 33 →				(100) 29,32,33	
West Virginia (BB-48)	16"	(40) 25, 30, 31, 34, 35	(70) 25, 30, 31, 34, 35 →				(25) 30,34,35	
	5"	(100) 25, 30, 31, 34, 35	((200) 25, 30, 31, 34, 35 →				(100) 30,34,35	
Tusaloosa (CA-37)	8"	(40) 7, 8, 9, 15, 16, 17	(70) 7, 8, 16, 17				→	(15) 29
	5"	(100) 7, 8, 9, 15, 16	(75) 8, 16	(150) 8, 16 →			(50) 26	(50) 29
Birmingham (CA-62)	6"	(75) 4, 5, 6, 18, 19, 20	(150) 5, 6, 18, 19 →		(50) 25 →			
	5"	(100) 4, 5, 6, 18, 19, 20	(75) 5, 19	(150) 5, 19 →		(25) 5, 19	(50) 25	
Mobile (CL-63)	6"	(75) 10, 11, 12, 13, 14, 27	(150) 11, 12, 13, 27 →		(50) 27 →			
	5"	(100) 10, 11, 12, 12, 14, 27	(75) 11, 12, 13, 27	(150) 11, 12, 13		(25) 12, 13	(50) 27	(75) 28

Ship	Gun				
Portland (CA-33)	8"	(50) 1, 2, 3, 21, 22, 23, 24	(50) 1, 2, 3, 4, 20, 21, 22, 23, 24		↑
	5"	(100) 1, 2, 3, 21, 22, 24	(200) 1, 2, 3, 4, 20, 21, 22, 23, 24		↑
Porterfield (DD-682)	5"	Screen	Screen	(150) 8, 16	(50) 14
Hall (DD-583)	5"	Screen	Screen	(150) 5, 19	(50) 14	Call fires 306 RCT
Irwin (DD-794)	5"	Screen	Screen	(150) 11, 12, 13	(50) 17	Call fires 305 RCT
Heston (DD-795)	5"	Screen	Screen	(150) 6, 18	(50) 18
Twiggs (DD-591)	5"	Stand by for counter battery fire between grid lines 83 to 85 →			↑
H. L. Edwards (DD-663)	5"	Stand by for counter battery fire east of grid line 85			↑
Isherwood (DD-520)	5"	Stand by for counter battery fire west of grid line 83			↑

(Continued)

Table 7.3. Continued

Unit	Gun Cal.	(Expend) Sect. S-150 or Dawn to S-35	(Expend) Sect. S-35 to S-15	1st Wave 600 Yards from Beach	1st Wave 300 Yards from Beach	Sugar Hour S-000	S+10	S+30
LCI(M) DIV D			Cover 900 yards left flank of Green T-1					
LCI(M) DIV E			Cover coast between Green T-1 & Red T-1					
LCI(M) DIV G			Cover 900 yards right flank of Red T-2					
LCI(M) DIV F			Cover Red T-1 to Red T-2					
LCS(L) DIV B			Cover Red T-2					
LCI(G) DIV A			Cover Green T-1					
Air Strikes		Bomb napalm 600 feet			Strafing 600 feet →			

Shima Attack Group. Watching from *Panamint*'s decks, Major General Bruce later remarked, "On the morning of April 16, the skies were clear; the sun warmed the chilled air; the seas were calm, the most magnificent weather conditions I've ever seen for an amphibious operation." Aided by capable planning, effective supporting forces, and a mature doctrine for joint amphibious warfare, the assaults went forward with great precision. Even though the landings would not be a problem for Bruce, the Japanese on Ie Shima would be.[23]

Chapter 8

IE SHIMA

Forge a Ring of Steel

THE MOST VULNERABLE TIME FOR A TRANSPORT is the period that encompasses the early phases of an amphibious operation. Its decks are cluttered with debarking troops, equipment, and ammunition. Landing craft are circling in the assembly areas as support ships execute their naval gunfire missions, restricting the ship's maneuverability. An invasion is run on a complicated set of timing tables that controls each aspect of the operation, all in support of one another. In the early phases of an amphibious assault, an attack by enemy aircraft would find a wealth of high-value targets with a diminished capability of defending themselves and could upset the timing of any number of critical events. This was indeed the scenario for *Tate* and Transport Squadron 17 on the morning of April 16, 1945, during the assault on Ie Shima, when eight enemy aircraft attacked the transport area. All of the Japanese planes were shot down by screening ships and friendly aircraft before doing any damage.[1]

Unknown to the crew of *Tate,* not far over the horizon to the north, one of the most desperate actions of the Pacific War was taking place at radar picket station number one. Beginning at 0827, the destroyer *Laffey* (DD-459) and a landing craft supply boat (LCS-51) were the focus of a ferocious and sustained attack by approximately 50 Japanese aircraft, 22 of which broke through the CAP. *Laffey* shot down 9, and the combined efforts of the CAP and both ships destroyed several others, but the effort was not enough.[2]

The intensity of the attacks on the plucky destroyer increased after it was eventually hit and set afire. Now an easily visible target without much of its firepower left, the *Laffey* was hit repeatedly. After more than an hour of continuous fighting, the ship was badly damaged from six kamikazes and four bomb hits. With its steering gear jammed, the wounded destroyer was steaming in circles, flooding and down at the stern. Its radar and gun controllers were disabled, and less than half of its armament was still operable. Even though the ship was apparently fatally damaged, its skipper rejected the suggestion that the situation was hopeless: "I'll never abandon ship as long as a gun will fire." Seventy-nine minutes after the attacks began, twenty-four Corsair F4Us finally swept the skies clear above *Laffey* and then guarded the crippled ship until help arrived. Rigged for towing, *Laffey* was moved to the relative safety of Kerama Retto.[3]

For its actions, *Laffey* received the Presidential Unit Citation, suffering 32 dead and 71 wounded in the third of ten major suicide attacks launched against the ships around Okinawa. In all, 165 kamikazes flew that day, and the destroyers on the radar pickets took the brunt of their attacks. At radar picket station fourteen, the destroyer *Pringle* (DD-477) was blown apart and sunk, and its companion, the destroyer minesweeper *Hobson* (DMS-26), was knocked out of the war. In what was a very expensive day for the navy, the carrier *Intrepid* (CV-11) was also hit by a kamikaze near Okinawa.[4]

The primary mission of the radar picket ships was to prevent enemy aircraft from reaching the transports. On April 16 only eight aircraft broke through the protective layers provided by the CAP and radar pickets to approach the invasion force off Ie Shima. All of them were shot down without causing any damage to the transports. From *Tate*'s perspective, the air attacks did not noticeably slow its landing or cargo operations. Unknown to *Tate*'s crew at the time was the price that had been paid for the ability to execute its mission without interruption. What was appreciated was the developing saga of the destroyers and the cost of shielding the transports. Profound respect was growing throughout the fleet for the destroyer crews on radar picket duty. These men were forging an enduring legacy in the navy's largest campaign in history.[5]

As four BLTs from the 77th Infantry Division hit the beaches of Ie Shima at 0800 on April 16, they met only sporadic sniper fire. Some of it came from covered slit trenches with firing ports in which the Japanese had buried themselves with food and water. Flamethrowers or explosives destroyed those positions that had survived the bombardment.[6]

The 1/306 and 2/306 quickly moved inland from Green Beach T-1, advancing abreast toward the airfields. By 1040 they were 2,000 yards inland. The island was heavily mined, and they were taking long-range machine gun and mortar fire from the heights of Iegusugu Yama. The unpronounceable mountain came to be called simply the "Pinnacle" by the infantry or the "Million Dollar Mountain" by those at sea with a good view of the enormous number of explosives being poured into it from the land, sea, and air. The 3/306 landed at 1015, moving inland and mopping up behind the advancing 1/306 and 2/306, who continued pushing hard throughout the day, overrunning the airfields before halting 600 yards north of Ie town.[7]

The 3/306 was having an easier time moving inland past the airfields to hook up with the rest of its regiment. As they advanced, they marked mines

and booby traps for the combat engineers to clear behind them. By late afternoon, the forward elements of the 306th RCT were running into prepared
positions on the outskirts of Ie town and continued working their way slowly
forward.[8]

The 1/305 and 3/305 moved inland from the Red Beaches T-2 and T-1,
respectively, and immediately ran into extensive minefields, which hindered
the use of their vehicles. By 0950, having reached their first objective, a coastal
road, the 1/305 began swinging east, sweeping a swath 800 yards from the
shore inland. After the initial light resistance, the advancing infantry began taking casualties from machine gun and rifle fire coming from Japanese defensive
positions in coral emplacements, caves, and fortified tombs.[9]

PFC Robert Howard of C/1/305 landed with the assault forces on Red
Beach T-2. A Browning automatic rifle (BAR) gunner, Howard had not gone
far inland before his unit came under machine gun and mortar fire. As he lay
on the ground preparing for the anticipated attack, the sounds of battle merged
into a deafening "continuous explosion." As a result, Howard could not hear
the amphibious tank behind him. "Suddenly, he felt the track of one of the
LVTs starting to run up his back. The track got hold of his pack and BAR and
turned the BAR into a pretzel." With his right foot caught in one of the track's
sprockets, he desperately tried to get out from under the moving LVT. "I
could feel myself being carried all the way up to the top of the sprocket where
there was a space, and then I was dropped off as [my] foot came loose inside
the tank track." In less than a year, Howard had graduated from high school,
entered the army, become a trained infantryman, gone into combat, and been
knocked out of the war after losing part of his foot.[10]

Also going ashore at Red Beach T-2 was the 304th Field Artillery Battalion,
the same unit that had run into trouble getting over the reef and across the
beach on Geruma Shima. As during the landings in Kerama Retto, the 304th
Field Artillery loaded their 105-mm howitzers into DUKWS, but this time
the terrain was more forgiving. The only artillery to be landed on Ie Shima,
they were in position by 1420, firing in direct support of the rapidly advancing
306th RCT.[11]

As night fell, *Tate,* with the rest of the transports, retired to the Hagushi
anchorage, using radar to navigate through the smoke screen. The majority of
Ie Shima was already under U.S. control, and five battalions of infantry were
building defensive positions around the periphery of Ie town under the shadow
of the obviously fortified Pinnacle.[12]

In the darkness, the Japanese probed the lines of the 1/305 and 3/305 for
weak points. Several small, reckless attacks and one company-sized assault were
driven off, killing 199 of the enemy. The Japanese, who attacked during the
night, used rifles, bamboo spears, grenades, and makeshift satchel charges at-

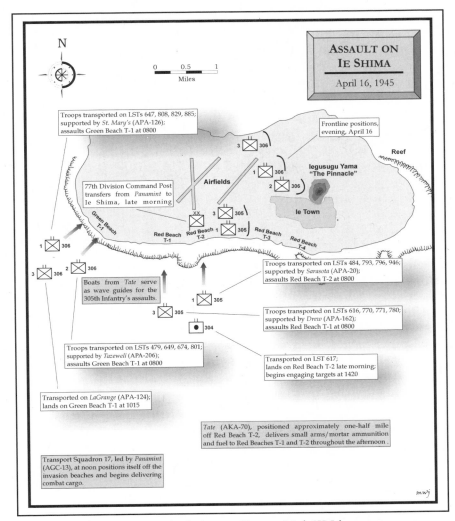

Map 8.1. Assault on Ie Shima, April 16, 1945. Courtesy Mark W. Johnson.

tached either to their bodies or to poles. Many were suicidal and blew themselves up while trying to take some Americans with them. One U.S. soldier had his arm broken by the flying leg of a fanatical infiltrator. The attacks were unproductive for the Japanese, but they signaled a new and more brutal phase to the fighting on the island.[13]

Ens. Albert Dorsey, who commanded four of *Tate's* eight LCMs, went to his squadron's flagship, *Chilton*, for briefings on the next day's amphibious operations. Seated with Dorsey during the meetings was the familiar face of famous war correspondent Ernie Pyle. To observe the preparations for the upcoming assault, Pyle had transferred to *Chilton* from the *Panamint*. One of Dorsey's assignments for the following day was to land Pyle on Ie Shima. More concerned with the management of his boats than spending time with a celebrity, Dorsey delegated the transportation of Pyle to one of his boat crews.[14]

On the morning of April 17, after the transports returned to Ie Shima, Ernie Pyle was transferred to *Tate* by one of the more than one hundred boats assigned to a boat pool for emerging transportation needs. Stationed close to the shore, *Tate* prepared to feed its combat-loaded cargo into the battle as soon as the assault troops moved off the beach. After arriving on *Tate,* Pyle had only a few minutes to get a quick cup of coffee and talk to the sailors. To the dismay of those around him, Pyle remarked, "You have not seen war until you have seen Europe." Certainly qualified to make such a statement, it still hurt the men of *Tate,* who had not picked their ship or their theater of operations. They had faced death and would likely do so again. Being killed on the beaches of Normandy was no different from being killed in any other operation. You were still dead. Pyle had a reputation for bringing recognition to the little guy, the common man dealing with the worst of the war. For Pyle, the common man was the infantry, and today he would leave the navy and its relative comfort and join the dogface soldiers in combat. Tonight he would sleep on the ground like a hunted animal with the men he loved.[15]

As the boat that would take Ernie Pyle to Ie Shima came alongside, Chief Machinist's Mate Norval W. Righter shook Pyle's hand and told him, "Goodbye and good luck." Pyle climbed into a jeep that was hoisted and then lowered into an LCM, where soldiers climbing down the cargo nets soon joined him. As the boat pulled away heading for the now secure Red Beach T-2, many of *Tate*'s crew lined the ship's rails for one last glimpse of the man they hoped would tell the story of their war experience.[16]

On the morning of the initial landings, the assistant commander of the 77th Division, Brig. Gen. Edwin H. Randle, went ashore to establish the division's advance command post. Randle colocated the group with the command post of the 305th Infantry. The command structure of the 305th had been decimated in the attack on *Henrico,* and its senior leadership roles were filled from below or through transfers from the division's other units. Having Randle and his staff on hand would help if the newly appointed officers of the 305th ran into trouble. Brigadier General Randle would control the ground fighting from on shore and be visited daily by Major General Bruce. Returning to the division's headquarters on *Panamint,* Bruce would utilize the ship's multiple command staffs and massive communications suite to control the joint land, sea, and air activities supporting the Ie Shima operation. This tactic proved to be, in Randle's words, "an efficient method of coordinating the combined arms effort." [17]

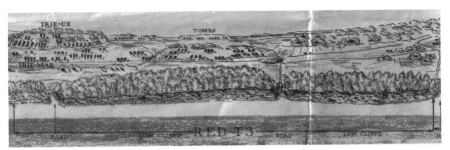

Photo 8.1. Combat landing chart panorama of Red Beach T-3, which was assaulted by the 2/307th on April 17, 1945. Courtesy Alvin L. Joslyn.

The next big move Bruce made from *Panamint* was to commit two of his three battalions that were being held in floating reserve, the 2/307 and the 3/307. At 1150 on April 17 they landed on beaches Red T-3 and T-4 under sporadic fire. Again a wave guide, *Tate's* Ens. Alvin L. Joslyn reported that his second assault in as many days occurred on "the beaches at the foot of the mountain. The bombardment was not as heavy this time, and we met some small arms fire on our way in." After the landings, Joslyn returned to LST 484, only a half mile offshore, and watched the fighting through his field glasses.[18]

Unlike the previous day's attacks with the amphibious tractors, LCVPs were also used to land the assault troops. Carpenter's Mate 3rd Class James Anthony was in one of the boats making a run to the beach. Before noticing that the soldiers were lying on the deck and the sky was clear, he thought he felt raindrops. Anthony then ducked below the gunwale as Japanese machine gun fire sprayed the area.[19]

After the war, Brigadier General Randle described the spectacle of the amphibious operation as seen from his command post. "The sea was like a chess board before the pieces are arranged—warships, LSTs, LCMs, all kinds of landing craft moving about, LVTs clanking and crawling over the fringing reefs." As Randle looked out to sea at the spectacle, he observed Ernie Pyle walking slowly up the hill from Red Beach T-2 to his command post. The Pulitzer Prize–winning Scripps-Howard journalist was wearing an ill-fitting fatigue jacket and a gray navy helmet. Weighing only 112 pounds, Pyle looked frail to Randle, who described him as having a "pinched, drawn look of one tired in mind and spirit." Randle speculated that the hard duty Pyle had pulled in the European theater had worn him down. In fact, Pyle had been ill and had spent time on board the *Panamint* recovering from a cold after a relatively quiet stint with the marines on Okinawa. While on board the attack transport *Charles Carroll* (APA-28) just before landing on Okinawa, Pyle composed a message for the ship's Easter Sunday plan of the day. Addressing the question that was surely on everyone's mind before the battle, he wrote these words:

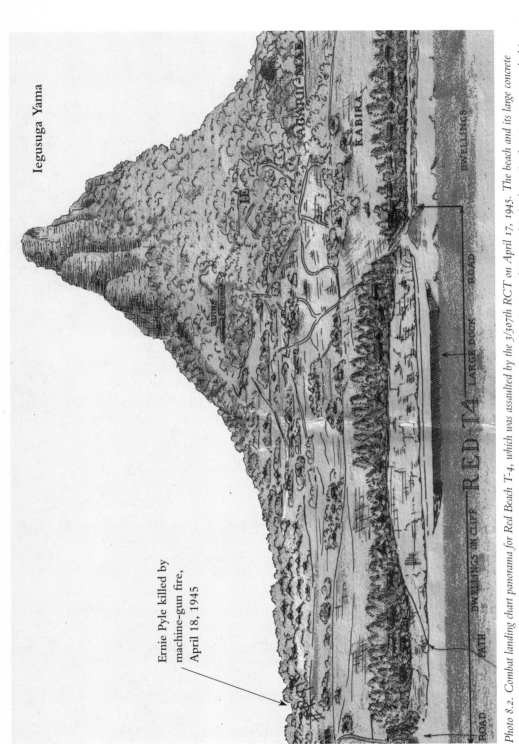

Iegusuga Yama

Ernie Pyle killed by
machine-gun fire,
April 18, 1945

Photo 8.2. Combat landing chart panorama for Red Beach T-4, which was assaulted by the 3/307th RCT on April 17, 1945. The beach and its large concrete wharf were vulnerable to direct fire from the looming heights of Iegusugu Yama. The approximate location of Ernie Pyle's death on April 18, 1945, was marked in

"At this point, it doesn't matter so much what we're fighting for. From now on, we are fighting for each other. You'll realize what I mean in a few days. The guy next to you is watching out for you. And you for him. We are truly a team. There is comfort in that. There are an awful lot of us in this together." Pyle wished everyone luck and ended with: "I'll need it, too." [20]

Pyle commented to Brigadier General Randle, "I just had to come ashore and see the infantry." He had felt at home with the army in North Africa, Italy, and France and preferred it to the other services. Pyle openly stated in writing, "I love the infantry because they are the underdogs. They are the mud-rain-frost and wind boys. They have no comforts, and they even have to learn to live without necessities. And in the end they are the guys that the wars can't be won without." [21]

Ernie Pyle did not have to wait long for a good look at what Ie Shima had to offer. Approximately 300 yards from Randle's command post, a huge explosion occurred where a bomb disposal squad was loading a truck with Japanese bombs that had been excavated from the road. All but one of the squad's men were killed. When Randle returned to his command post after investigating the blast, Ernie Pyle was off exploring a cave. Randle was miffed, and when Pyle returned, Randle saw to it that the writer was escorted at all times. [22]

On the morning of April 17 the 305th and 306th Infantry, supported by artillery, began attacking toward Ie town. They encountered pillboxes, machine gun nests, and more minefields. The 1/305 advanced 800 yards along the coast, securing the area behind Red Beaches T-3 and T-4 by noon. At 1300 the fresh 2/307 and 3/307 jumped off, passing through the 1/305, and attacked toward Ie town. Encountering steadily increasing resistance, the 307th was able to advance only 400 yards in two hours. Beyond the dunes, the ground behind the beach sloped gently uphill and offered the Japanese an excellent view of the U.S. movements on the Pinnacle and the intervening high ground. Besides those on the Pinnacle, the strongest enemy positions were about 700 yards to its southwest on a prominent ridge topped by a large concrete building. These key positions, called Bloody Ridge and Government House, were the scene of tenacious and costly fighting. [23]

As the 307th gained a foothold in Ie town, they came up against well-organized positions protected by wire and minefields. Some of the mines were wooden boxes full of explosive picric acid and could not be located with magnetic detectors. Every logical access point seemed to be booby trapped with improvised devices. As a house-to-house fight ensued, the mined streets of the town prevented the use of self-propelled guns and tanks from the 706th Tank Battalion, which had followed the 307th RCT ashore on Red Beach T-4. Engineers who were attempting to clear paths through the town for the armored vehicles were coming under machine gun fire. By late afternoon, the Japanese were pouring a barrage of mortar and machine gun fire into the Americans in front of Bloody Ridge. Unable to consolidate their position under the circumstances, the 307th withdrew for the night to a point 400 yards inland.[24]

Tate's boats were having a busy day. Having already participated in the landings of the 307th RCT, the boats were now fully engaged in attack cargo operations. All of the available LCVPs were loaded with hot cargo consisting of two prestaged cargo nets full of small arms ammunition, 60-mm mortar rounds, or fifty-five-gallon drums of gasoline. For the first time the ship was performing its primary mission of feeding combat-loaded cargo directly into battle. *Tate's* cargo of gasoline was critical to sustaining the operations of the 706th Tank Battalion. After landing, the armored vehicles were driving straight into the fight that was raging on the outskirts of Ie town. Four of *Tate's* LCMs each picked up an M-8 howitzer motor carriage from an attack transport and then landed them on Red Beach T-4. The M-8 self-propelled guns were followed ashore by the more powerful M-18 Hellcat tank destroyers.

Both the M-8 and the M-18 had lightly armored, open-topped turrets for better gunfire observation, but at the expense of crew protection. Designed for light close-in support, the M-8s sported a short-barreled, low-velocity 75-mm gun. Fast and maneuverable, the M-18s sported a long-barreled, high-velocity 76-mm gun that was originally intended for use in the open terrain of Europe. On Ie Shima, the M-18s were fighting at close range against fortified targets in broken terrain and among urban rubble, where their vaunted maneuverability was of little value. The new tank destroyer design had captured Ernie Pyle's interest, and he wanted to see them in action. He had already observed the landing and advance of the 307th RCT toward Ie town. Roaming about Red Beach T-2, Pyle watched from a distance as the Hellcats rumbled ashore on Red Beach T-4 before heading toward the ominous sounds of battle. He hoped that tomorrow he would get a closer look at the new M-18s.[25]

For Machinist's Mate 2nd Class Milton Buswell, the war had already provided many riveting memories. He had witnessed torpedoes heading for his previous ship and a kamikaze passing overhead at arm's length, and now he spotted a white horse standing chest deep in the water off Ie Shima. The frightened animal was seeking refuge in the sea. Seemingly part real and part apparition, the horse became a visual curiosity against the backdrop of the aircraft making bombing and rocket runs on the Pinnacle.[26]

As soon as the assault troops were on dry land, beach parties with hydrographic personnel began surveying. They determined the most suitable routes for the boats that were carrying supplies and additional troops. In charge of the Hydrographic Survey Group, whose primary asset was the survey ship *Littlehales* (AGS-7), was Cdr. Ira Sanders. The hydrographers quickly surveyed and marked a narrow, crooked channel to an existing concrete wharf with a ramp on Red Beach T-4, which provided direct access to ships as large as LSTs carrying full loads of the badly needed M-18s. The four roads leading from Red Beach T-4 inland toward Ie town were the key supply routes for the ongoing battle. Sanders was instrumental in the formation of mobile hydrographic units that were proving so useful in supporting amphibious operations. Conducting surveys as soon as the troops landed, they charted and designed anchorage layouts, surveyed and cleared channels, and established aids to navigation. The mobile hydrographic units made it possible for the logistical tail of reinforcements and combat-loaded cargo to be landed effectively and fed into battle.[27]

Tate was now the closest ship to the beach, and its cargo details were in high gear. After the chief boatswain's mate in charge of cargo operations became ill, Chief Storekeeper William Newton took over and controlled the operation with hand signals. The booms moved the cargo from the holds to the boats as the winch operators followed the simple gestures. An upward-pointed twirling finger raised the cargo skyward until a clenched fist stopped the hoisting. A downward twirling finger lowered the load. As the winches whined under the load of the heavy cargo, their drums played out or pulled in cable running through metal blocks at the tops of the king posts. Ropes attached to the boom ends via a block and tackle swung the booms to and from the open holds. An arm held straight out with a finger from the opposite hand pointing up under the arm raised a cargo boom. A finger pointing down to the top of the arm lowered the boom.[28]

The initial supplies and equipment went immediately to the assault troops ashore. As things became more organized on the beach, the flow of cargo was increased. Boats mounted signs and flags denoting their type of cargo. A shore party commander managed the flow of boats to and from each beach, while a reef beach master used control boats to guide the boat traffic over the hazards marked by the Hydrographic Survey Group. The shore beach master managed the beach up to the high-water line and ensured that the cargoes were unloaded and staged in the right areas to avoid congestion.[29]

The man in charge of managing the ship-to-shore signals for *Tate*'s ongoing cargo operations was Chief Signalman Wade V. Waidner. In 1928, at the tender age of sixteen, Waidner had enlisted in the navy. By 1945 he was one of the experienced chief petty officers whom Lt. Cdr. Rupert E. Lyon called the "backbone" of his ship. Before joining *Tate,* Waidner had served on the amphibious command ship *Ancon* (AGC-4) during the invasions of Casablanca, Sicily, and Salerno. For his actions during the Italian campaign, he received a "citation for his display of initiative, efficiency, and courage outside of his regular duties during the course of battle." Chief Waidner had been a firsthand witness to the evolution of amphibious warfare from the confusion of the Casablanca landings in November 1942, where loitering transports were torpedoed, to the now seemingly routine combat cargo operations off Ie Shima. In less than three years, Wade Waidner had slogged ashore on the beaches of three different continents, while dodging death from above and below the waves.[30]

Tate's boats were running directly from ship to shore, and they quickly found out the beaches were still far from being safe. Seaman 1st Class Leroy Kemske had just finished unloading a cargo of fifty-five-gallon drums of gasoline onto Red Beach T-4 when a sniper fired on his boat crew. Instinctively Kemske hid behind the fuel drums. After realizing his first choice of protective cover was not a wise one, he scampered across the beach and up the ramp of his LCVP, which was getting under way. Seaman 1st Class Wilmer Bosarge's nearby LCM was also carrying a load of gasoline drums. Fearing a single bullet could explode their cargo, the beach master ordered them to wait offshore until things cooled down. Gunner's Mate 3rd Class Mark Johnson was on another one of Tate's LCMs off the same beach when a bullet struck a bulkhead inside his boat's well deck. With daylight fading, the boats tied up alongside an LST to spend the night, intending to unload in the morning, when the beach would, they hoped, be more secure.[31]

Transports were not to delay their night retirement departure to recover landing craft. Any boats that had not yet been hoisted would remain behind. Each transport was to leave one officer behind for each six boats not recovered. Signalman 2nd Class Willard D. Whitcome was on one of the unlucky boats left behind for three nights in a row. Anchored offshore and sleeping atop a kapok lifejacket on the boat's open deck, Whitcome listened to the sounds of combat ashore. Eventually running out of food, the boat crews begged for rations from some of the larger vessels. After the Japanese fired a few mortar rounds at the sounds of the boat engines, the LCVP crews switched over to the boats' underwater mufflers. These devices caused a loss of horsepower but dramatically reduced the noise and the likelihood of drawing enemy fire.[32]

On the night of April 17–18 the Japanese again attempted to infiltrate the U.S. lines on Ie Shima. After hiding in bypassed positions, some of the enemy approached from the rear. Daylight found forty-four Japanese bodies littering the lines around the 305th's positions. The 307th also fought off a strong counterattack. Supported by heavy mortar fire, five Japanese with satchel charges strapped to their backs rushed the U.S. positions and were killed in a brief but intense fight that wounded six Americans. During the fighting, some of the U.S. soldiers thought they heard a baby crying. In the morning they discovered that some of the bodies in front of their position were women. One, who had a baby on her back, was holding a spear, and both were dead.[33]

In the trenches that night, a popular topic of discussion was Ernie Pyle's joining the 77th Division. A soldier on the front line can easily feel insignificant and temporary. With only the companionship of his buddies under the umbrella of his regimental family, he can feel detached from the world that first nurtured him and then sent him to war. Knowing that Ernie Pyle was sharing the same dangers, sleeping in the same dirt, and eating the same bad chow was comforting. Ernie was a conduit home through which the truths of a soldier's existence were portrayed. The next column Ernie wrote would be about the 77th Division on Ie Shima. He would surely write that the fighting in the Pacific was just as brutal as that in Europe. In World War II it was a commonly accepted notion that no one could tell the common soldier's story better than Ernie Pyle, and his presence with the 77th Division was a source of great pride. A soldier in the 305th remarked:

> This puts us in the same class as the Marines. They do the same kind of work that we do, but do the people at home ever hear about the glory of the Infantry? They do not. Whenever they hear of a lot of fighting being done they think of only the Marine Corps. Somebody said once—I read it—that the Navy gets the pay, the Marines get the glory, but the Infantry does the dirty work. The Marines never go into battle without carrying a press agent along with them. Well now the folks at home will get some straight dope on the Infantry. Ernie Pyle will be our press agent.[34]

On April 18 the attacks by the 305th and 307th RCTs on Ie town resumed. The 306th RCT moved to the north and northeast of the Pinnacle. To Major General Bruce it "was the age-old, but still workable, plan to forge a ring of steel around the enemy['s] position, then squeeze." The two regiments that were fighting through the rubble of Ie town now had the support of tanks and self-propelled guns firing directly into the fortified positions. Nevertheless, the numerous minefields were still hampering the armored vehicles as the advance stalled in front of the high ground of Bloody Ridge. To help relieve some of the pressure on the 307th, the 305th attacked the eastern side of Ie town. The fighting was intense and progress was slow. Both regiments halted to construct defensive positions for the night. Completing their move around the Pinnacle, the 306th now faced the dirty business of rooting out the determined enemy forces, who were ready to die in a seemingly infinite number of hiding places:[35]

> The Japanese on Ie Shima were using the defensive methods that had characterized their fighting on other Pacific islands: a house-to-house, cave-to-cave, yard-by-yard linear defense, supported by vicious counterattacks of from platoon to company strength; ingeniously concealed detachments that harassed rear elements after assault troops had passed

by; and night infiltrators who even reactivated mines that had been collected by American troops during the day.[36]

Securing Ie Shima was proving to be a tough job, partly because of the island's terrain. Unlike the flat atolls that had been attacked across the Central Pacific, Ie Shima's Pinnacle offered the Japanese an excellent vantage point (similar to Iwo Jima's Mount Suribachi) from which to observe the movements of the U.S. forces. Plus, the position of Ie town in the mountain's southern foothills enabled the Japanese to build a network of formidable defensive fortifications.

Ernie Pyle spent an amazingly peaceful night. He stated that "he hadn't heard any ruckus" even though night fighting killed a number of Japanese within fifty yards of where he slept in a captured Japanese bunker. Following a breakfast of cold C rations, Ernie was anxious to move forward and observe the fighting. After traveling approximately one mile by jeep from the command post to Red Beach T-4, Pyle had a few minutes to kill before his scheduled trip to the front. He spent the time walking on the beach, where he crossed paths with *Tate*'s Gunner's Mate 3rd Class Mark Johnson. Johnson did not recognize Pyle, who seemed nonmilitary and out of place as he greeted him with a "Hi, sailor!" Another seaman pointed out to Johnson that he had just spoken to Ernie Pyle. Then, looking back at the famous journalist, Johnson saw him boarding one of four LSTs that were busily unloading the heavy construction equipment intended for use on the airfields. Pyle went to the LST's mess deck for a cup of coffee and joined *Tate*'s Seaman 1st Class Wilmer Bosarge, who was eating breakfast after a long night on his LCM. Sensing that Bosarge did not recognize him, Ernie Pyle introduced himself. After a brief chat with Bosarge and his messmates, Pyle excused himself by saying, "Boys, I have got to work now."[37]

The commanding officer of the 305th RCT, Lt. Col. Joseph B. Coolidge, arranged to take Pyle in his command jeep with another officer and two NCOs to visit the 307th RCT, which was now attacking Ie town with the support of the M-18 tank destroyers. The 307th was fighting just over a series of sandy hills north of Red Beach T-4. Coolidge's jeep traveled down a road that had been cleared of mines—but not of all resistance, as he believed. A Japanese soldier with a machine gun was hiding in a rocky enclosure with a clear view of the road. Spotting Coolidge's vehicle, which was flying a command pennant, he opened fire. In a chaotic tumble, the jeep's five occupants instinctively bailed out of the vehicle away from the gunfire, diving into a ditch, all unhurt. Gathering himself on the side of the road, Ernie Pyle must have thought that not everyone had made it safely to cover. As he peered over the edge of the roadway to see whether anyone needed help, another burst of machine gun fire stitched along the roadside. Pyle was struck in the left temple just below his helmet. As the bullet passed through his brain, it destroyed a unique combination of human understandings. The balance of Midwestern sensibility and appreciation for the common man's experience in war that had produced a Pulitzer Prize was tragically extinguished. Also lost were the tortured memories of a man who had seen untold suffering and yet found a way to distill its essential human elements into poignant prose. America's most prominent war correspondent lay dead in a ditch on an island that almost no one in the United States even knew existed.[38]

On the morning of April 18 *Tate* and Transport Squadron 17 returned to the waters south of Ie Shima from the haven of a night anchorage at Nago Wan off northwest Okinawa. Nago Wan was not only closer but also quieter than Hagushi, where battleships firing through the night, directly over their ship, shook *Tate*'s crew repeatedly. The ship spent one more night at Nago Wan before returning to the larger Hagushi anchorage farther south. Frequently operating within a smoke screen, *Tate*'s captain was satisfied with the dependability of his surface search radar for navigation. However, the relaying of bogey reports from the air search radar was still a concern. Dissemination of these reports by radio was taking from one to two minutes after the initial contact. While anchored under smoke, *Tate* received a radio report of a Japanese aircraft five miles to port when, in fact, the plane was passing low over its starboard side. When later assigned duty as a radar guide, *Tate* was able to reduce the time for bogey reporting to thirty seconds.[39]

On April 18 the news of Ernie Pyle's death spread through the fleet in the same way that news of Roosevelt's passing had the week before. Again stunned by the loss of such a popular soul, the crew of the attack cargo ship continued landing its combat-loaded cargo onto Red Beaches T-3 and T-4. However, the two beaches were still far from safe. Occasional mortar and machine gun fire from Ie town, Bloody Ridge, and the Pinnacle onto the beaches and their exit roads was causing a great deal of congestion. Snipers continued to be a problem in the supply staging areas and late in the day caused a temporary halt to the supply operations.[40]

Carrying vital supplies, the LSTs continued landing at Red Beach T-4 after negotiating the channel that the hydrographic surveyors had marked. The sandy beach required tractors and bulldozers to tow the wheeled vehicles inland before the completion of the causeways on April 20. Continued air attacks and squally weather added to the confusion, as heavy demands for tank, artillery, and self-propelled gun ammunition continued.[41]

For three days *Tate* continued unloading its cargo, then retired each night with the squadron to Okinawa to anchor. On April 19 the remainder of the 305th RCT's fourteen officers and 225 men on board *Tate* finally landed. Some of these men were combat engineers who were needed for demolition work to eliminate the numerous mines and booby traps on Ie Shima. One of the engineers, a technical sergeant, had been sent to the command ship the day before for commissioning as a second lieutenant. He was a favorite among *Tate* sailors he had befriended during the past month. After seeing *Dickerson* getting hit and then exploding, he was the first in a group of speechless spectators to speak, saying simply, "Some fun." Sadly, his jeep hit a land mine while exiting a supposedly cleared section of the beach, killing the new officer and the vehicle's other occupants.[42]

Despite the chaos of a congested beach that was still taking occasional hostile fire, *Tate*'s boat crews kept a steady flow of combat cargo moving ashore. Some of the returning boats transported casualties to medical facilities afloat. During one of these trips Ens. Alvin Joslyn saw Ernie Pyle's body laid out "on the beach shot through his head." The troops assigned to retrieve Pyle had to wait until after sunset to reach the spot where he had been killed. Pyle's body was placed on a tank and transported to a casualty collection point on Red Beach T-4.[43]

On April 19 naval gunfire support ended as the shrinking area occupied by the Japanese and the proximity of the Americans made it unsafe to use the navy's guns. The three battalions of artillery on Minna Shima, plus the one battalion of howitzers just north of Red Beach T-2, were now providing all of the artillery support. *Tate*'s cargo had included an artillery spotter plane that had been assembled on its decks and shipped ashore to Minna Shima. Flying from a crude airstrip on the small island, the spotter aircraft conducted registration missions as the artillery sighted in targets and reference points. On Ie Shima, the engineers had also made one of that island's main airstrips operational. *Tate*'s contribution to aviation included more than building and landing a single spotter plane. One of its boats picked up a U.S. pilot who had been shot down by friendly fire and transported him unhurt to a nearby destroyer escort.[44]

Unhappy with the progress ashore, Major General Bruce sailed around the eastern portion of Ie Shima on April 19 in a navy patrol boat to reconnoiter the terrain. That perspective, which was impossible to gain with aerial photography, gave Bruce an idea of what the infantrymen saw from ground level. He then decided to shift the main effort from south of the Pinnacle to the north using the entire 306th RCT while the rest of the division tightened its hold around the base of the mountain. As Bruce was conducting his survey, his remaining reserve, the 1/307, boarded landing craft from the attack transport *Mountrail* to feign a landing on northern Okinawa to draw pressure off the marines who were fighting there. The troops returned to *Mountrail* and would be the only available battalion in the 77th Division not to fight on Ie Shima.[45]

Beginning on the morning of April 20, the 306th RCT, supported by artillery, began clawing its way to the top of the Iegusugu Yama, using flamethrowers, grenades, and satchel charges. At 0850 an intense artillery barrage hit the enemy's positions for ten minutes before abruptly stopping. The plan was to draw the Japanese out of their positions directly in front of the stationary Americans. Ten minutes later, a second, heavier concentration of artillery struck the Japanese positions for fifteen minutes. Just as the second bombardment ended, all three of the 306th's battalions attacked. Enemy resistance from mutually supporting pillboxes, deep caves, and tunnels was stiff, and the fighting in the rocky terrain occasionally erupted into hand-to-hand combat. By noon the 306th was 200 yards from the summit of the Pinnacle. Here they paused to reorganize and call for more artillery fire. The Japanese resistance ended with a final stand in a cave twenty feet below the summit. By the end of the day, the 306th held the summit and the entire northern half of the mountain. In a testament to the severity of the fighting, the Japanese casualties for the day were reported as 1,006 killed, with only 3 taken prisoner.[46]

One particular incident was typical of the style of fighting on the Pinnacle. An engineer capped, fused, and lit a satchel charge and threw it into an enemy emplacement, but it did not explode. Thinking the charge had been a dud, he repeated the procedure twice with the same result. A nearby engineer officer conjectured that the Japanese were pulling the fuses out of the charges, so they rigged up a fourth satchel charge with about a dozen fuses of different lengths. Only a handful were then capped and lit. After throwing the improvised contraption into the Japanese position, the engineers crouched behind an embankment and "could picture the Japanese in there furiously pulling out the fuses, wondering which one was live." A huge explosion followed, no doubt the cumulative effect of the makeshift bomb, the previous three charges, and the Japanese ammunition stored in the emplacement.[47]

The success of the 306th on the Pinnacle proved to be the key to breaking the Japanese resistance on Ie Shima. As a result, the regiment received a flattering tribute in a divisional report:

The attack of the 306th Infantry was as close to being a perfect Fort Benning demonstration problem as one could expect to see in actual combat. Maximum use was made of organic and attached supporting weapons on a ridge overlooking the advance, and their fire was closely coordinated with the steady advance of the infantry: 37-mm guns emplaced in positions from which gunners had good observation of the terrain were used to blast pillboxes and to designate targets with tracers for more powerful guns of the SP Guns M18 and the medium tanks. The Infantry advance frequently was accomplished only by creeping, crawling, and infiltration, but it continued steadily forward. Engineers and infantry regiments and tanks opened a lane through the minefields,

which ringed the mountain, and through this bridgehead, succeeding
waves of tanks and infantry poured to fan out on the other side of the
field and resume the offensive.[48]

For the fourth consecutive day, the fighting continued in the jumbled mess
of rubble of Ie town. On the slopes of Bloody Ridge, the 305th and 307th
regiments gained important ground. Major General Bruce notified the commander of the Tenth Army, General Buckner, that "Base of Pinnacle completely surrounded despite bitterest fight I have ever witnessed against a veritable fortress."[49]

On April 20, as the fighting on Ie Shima raged, *Tate* was completing its
cargo operations. From the ship's decks, *Tate's* crew had a clear view of the
fighting, which was now advancing up the slopes of the Pinnacle. The frequent
explosions and flamethrower attacks, which were moving ever closer to the
mountain's summit, demonstrated that the battle was reaching its climax. That
afternoon, with its five cargo holds finally empty, *Tate* returned to the Hagushi
anchorage, riding high in the water. The ship bade farewell to Ie Shima and
the troops it had helped land and support. As *Tate* steamed away from the
island, the white horse was still standing in the water. After four days in the
water, the animal had not changed its mind about the war.[50]

The night of April 20–21 witnessed one last desperate counterattack by
the Japanese. After several small probing attacks, the enemy assaulted G/2/307
south of the Pinnacle in Ie town with three columns from different directions.
The Japanese advanced right through their own mortar barrage without regard
for their own safety and slammed into G/2/307, pushing it back into the battalion command post on a small hill. All available U.S. personnel helped repulse
the attack. "Clerks, cooks, drivers, engineers and the battalion commander
and staff formed a line around the crest of the hill and managed to stop the
attack after an hour of vicious fighting. Many of the Japs got within 15 yards
of the CP [command post] center before being shot down." The Americans
used a plentiful supply of grenades and three tanks to help blunt the attack.
Found within G/2/307's lines were 280 dead Japanese, 52 more lay in front
of E/2/307's lines, and another 32 were in front of F/2/307's position. A high
percentage of the dead Japanese were officers and NCOs. Found among the
dead were eight women. Again, the use of suicidal attackers wearing satchel
charges was costly for the Americans. The Japanese losses from the night attack
virtually ended the resistance around Government House.[51]

The night action also resulted in the only Medal of Honor for actions
on Ie Shima. Pvt. Martin O. May, H/2/307, was posthumously awarded the
distinction for manning his machine gun position with the utmost tenacity
on Bloody Ridge. May held that position doggedly for three days, single-

handedly breaking up two Japanese attacks: the first with machine gun fire and the second with grenades after being mortally wounded by the mortar fire that destroyed his machine gun.[52]

The hard fighting continued on April 21, with supporting artillery fire continuously pouring into an ever-shrinking area of resistance. After finding five volunteers to accompany him, Capt. Stephen K. Smith of the 306th RCT set out for the summit of Iegusugu Yama. Scrambling past their hunkered-down comrades, the soldiers climbed up the steepest side of the mountain. While ascending the final fifty feet up a nearly vertical cliff, they came under sporadic sniper fire. Upon reaching the summit, they quickly unfurled Old Glory. Once again, the 77th Infantry Division was living up to its motto, "Ours to Hold It High." Waving their flag for the benefit of all of those who were fighting within sight of the mountain's peak, the flag party came under intense fire from several directions. Forced to descend the peak, the six men retraced their steps to the relative safety of their own lines. By nightfall, Ie Shima was declared secure. The fighting on the island continued at a diminishing rate for four more days, but now it took place underneath a U.S. flag that was fluttering from the hard-won summit of the Pinnacle.[53]

In combat that was similar to what was taking place on the main island of Okinawa, the 77th Division's 302nd Combat Engineer Battalion "destroyed 559 caves and pillboxes, 2,156 large mines and many smaller ones and destroyed 405 fifty-five-gallon drums of gasoline rigged with detonators." The Japanese proved extremely efficient in their use of small arms and mortars, while also being masters of concealment. A formidable enemy, they were fighting a losing battle and were hoping only to inflict a heavy toll on the Americans.[54]

For the 77th Division, the cost for the conquest of Ie Shima was 239 dead, 897 wounded, and 19 missing. The Japanese lost 4,706 killed, including their civilian casualties. Only 149 of the island's garrison of Japanese soldiers survived as prisoners. Major General Bruce called the Ie Shima operation a "masterpiece of planning and execution" and gratefully issued General Order 56: "Ie Shima is captured. Thank you, tough guys." Construction crews were turning the island into an unsinkable aircraft carrier. Bruce wrote of this effort in a letter home to his family not long after the fighting ended. "Work has been started on the flying field (Ie Shima off Okinawa) and I hope it won't be long before planes, 325 miles from Japan, will be striking, striking, striking."[55]

For the men of the 77th Division, who welcomed the idea of having Ernie Pyle in their midst as a chance to gain some overdue recognition, it was disheartening to realize that such acknowledgment was coming from Pyle's death rather than his reporting. The brutal expediencies of war usually require a burial without a coffin. Wanting to make an exception for Pyle, Cpl. Landon Seidler crafted a crude coffin out of ammunition packing cases. On April 20,

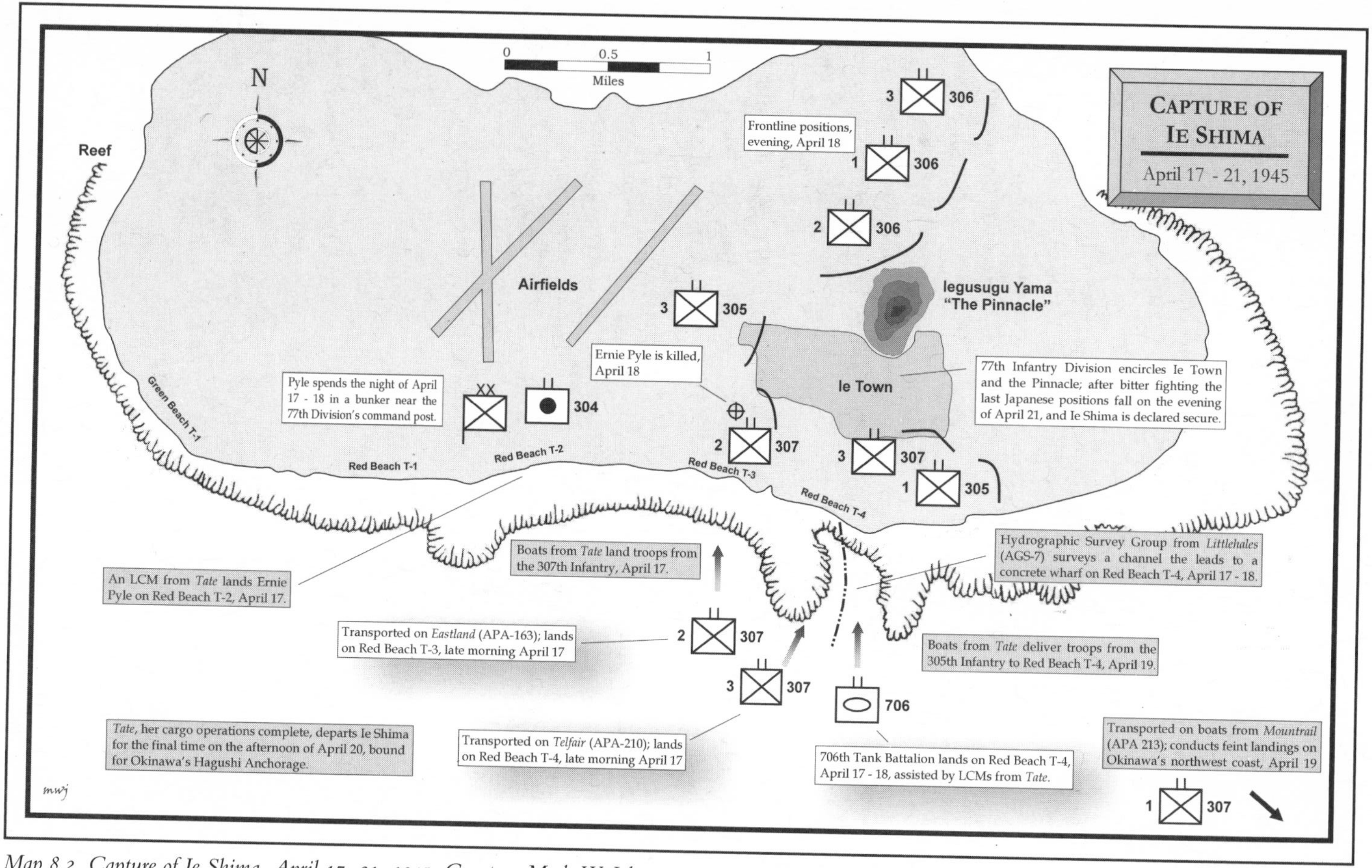

Capture of Ie Shima
April 17 - 21, 1945
0
0.5
1
Miles
N
Reef
Airfields
Iegusugu Yama
"The Pinnacle"
Ie Town
Green Beach T-1
Red Beach T-1
Red Beach T-2
Red Beach T-3
Red Beach T-4
3 306
1 306
2 306
3 305
1 305
2 307
3 307
304
XX
Frontline positions, evening, April 18
Pyle spends the night of April 17 - 18 in a bunker near the 77th Division's command post.
Ernie Pyle is killed, April 18
77th Infantry Division encircles Ie Town and the Pinnacle; after bitter fighting the last Japanese positions fall on the evening of April 21, and Ie Shima is declared secure.
An LCM from *Tate* lands Ernie Pyle on Red Beach T-2, April 17.
Boats from *Tate* land troops from the 307th Infantry, April 17.
Hydrographic Survey Group from *Littlehales* (AGS-7) surveys a channel the leads to a concrete wharf on Red Beach T-4, April 17 - 18.
Transported on *Eastland* (APA-163); lands on Red Beach T-3, late morning April 17
2 307
3 307
706
Boats from *Tate* deliver troops from the 305th Infantry to Red Beach T-4, April 19.
Tate, her cargo operations complete, departs Ie Shima for the final time on the afternoon of April 20, bound for Okinawa's Hagushi Anchorage.
Transported on *Telfair* (APA-210); lands on Red Beach T-4, late morning April 17
706th Tank Battalion lands on Red Beach T-4, April 17 - 18, assisted by LCMs from *Tate*.
Transported on boats from *Mountrail* (APA 213); conducts feint landings on Okinawa's northwest coast, April 19
1 307
mwj

Map 8.2. Capture of Ie Shima, April 17–21, 1945. Courtesy Mark W. Johnson.

1945, Ernie Pyle was buried in a row of graves, with an infantry private on one side and an engineer private on the other. Always a champion of the common foot soldier, Pyle was laid to rest among the men he loved and respected the most. Those attending the brief service, conducted by Chaplain Nathaniel B. Saucier, were required to carry arms and keep their helmets on since the fighting continued nearby. Some respectful soldiers erected a simple wooden sign on the spot where Ernie fell; the lettering was painted on with a cotton swab on a stick. The inscription, composed by Major General Bruce, who was present for the ceremony, read: "At This Spot, the 77th Infantry Division Lost a Buddy, Ernie Pyle, 18 April 1945."[56]

On July 2, 1945, a permanent concrete marker with two brass plaques was unveiled on the spot of Pyle's death. One of the plaques carried the original inscription by Major General Bruce; the other the emblem of the Liberty Division. Brigadier General Randle, with whom Ernie spent his last night peacefully oblivious to the fighting around him, dedicated the monument. *Tate* played a role in taking Ernie Pyle to his death. The same was true for some of the soldiers *Tate* carried into battle in the Ryukyu Islands. Whether the ship would do the same for any of its own men was an uneasy question stirring in the minds of the crew.[57]

Chapter 9

CROSSING THE LINE

Peace-Lovin' Civilian

As *Tate* lay anchored in the Hagushi anchorage on April 21, 1945, the crew began preparations for departing Okinawa. *Tate's* role in Operation Iceberg was now complete. The ship would return to a secure area to resupply, embark troops, and load cargo for its next mission. Spending one last long night with the men sleeping at their guns, the ship sounded general quarters twice as Japanese night bombers got in some parting shots. From the sea, the spectacle of the island of Okinawa was foreboding. "There was constant artillery fire and flares. One could see the shells, red hot from the guns, soaring off towards the front, losing their color as they went." The land battle had turned into a World War I–type meat grinder, with entire battalions covering a front only 600 yards wide. The infantry and marines were fighting at close quarters in a sea of mud, while artillery and combat engineers targeted countless enemy strong points for reduction. The 77th Infantry Division, now victorious on Ie Shima, would soon be transferred to Okinawa and fed into the battle for Shuri Castle, the costliest and most desperate action of the Pacific War's bloodiest land battle.[1]

Tate was fortunate in suffering no serious casualties during four weeks of nearly continuous action. The ship's newspaper, the *Hot Tater*, reported that the ship's dog, Penny, was wounded when she was struck by a piece of shrapnel that lacerated her left foreleg. Bleeding badly from a nicked artery, the dog was taken to sick bay. After fifteen minutes of treatment, Penny was "walking again as if nothing had occurred." The dog "took it like a hero," and the ship's medical records noted that "Penny received proper medical attention and was released to duty—our first casualty in the pet line."[2]

Ens. Albert Dorsey spent five days in sick bay after the operations at Ie Shima ended. Dorsey sustained an injury while serving as the officer on fly-catcher patrol. His boat was underneath the guns of the heavy cruiser *Tuscaloosa* when it unleashed a salvo into Ie Shima. Doctor Heinan's diagnosis was a vertigal rupture of both ears. In addition to the hearing loss, Dorsey had symptoms similar to seasickness. Technically not a battle casualty, Dorsey was still laid up in considerable discomfort.[3]

On April 22 *Tate* got under way for Saipan in the Marinas Islands, sailing directly astern of the attack transport *Sarasota,* which carried the officer in tactical command of Transport Division 50, while most of Transport Squadron 17 remained at Okinawa. *Sarasota* and *Tate* were the first two ships in the port column of a convoy containing several auxiliaries and merchant ships, plus a screen. Designated as Task Unit 51.29.20, the convoy zigzagged at fourteen knots into the open sea, away from the continuing air attacks around Okinawa.[4]

One of the convoy's escorts was the severely damaged destroyer *Laffey,* which had undergone temporary repairs at Kerama Retto. After restoring the ship's steering and some of its firepower, *Laffey* was seaworthy enough to head for a stateside repair yard. Its shattered five-inch turrets and burned superstructure were stark reminders of what *Tate* was leaving behind.

Because of the threat of submarines, the convoy exercised a dawn alert on April 23, and battle stations were manned from 0445 until sunrise. This was followed by tactical maneuvers in the mid-morning for a report of a bogey that proved friendly. That afternoon the convoy conducted evasive maneuvers while the screen investigated a potential submarine contact. When no submarine was detected, the ships continued on to the southeast.[5]

Three days of uneventful cruising ended with the sighting of several friendly patrol aircraft. Like birds signaling the welcome approach of land to weary sailors, the planes meant that *Tate* was soon to be snugly secure in a U.S. facility, far removed from the big show at Okinawa. For the crew of the battered *Laffey,* it was debatable as to "who was escorting whom." The commander of Transport Division 50, Capt. Royal W. Abbott, put the matter to rest shortly before their arrival at Saipan when he told *Laffey,* "It was an honor being escorted by you."[6]

On the morning of April 27 the *Tate* anchored off Saipan before it was to sail on to Guam. For the past week, *Tate*'s crew had lived off a steady diet of lamb stew and rice, but now that too was gone. Due to the shortage of food, *Tate* remained at Saipan for provisioning. Evening fell before the ship could launch an LCVP to obtain food. Machinist's Mate 2nd Class James Baker was on the boat sent ashore. His last meal had been only a light breakfast of toast and coffee. Upon arrival on shore, Baker's boat crew found the Supply Department closed for the day. *Tate*'s skipper radioed the port director asking for an emergency issue of enough food for two meals. When the supply clerks showed up to load the boat, they asked where *Tate* had come from. After hearing the stories of the kamikazes off Okinawa, the clerks took mercy on the men and turned loose as much food as they could load onto their boat without charging the ship for most of the stores.[7]

Photo 9.1. Lewis A. Crew, an officer in Tate's landing division. After Okinawa, he longed to return to Pontiac, Michigan, and become his state's "top peace-lovin' civilian." Courtesy Lewis A. Crew.

The arrival at a forward base such as Saipan enabled *Tate*'s men to receive their much-anticipated and overdue mail. Ens. Lewis Crew hit the jackpot at mail call and then wrote to his future wife, Alice Bueschlen, "Big day again today! The first of the week brought some sixteen letters and today brought nineteen more. Oh happy happy day!" While *Tate*'s location was a military secret, Bueschlen guessed, based on the news reports of the immense scale of the campaign, that *Tate* was at Okinawa. Crew responded to her inquiry in a way that dodged the censorship issue: "My dear Watson you are more than clever to figure out where we *were*. We were there in the thick of it, and as the result, I'm ready to return to Michigan and become its top peace-lovin' civilian. I have had my fill of this heroism and fight fight stuff." Crew was hoping the U.S. Army Air Forces could end the war without any further help from him. Making no mention of his location he also wrote, "The B-29s are plentiful out here, they really look sweet gliding gracefully through the air. If they keep up their infernal pounding on Japanese installations it might turn into a second Germany." The young officer, who had lost weight during the Okinawa campaign, was looking forward to "a week or so of well earned rest" and a chance to go ashore on an island with no fighting. He was also relieved they were no longer remaining blacked out at night: "It is indeed very relaxing to be away from all this boom boom stuff."[8]

Like so many of the men in the service, Ensign Crew had never really traveled before the war. His family had not ventured far afield from their Midwestern turf. Crew's mother, a Canadian from Ontario living in Pontiac, Michigan, wrote to her son asking him whether the stars shone as bright in the Pacific as they did in Michigan. To answer her, he responded that he would have "to send her a chunk of the beautiful and gorgeous moon that shines so brilliant tonight."[9]

Tate's crew spent five pleasant days at Saipan, but it was not all rest since they were busy preparing for their next mission. The ship was ordered to transfer "all the ship's boats except two LCVPs to the PhibPac Replacement Pool." Then, on May 2 *Tate* got under way for Guadalcanal, in the Solomon Islands, cruising singly without an escort. Even though a long way from the front lines of the war, it was still unsettling to sail without protection from enemy submarines. While alone at sea over the next few days, *Sarasota* and the attack cargo ships *Trousdale* (AKA-79) and *Lumen* (AKA-30) were spotted also traveling on the same track.[10]

As *Tate* put additional miles between it and Okinawa, the crew reflected on its month of combat off Okinawa. They wondered whether the war had changed them and what memories they would carry through the years. At some point all warriors of the sea find themselves at the rail, gazing across the water, asking themselves questions, both simple and profound. There is a brutal honesty at sea. With nothing but a thin piece of khaki or denim between your breast and the endless horizon, a man can feel quite vulnerable.

Reflecting on his ship's performance off Okinawa, Ensign Crew wrote home, "I'm inclined to believe that our ship benefited muchly from our last deal [Okinawa]. The addition of the proper naval courtesies to officers by their men as well as [their] full cooperation has been highly appreciated by all of us. Before it just wasn't there." The mass production of ships and the rapid training of crews did not always produce a ship in its purest definition. Even the navy's well-founded rules and traditions were to some men hollow standards that they only reluctantly followed when compelled to, without appreciating the benefits of prompt obedience.

For the most part, the crews of many navy ships in World War II, especially in the amphibious forces, were at heart civilians in uniform. For *Tate,* it took the shared experience of prolonged combat for its men and equipment to gel into a ship. With officers sharing the same dangers as the enlisted men and the ship emerging from the thick of the action without a serious casualty, the crew developed a heightened faith in the ship's leadership. What many men realized was that the navy regulations they had disdained at first now offered a great deal of comfort and security in perilous times. As *Tate* headed for the equator, its proud crew believed in themselves and their ship.[11]

On May 7 two additional lookouts, both officers, were posted on *Tate's* bow. One was clad in a survival suit and the other in only an athletic supporter and a talker helmet. Instead of looking through binoculars, they were using two spent 40-mm shell casings. They were not looking for Japanese but rather for Davy Jones. *Tate's* crew was preparing to enter the royal domain of Neptunus Rex, ruler of the raging main at longitude east 163 degrees, 28 minutes. For the next four hours the pecking order of the now veteran warship was capsized, and the distinction between officer and enlisted man blurred. The only valid class distinction was between the trusty and honorable shellbacks, who had previously crossed the equator, and the unworthy, spineless, slimy, squirming pollywogs—or, more disdainfully put, wogs—who had not.[12]

The shellbacks, who made up less than a fourth of the crew, reveled in their role as the initiating tormentors of the pollywogs. The honor of earning the title of shellback did not come easily. The order of the day was prolonged and humorous tyranny. Herded about the ship, the persecuted wogs endured the whims of the Royal Court and its numerous henchmen, dressed as pirates. As they went from ordeal to ordeal, the wogs ran a perpetual gauntlet of whippings with pieces of wet canvas hoses. If a wog was left any hair at all, the Royal Barber's treatment made baldness preferable. The Royal Dentist inserted a battery-powered device into each wog's mouth and, while flouting implements of extraction in his face, gave him an electric jolt. The Royal Surgeon had his patients held down on an operating table while performing frightening medical rituals. The Royal Kotex, a large wad of linen soaked with ketchup, was rubbed into their faces. Mandatory appearances before the Royal Court, which was made up of the saltiest of *Tate*'s sailors, resulted in arbitrary judgments and additional punishment such as time in the pillory, or Royal Brig. All of the wogs were found guilty of some crime, as Electrician's Mate 3rd Class Israel Kampel found out during his appearance before the Royal Court. In a humorous mockery of his Jewish-Polish accent, Kampel was accused and found guilty of impersonating an Irishman. By the time it was over, many of the men—covered in grease, slime, and foodstuffs—were hard to recognize. Ironically, one of the wogs was an enlisted man named Joe Neptune, but his royal surname earned him no special favors.[13]

The newly minted shellbacks paid dearly for their coveted new title. Ensign Crew wrote a week later that "my outer extremities are still bluer than a blueberry pie from the incessant whopping I took." Although bordering on abusive, their initiation into the solemn mysteries of the deep, by which they earned the shellback title, is one of the fondest memories of *Tate* veterans. It was also an opportunity for the ship's crew, who had so recently escaped the fury of war, to really blow off steam. The high jinks further cemented the bonds that had so recently turned *Tate* into a highly effective fighting ship. *Tate*'s crew was now fully initiated as both shellbacks and combat veterans.[14]

While the new shellbacks were still washing off the residue of the equator ceremonies, Hitler's death and Germany's surrender were announced. As *Tate* crossed the equator for the first time, it also crossed into a New World, a world with a defeated Germany. The victory in Europe was good news, but the Pacific War still seemed all too close. At best, it was believed that some of the resources going to Europe would now go to the Pacific to help finish the job there. Although grateful for their survival, the crew realized that Okinawa was just a beginning. Standing at the rail and gazing at the horizon, a sailor could easily imagine that the worst was yet to come. On May 12 *Tate* arrived at Guadalcanal, where the first major campaign in the Pacific War had begun three years before and where Lt. Cdr. Rupert Lyon had helped save the burning *Celeno*.[15]

The next day was Mother's Day. Ensign Crew and another officer attended church services in a thatched memorial chapel built by the island's natives to honor the U.S. servicemen who had been killed during the fight for Guadalcanal. Standing next to a military cemetery, the chapel, which had been the subject of a short article in *Time* magazine the week before, provided an evocative contrast between war and religion. In the article, a marine who was stationed at Guadalcanal stated that, after observing the "simple life and the love of God these natives display, it makes you wonder just which race is ignorant or savage."[16]

Following an experience such as Okinawa, the desire for religious worship was common, as the soldiers struggled to put their experiences into perspective. They sought much-needed comfort and strength to face a future that likely promised more of what they had already endured. Author of *Away All Boats*, Kenneth Dodson perhaps said it best:

The war leaves a stamp on you. You take a bath and don't feel clean.
You want a spiritual purge of the whole stinking business. You feel
you'd like to be baptized and have communion. You want to lie on
the grass and watch the cumulus swimming by in the blue of the sky.
You want to have your arms around one very near and dear to you, and
snuggle your head deep beside your beloved and feel the tenderness of
her lips on yours and the clean warm living scent that is her. And then
sleep, and there shall be no more war, no parting, no killing, no smell
of death: just peace.[17]

On May 16 *Tate* moved to Tulagi to take on board sixteen landing craft, fuel, and provisions. The voyage was short, but it crossed Iron Bottom Sound, the infamous graveyard of warships named by the hydrographic survey ship *Oceanographer* (AGS-3), which had charted the area in 1943. After a pleasant six days and ample liberty in the Solomon Islands, *Tate* got under way again early on May 18. Carrying 2,100 tons of cargo, 7 marine officers, 3 navy officers, 20 navy corpsmen, and 120 marine enlisted personnel from seventeen different units, *Tate* headed for Guam via Eniwetok.[18]

On May 20 *Tate* again crossed the equator, and the newly initiated shellbacks got their turn on the other end of the wet hoses, as they initiated the pollywog passengers the ship was transporting. Since he was now the Royal Chief of Police, Motor Machinist's Mate 2nd Class John Borenski felt he got some measure of revenge for the licking he had taken two weeks before as he "filled the brig" with lowly wogs.[19]

The cruising routine was relaxing and offered many diversions to a ship that was used to repeatedly going to general quarters. One of the most enjoyable activities was watching movies. The ship had only "one projector and there is a gruesome gap between each reel" as the film was changed, but movie time in the mess hall remained a popular event whenever new films were obtained and the ship's routine allowed the crew to view them. The cinematic entertainment available during this time included *Meet Me in St. Louis* (with Judy Garland), *Practically Yours* (with Claudette Colbert and Fred McMurray), *Marriage Is a Private Affair* (with Lana Turner and John Hodiak*)*, *Laura* (with Gene Tierney), and *None but the Lonely Hearts* (with Cary Grant).[20]

An additional but nonregulation diversion in *Tate*'s routine was occurring below decks, as several of the sailors gained access to the number three cargo hold via an inspection ladder. While loading cargo in Guadalcanal, the marines posted four guards with rifles around the number three hatch forward of the deckhouse. The armed marines were guarding the transfer of liquor crates from their officers' club and making sure it was securely stowed on board *Tate* without any pilfering. Carefully lowered and placed in the bottom of the hold, the crates of precious cargo were then buried under additional items, including jeeps and trucks. Once the hold was full and its hatch secured, the marines assumed their liquor was safe. Some of *Tate*'s sailors—those who had loaded the liquor—knew otherwise. They had volunteered for the hard labor of the cargo detail in order to control the placement of the liquor. Several of the crates were within an arm's length of an inspection ladder enclosed with vertical safety ribs. The crates were easily opened and emptied, and the liquor turned out to be brand-name whiskey. An underground railroad of "bilge rats" transported the stolen goods bottle by bottle through the bowels of the ship. Their interest was not so much in drinking as it was in selling the liquor, which could bring as much as $100 a bottle in the forward locations. The battle-hardened marine veterans of Guadalcanal had violated two of the most important principles of war: They were unfamiliar with their foe and with the terrain on which they were engaged.[21]

Tate slipped through the east channel of Eniwetok Atoll in the Marshall Islands on the morning of May 22 and anchored. The ship spent the next two days in the large lagoon before receiving a visual message to remain there until told to sail to Guam. After another seven days of swinging on its hook, *Tate*, under the direction of the commander of Transport Division 50 on board *Sarasota*, conducted a battle problem with several other ships. The exercise included damage control drills and the tracking of aircraft.[22]

Another five tedious days passed before *Tate* was finally directed to get under way for Guam. Steaming at fifteen knots, the ship took immediate advantage of its freedom, exercising at general quarters and conducting practice firings. Arriving at Guam on June 4, the ship moored to a buoy in Apra Harbor to await docking space. On June 6 *Tate* transferred the landing craft it had picked up at Tulagi to Guam's port director. That evening the ships in Apra Harbor went on alert and made smoke, but no threat materialized.[23]

On June 8, *Tate* finally moored pier side in Apra Harbor, and navy construction battalion (CB) personnel soon began unloading its cargo. When the marines found their liquor was missing, they performed a thorough search of the ship. The search detail consisted of an armed marine officer escorted by one of *Tate*'s officers. The marine was steaming mad as he rummaged around in the enlisted men's lockers. There was some concern among the innocent that a hot bottle might be in their locker without their knowledge and they would have no way to explain its presence. The innocent sailors had nothing to worry about since the liquor had been stashed in a cargo net hanging inside one of engine room's air vents. To those unfamiliar with the nooks and crannies below decks, the hunt was futile. After finding nothing, the frustrated marine lieutenant confronted *Tate*'s captain. Lieutenant Commander Lyon bristled at the suggestion that he was running a dishonest ship and ordered the marine off his ship. The frustrated lieutenant departed *Tate,* knowing that this time the navy had gotten the best of the marines.[24]

There were other secrets below decks as well. While the officers had the privilege of freshwater showers, the enlisted men scrubbed down with salt water. In the engine room, a secret freshwater shower had been rigged up for use by a select few of the enlisted. Blocks of cheese and other food items that had been liberated during cargo operations were also squirreled away in the engineering spaces. The most forbidden of all activities was gambling. Because a big winner would have to guard his cash against possible sore losers, officers did their best to bust up any card or crap games where money was found on the deck. The potential for serious morale and disciplinary problems resulting from gambling mandated its strict prohibition.[25]

After four days only 408 of the 2,100 tons of cargo had been unloaded. The CB stevedores were complaining about their work, griping that it was unfair that they were still stuck on Guam while many of the ships they had unloaded had gone stateside. Having spent a month at Okinawa unloading their own cargo at sea into boats, *Tate*'s captain had no sympathy for the stevedores, who were laboring in relative safety. After a meeting of all of the relevant ships' officers, it was agreed *Tate*'s crew would finish the job themselves. Lieutenant Commander Lyon informed the port commander of his decision and issued rifles to his deck force. They then ordered the grumbling CBs out of the cargo holds and ashore. The remaining cargo was then expeditiously unloaded.[26]

To the cargo gangs, now veterans of hard service in forward areas, unloading the ship at a pier in Guam instead of into boats bobbing in hostile waters was an easy job. The captain had two sound motives for removing the CB stevedores. The first was to prove that *Tate*'s crew was more efficient than the CBs, a demonstration that further improved their pride and cohesion. Second, he wanted badly to execute his next set of orders, which were contingent upon *Tate*'s unloading. The ship was to proceed directly to San Francisco. They were going home.

Chapter 10

THE GOLDEN GATE

A Virgin Visits Frisco

ALONG WITH THE BATTLE DAMAGE to the number five cargo hold, *Tate* had developed a significant leak in the packing around its propeller shaft that required attention in a stateside shipyard. Just two hours after finishing the unloading of its cargo in Guam, the ship was under way, moving away from the war at fifteen knots toward the United States. *Tate*'s transport quartermaster, marine 2nd Lt. Dewey Maltsberger, flew ahead to arrange for the repair of his ship. For five days, the ship and its anxious crew plodded closer to home. Spotting a small flag target on June 18, 1945, the ship exercised at general quarters for a session of target practice on the floating object. Additional gunnery practice was conducted on the following two days, using the smoke from a five-inch shell burst as a target.[1]

On June 19 *Tate* crossed the International Date Line without ceremony. To the veteran crew of several line crossings heading home, the event was now insignificant. Two days later *Tate* replied to a distress call from the cargo ship *Colgate Victory,* who requested medical treatment for a member of its crew. *Tate* stopped and dispatched its medical officer, Lieutenant Heinan, by boat to render treatment. Returning after less than an hour, the doctor followed the patient's progress as the two ships remained within signaling range for the next day.[2]

Tate's navigator, Lt. (j.g.) Paul Leahy, who had gotten off to a shaky start during the ship's early days, was now setting a standard for professionalism for the entire crew. Immaculate, impeccably precise, and well respected by his peers, Leahy was the very model of a naval officer. His credibility with his captain earned him the latitude to recruit men of good character and intellect for his navigation department. One such man was John C. Raynor, a member of an LCM crew. During a stint at the ship's helm, Leahy recognized Raynor's aptitude for navigation. Raynor gladly accepted the invitation to study under Leahy, who became his mentor, encouraging him to pursue a college education after the war. Working on the bridge and in the chartroom presented a completely new perspective to the young sailor, who quickly achieved the rating of quartermaster 3rd class. It also put him in frequent contact with the ship's command structure. While working a night watch, his captain told him, "Raynor! Go get Mr. Leahy and bring him here now! I do not want him to dress or shave. I want him here now—as he is!" Lieutenant Commander Lyon certainly appreciated Leahy's professional decorum, but on this occasion the savvy mariner wanted an experienced navigator and not a naval officer. Raynor could only chuckle to himself as he hustled to Leahy's quarters to awaken him. Enlisted men never got this kind of entertainment working in the boats.[3]

The long cruise gave Gunner's Mate 1st Class Hubert Six plenty of time to make his daily diary entries. Several days after leaving Guam, he found himself unable to sleep and wrote the following: "On our way to the states. I am thinking a lot of home. Lonely and I have lots of dreams." Several days later he penned this: "Still underway for Frisco thinking and wondering if my wife will be able to come see me, I hope so." Six later changed his mind about sending for his wife: "I am glad to get to go home. I have been thinking about how surprised the home folks will be to see me." Events would alter Six's plans, and he would neither go home nor see his family.[4]

About 500 miles west of California, *Tate* received a dispatch from the commander of the Western Sea Frontier, ordering the ship to divert to Seattle due to shipyard availability. This was disappointing news, for there was no West Coast port as glamorous as San Francisco. On June 28 the disappointment eased as a sunrise illuminated the mountains of the Olympic Peninsula, providing the weary crew their first view of the United States. The ship sailed on to Seattle, where it docked for a few hours before moving to the Everett-Pacific shipyards in Everett, Washington. They were finally stateside.[5]

Liberty for all hands was granted in two ten-day periods. For those from the eastern United States with the means to make it home, this meant spending much of their leave traveling by train or air. The time at home was a short, but cherished, chance to reconnect with friends and family and enjoy the simple pleasures of life.[6]

Gunner's Mate 3rd Class Uel Smith was one of those heading home. Fearing a train would be too slow, Smith flew to Chicago to be with his wife, Darlene, who was expecting their second child any day. He arrived just in time for the birth of his son on the Fourth of July. The happy event was short lived as Smith had to depart the next day by train for his return trip to Seattle. Since he had been able to spend only a few days with his family since joining the navy in 1943, Smith was fortunate to be home when his son was born. Such was the life of a sailor at war.[7]

Some of the men took home stories of the fighting at Okinawa. Others chose either not to talk about it or to downplay the events of the last few months. When the time came to depart, they certainly had a better idea of

Photo 10.1 Uel and Darlene Smith during one of the few opportunities the war gave them to be together. Courtesy Uel Smith.

what lay ahead than they had the last time they left home—probably more desperate combat against a suicidal enemy, interspersed with tedious duties and hardships. For some, this made parting easier; for others, it made it harder.

For those who remained on the ship because they lacked the means to go home, the local bars offered a chance to chip a bit of paint off their personal decks. Some of *Tate*'s crew found themselves elbow to elbow at a bar with survivors of *Henrico*. The discussions in the smoky bar were sobering. Listening to the survivors' version of the events of April 2, 1945, the men came to grips with a grim reality. The terrific explosion they witnessed had caused great carnage, decapitating *Henrico*'s leadership, killing everyone on the bridge, and leaving only a junior officer in command. Knowing the same type of aircraft had also attacked *Tate* made the new knowledge even heavier to carry.[8]

The extended maintenance period allowed the delivery of the ship's paper-work, which had been following the ship from port to port across the Pacific, seemingly always one step behind. One unpleasant issue included in the ship's old business required the skipper's attention. Confronting Radioman 1st Class Charles Gries, Lieutenant Commander Lyon asked Gries directly, "Did you send a personal message for an army colonel in the 77th Division?" Gries answered, "Yes, it occurred while at Leyte." When requested by the colonel to do so, Gries had agreed to send the message when he made a trip to the flag-ship to pick up *Tate*'s mail. Lyon informed Gries that the message had changed the colonel's life insurance beneficiary from his wife to his daughter. The colonel had been killed at Okinawa, and now the officer's wife was protesting the settlement. Lyon made it clear that no more personal messages were to be sent regardless of the rank of the requestor. This was yet another sad affair in the countless lives that were touched by the war.[9]

After Rupert Lyon finally received his promotion to full commander, he commented, "I am going to get a commander's hat with its scrambled eggs and have my portrait made. Then I will pitch the hat into the sea and never say the word 'navy' again." Lyon never threw his hat overboard, but the remark clearly revealed how weary he was becoming of his service at sea. On July 19 *Tate* sailed, carrying 3,620 tons of general cargo, three army officers, and eighty-five enlisted personnel. Moving through intermittent heavy fog banks in the Straits of Juan de Fuca, the ship entered the Pacific Ocean. *Tate* was ordered to return to Guam after making one last stop to pick up a full complement of landing craft. To the delight of the crew, that stop was San Francisco.[10]

Tate had acquired a new exterior. Having been repainted piecemeal during the last eight months, the remnants of the camouflage wave pattern decorating the ship's hull when it left the Carolinas were now completely gone. On January 1, 1945, the Pacific Fleet discontinued its use of the geometric dazzle painting schemes that had been designed to obscure a ship from surface and submarine observation. Now that the main threat was from aircraft, a solid shade of neutral gray paint was used to help reduce aerial detection. Since the veteran ship was sporting a new paint job, the seemingly continuous work of the chipping and painting details dropped off. As *Tate* steamed south along the West Coast with a bellyful of cargo, Ens. Lewis Crew proudly compared his ship to a new luxury car. He described it as "quite heavily loaded and riding just like a Packard. She has a very distinctive coat of real dark battleship gray [paint]."[11]

As *Tate* cut through a fog bank, anxious men lined the forecastle, looking for an unmistakable landmark. Almost as if arranged, the ship emerged from the fog, sailing toward a majestic symbol of American culture—the Golden Gate Bridge. As the warship passed under the famous bridge, Chief Electrician W. Earl Gilmore was deeply moved. To him, both his ship and the bridge were examples of U.S. industry and ingenuity.

Tate spent four days in San Francisco Bay, where it picked up eight LCMs, fifteen LCVPs, and one LCP-L from the Naval Landing Force Equipment Depot in Albany, California. *Tate* also embarked six navy officers and 125 enlisted passengers from miscellaneous units for transport. With the ship suddenly needing some unexpected engine repairs, most of the crew had ample time to go ashore. The port lived up to its reputation as a liberty paradise, and for some of the men from California it offered a chance to visit family in the area. One of these men was the captain, a native of San Francisco.[12]

Commander Lyon gave officers Paul Leahy and Wendell M. Stewart the use of the ship's jeep and directions to his nearby home, along with an invitation to stop by for a drink. The two young officers accepted and were impressed with Lyon's beautiful residence and his delightful wife, Leona. Even more impressive to them were the Lyons' two attractive daughters, whom the officers then took out on the town. Lyon's trust in the young men evidently extended to more than their abilities as naval officers.[13]

Tate's mischievous monkey, Josephine, also rated liberty and ended up in a bar with some of the sailors. As friendly patrons offered her drinks, Josephine made a game of hopping across the barstools. The discerning primate was not interested in anything alcoholic until someone gave her a shot of scotch. The monkey again tried to jump the barstools. The comical results left everyone in the bar laughing hysterically.[14]

Upon returning to his ship, Commander Lyon found two enlisted men working in his cabin on a wooden bunk rail that he had requested. Wanting to please their popular captain, the men had built the rail out of redwood purchased in San Francisco. They were polishing the finished rail when Lyon entered and asked, "What's this?" The carpenter responded, "Well, sir, knowing that you are from redwood country, we wanted you to have a piece of

Photo 10.2 (Left to right) Quartermasters Marcel E. Hotte, Alfred S. Coslett, Blaine Lakes, and Donald L. Patrie enjoy liberty in San Francisco. All four men were in the navigation department. Courtesy Alfred S. Coslett.

California with you wherever you went." Shipfitter 2nd Class William Poli-kowski told his skipper, "The only important thing, sir, is that you are satisfied." Stunned by the gesture, the tears in Lyon's eyes assured the two seamen that he was indeed satisfied.[15]

Tate again passed westward beneath the Golden Gate Bridge across the Pacific toward the war. When he penned his thoughts for the ship's newspaper, Chief Electrician Gilmore effectively captured the spirit of the crew, who had defended their ship:

A Virgin Visits "Frisco"

A huge dark gray ship, one of our Navy's auxiliary cargo type, slid her nose then her eyes, and finally her long trim body from under a thin light fleecy blanket of fog one evening and beheld a sight that will remain for a long time on file in the office of memory of the men nestled so proudly within her bosom. For some, the original, but for others a carbon copy. The stage before them had been set many years before and had been gazed upon by millions of ships and peoples from all over the world. The leading role of this scene is played by the original star as should and ever shall be—a star as brilliant as her name, paralleled only by the Statue of Liberty—the Golden Gate Bridge, gateway to life, liberty, and the pursuit of happiness of millions of free peoples all over the world.

This little ship was a newcomer to the waters that flow beneath the Golden Gate Bridge, but not a newcomer to war. She's only eight months old, but since her body received its first impulse of live steam and electrical energy, thousands of nautical miles have slid beneath her trim bottom, irritated at times by the ocean parasite, the agitating and obnoxious barnacle. She's seen action off the Philippines, Okinawa, Ie Shima, and Kerama Retto, where the kamikaze has not been taught to show respect to the female sex, gender of which belongs to all our ships of the Navy. The men in her life and who live within her are bound with decency and respect for this maiden of the amphibious fleet. They fight with fury to protect her from the lustful raping kamikaze.

So, one can imagine her thrill of drawing water beneath this golden bridge and then come, to rest at anchor just beyond another bridge which is a symbol of America's ingenious engineers, the Oakland Bay Bridge, eight and one quarter miles in length, if only for a day or so. Thus she was afforded the opportunity to show her appreciation for the men she loves, to allow them a brief respite from war.

For one it was a twenty-four-hour paradise with his bride of five years, who was fortunate enough to get the last available seat on a bus to Frisco's southern neighbor, the incomparable metropolitan Los Angeles.

This little lady of the amphibs said "So long" a few days later. "So long, but I'll be back soon."

Her prayer is: "Almighty God, protect the freedom-loving men who go to sea with my sisters and me, men who protect us from our enemies. Speed the day when our missions are of peace and there are no enemies, and our cargoes are implements of civilization and not implements of war." [16]

The anxiety created by thoughts of what might lie ahead was already palpable. *Tate* had barely cleared the channel markers west of San Francisco Bay when a lookout reported a submarine on the surface. The ship went to general quarters. When the "submarine" turned out to be two whales, the whole event was laughed off. Even more amusing were some of the passengers on their first sea voyage manning the rails to feed the fish. Others stayed close to the lifelines, expecting an emergency. The green-gilled passengers were a source of amusement to the old salts of *Tate,* who were easily falling back into their accustomed routines. With the ship in great shape, they had time to enjoy the recreational activities that duty and circumstances had precluded over the last few months. The ship's band and glee club finally got to practice. One of the songs rehearsed was the "*Tate* Marching Song":[17]

Tate Marching Song

Sail on, you men of the *Tate,* with strength to win
Battles with fate, we will fight 'til our
Job is done, then homeward we will come
As we fly our colors bold and gay
May our motto be anchors aweigh and we'll
Fight for the right to win victory for the USA.[18]

The scuttlebutt from the message traffic fostered optimistic speculation. In a letter home, Ensign Crew wrote, "The news from Tokyo is looking up of late. In fact, some of the big 'goldies' are beginning to be a bit dubious as to whether an invasion will be necessary. I certainly hope not." The thought of returning to another Okinawa–like experience was on everyone's mind. In addition, they believed that the Japanese homeland would require conquering, just like Germany. Even the most optimistic imagination dared not dwell on the thought of invading Japan's main islands.[19]

On the morning of August 6, *Tate* anchored in Eniwetok Atoll and off-loaded six navy passengers. That afternoon the ship went to general quarters for twenty-five minutes when the whole atoll went on alert for an air attack that never materialized. It was an unwelcome reminder that the ship was indeed back in the war. On this same day, the fundamental energy of the universe was unleashed on the city of Hiroshima by a single B-29 bomber that dropped an atomic bomb. The Japanese were experiencing the culmination of the greatest industrial military effort in history and the vengeful wrath of a democracy aroused.[20]

After five days of swinging at anchor, *Tate* sailed for Guam. Along the way, all of the gun crews conducted antiaircraft drills on a towed sleeve. The night before arriving at Guam, Radioman 3rd Class John J. O'Neil was standing watch in the radio shack. O'Neil was searching the airwaves for music when he started receiving a diplomatic channel whose chatter implied that Japan's surrender was imminent. O'Neil notified the officer of the deck, who called the captain and the executive officer to the radio shack. Together they listened to the news, concluded it was real, and speculated that the war would soon be over. As the word quickly spread throughout the ship, the men on board the *Tate* optimistically began anticipating the end of the war.

The next morning, not far from Guam, the destroyer *Hopewell* (DD-681) came close along *Tate*'s port side with many of its crew on deck, waving and yelling. Someone on the destroyer threw onto *Tate*'s deck a rolled-up newspaper carrying the news of the atomic bombing of Japan. *Tate's* crew speculated on the impact of this new weapon and its possible link to the news that the war would soon end. Quartermaster 1st Class Alfred S. Coslett discounted the effects of the bomb, comparing it to the poison gas used in World War I. Quartermaster 2nd Class Donald Patrie disagreed, arguing that a single bomb that could destroy a whole city would have "effects that would live forever." To men who were facing a possible invasion of Japan's main islands, the new weapon seemed a logical method for clearing the beachheads before a landing. The ship arrived at Guam early on August 14 and waited for heavy traffic to clear before entering Apra Harbor and mooring alongside the refrigeration ship *Aldebaran* (AF-10).[21]

On August 15, 1945, the moment *Tate's* crew had been waiting for came to pass. An excited voice blared out over the ship's loudspeaker system, "Now hear this! The Japs have surrendered! The war is over!" Moments later, all of the ships in the crowded harbor began blowing their horns. Transports, auxiliaries, destroyers, cruisers, and a battleship joined in the awesome audio display celebrating the end of the costliest war in history. The chorus lasted for more than an hour as "joy reigned supreme."[22]

All of the men who were not on duty spilled onto the decks for an impromptu celebration. Ens. David Waller joined the party wearing only his shorts, and Ens. Alvin Joslyn was adorned with only a damp towel and a smile. Commander Lyon addressed his men over the ship's loudspeakers. A talented public speaker with the flair of a politician, Lyon made a stirring speech about the end of the war. Then, moving from profound eloquence to the practical, he hinted that the large quantity of beer on the ship that had been destined for delivery to the army might not arrive as scheduled. It was a hint that needed no interpretation. He further ordered his supply officer to ice down the beer before issuing each man two cans for dinner. The recreational fluids were soon flowing freely. Although Lyon cautioned the men to do their drinking below decks, the sailors of *Tate,* not wanting to be selfish with their good fortune, tossed beers to the crew of *Aldebaran,* which was moored alongside.[23]

The party lasted well into the night, and some of the men went ashore to celebrate and play baseball. The beer was tropical issue and thus contained a preservative that gave it a greenish tint. The sailors iced down the beverage inside 40-mm ammo cans that doubled as coolers. Some of the men who did not drink traded their share of the beer for Cokes or cash. The combination of alcohol, preservatives, and the sudden relief from stress prompted some of the men to abandon their inhibitions. One sailor climbed the wreck of a Japanese observation tower, where he found some abandoned gear. Pitching out the equipment, he created quite a display as the items crashed to earth. Military decorum gave way to spontaneity, and the men indulged themselves.[24]

Pulling a four-hour security watch, Shipfitter 2nd Class J. C. Bostic discovered that, after having a few drinks, the first thing many of the enlisted men wanted to do was fight. Moreover, there was little hope of bringing the situation under control. Near the end of his watch, he was jumped and beaten but never saw who hit him. With his face cut and one eye swelling shut, he went to the sick bay, only to find it filled with men injured while fighting. With his watch now over, Bostic gave in to the mood and, when offered some hidden liquor, got drunk. Climbing into his bunk still in uniform and in bad shape, he awoke to find that his .45-cal. pistol had been stolen right out of his holster. This was the first—and last—time in his life that Bostic ever drank.[25]

Some of the officers were also feeling the urge to vent their frustrations. When the executive officer, Lieutenant Commander Boland, found his skipper on the enlisted mess deck amid a bustling party, the captain handed him a can of beer and asked him to toast the enlisted men. Boland, whose strictly by-the-book, spit-and-polish, quick-to-the-whip personality had often come up against Lyon's fight-hard-and-play-hard style of command, refused the request. Lyon bristled, grabbed Boland by the shirt, and demanded, "You'll drink to these men if I have to pour it down you!" Reluctantly Boland guzzled down the beer, nodded, and then briskly went topside. The sailors who witnessed the event did not miss its implications. Boland had also refused to participate in the equator-crossing ceremony, a point that also chafed Lyon. Their captain's reputation as an amiable father figure of unquestioned strength and courage was a source of great pride to the crew. The scuttlebutt was that, before the war, Lyon was a sparring partner for former heavyweight boxing champion Jack Sharkey. The idea of Lyon teeing off on the executive officer was a source of much speculation and amusement among the enlisted men.[26]

As the celebration continued into the night, an officer, feeling no pain, showed up on the bridge during the midwatch and demanded—in the saltiest language—to get up a head of steam and head for home since the war was over. He was gingerly put to bed without incident. No one wanted to see anyone get into trouble on the day they had prayed for since the beginning of the war.

Back home in the United States, V-J Day spawned the biggest celebration the country had ever seen. The same could be said for the crew of *Tate*. Radioman 3rd Class John O'Neil, the first member of *Tate*'s crew to hear of the war's impending end, finished another night of radio watch before enjoying a cup of coffee and two beers for breakfast. It was a great day, he felt, to be in the service of the United States.[27]

Daylight revealed to *Tate*'s skipper that the festivities had resulted in a bit more of the fog of war than anticipated—his ship was surrounded by floating beer cans. Commander Lyon stated he had other ideas about how he would

Photo 10.3 Happy servicemen swarm over one of the two specially marked Betty bombers that carried the Japanese surrender delegation to Ie Shima.

leave the navy and ordered the fire hoses manned and the evidence sunk. The remaining passengers disembarked, and the ship shifted pier side to commence discharging its cargo with the help of CB stevedore teams.[28]

The ship's newspaper, the *Hot Tater,* issued a victory edition with a sketch of a rising sun with the caption "The Sun Shall Rise No More." The symbolism was obvious. The men thought the war was over, but officially it was only a cease-fire. The articles of surrender were yet to be formalized and signed by authorized Japanese emissaries. On Ie Shima, the island *Tate* had played a key role in conquering, a remarkable drama was unfolding. Men from the United States and Japan were risking their lives on a mission of peace. Gen. Douglas MacArthur, the supreme commander of the Allied forces in the Pacific, sent a message from his headquarters in Manila detailing the next step on the road to peace. The Japanese were to send a "competent representative empowered to receive in the name of the Emperor of Japan certain requirements for carrying into effect the terms of the surrender." The representative was to fly to Ie Shima in a specially marked aircraft painted white with large green crosses on the top and bottom of each wing and both sides of the fuselage. The aircraft, code-named Bataan, was to approach Ie Shima from the north and circle the airfield at one thousand feet. Radio frequencies were preestablished. Finally, six hours prior to departure, the Japanese were to broadcast their flight plan in English.[29]

On August 19, two days after the date MacArthur requested, a combined military and diplomatic delegation left Japan in two Betty bombers marked in compliance with MacArthur's message. Aware that elements in the Japanese military preferred to fight to the death, they first flew northeast and then south instead of directly to Ie Shima. Spotting several approaching aircraft, the Japanese were relieved to see they were American P-38 fighters assigned as their escort.[30]

On Ie Shima, nearly five thousand servicemen and more than fifty journalists and photographers gathered for the historic event. At 1230, the two Japanese Betty bombers appeared. They were flanked by two B-25s and four P-38s, with a single B-17 trailing after the group. The first Betty landed after circling overhead three times before being followed down by the second bomber. As Maj. John D. Fleming of the Army Garrison Force watched, he wondered whether these same Betty bombers had ever visited Ie Shima before under less favorable circumstances. Ie Shima was the closest land-based airfield to the Japanese home islands and was to play a vital role in the final assault on them. This fact was painfully obvious to the Japanese, who conducted frequent bombing raids against the island's airfields. As the Japanese delegation debarked from their aircraft, they formed two rows and faced the U.S. Army representatives. Major Fleming got a good look at the seventeen Japanese representatives and their aircrews. Later he noted in his diary that the head of the Japanese delegation, Lt. Gen. Torashiro Kawabe, the vice chief of the Imperial Army's general staff, was a "squat and sullen man." The Japanese neither bowed nor saluted either among themselves or with their American counterparts. In less than an hour, the Japanese delegation was transferred to a C-54 and flown to Manila to receive the terms of surrender.[31]

On the evening of August 21, the Japanese representatives returned to Ie Shima and boarded their aircraft for an immediate departure to Japan. As the first Japanese bomber taxied down the runway, it ran over a small embankment and was damaged. Although the damage was minor, it necessitated the plane's remaining overnight for repair by U.S. ground crews. "Irked at the turn of events," Lieutenant General Kawabe ordered nine of the delegation to depart immediately in a single plane for Kyushu, while the others would return the next day. When Kawabe's aircraft ditched along the Japanese coast due to a fuel leak, the Japanese delegation waded ashore through shallow water. Avoiding contact with Japanese military forces, the delegation carefully made its way back to Tokyo. The mission was successful, and the arrangements for the formal surrender ceremony were on track.[32]

While Tate's crew was unaware of the events that were taking place on Ie Shima, there was still plenty of work to be done as the ship continued unloading cargo for eight days. The ship then moved to Guam's outer harbor, where its remaining cargo was discharged using landing craft tanks. On August 26 the Tate sailed to rejoin its squadron in the memorable waters off Okinawa. There the veteran ship and crew would meet their old friends and find out who had survived.[33]

Chapter 11

CHINESE ODYSSEY

Mighty Sick of the Pacific

CUTTING THROUGH THE WAVES OF THE CENTRAL PACIFIC, *Tate* was steaming toward Ulithi to join Transport Squadron 17, bound for Okinawa. Sailing alone, the ship was still under orders to zigzag as protection against submarines. Arriving the next day, *Tate* dropped anchor in Ulithi's northern anchorage. On the morning of August 28, 1945, as the crew prepared to sail, the ship's throttle broke. As a result, *Tate* missed sailing with the squadron. Reassigned to a new convoy consisting of a refrigeration ship, an LST, seven merchant ships, and two destroyer escorts, they departed the next day into steadily worsening seas.[1]

From the starboard of the front row of three columns of ships, *Tate* launched a boat into heavy seas to transport a neurotic sailor from the destroyer escort *Raymond* (DE-341) to *Tate* for medical treatment. Watching the boat disappear behind the building waves provided a daunting reminder that they were still facing plenty of dangers. The stricken sailor on *Raymond* had broken down in the face of these same hazards. Now some men from *Tate* were facing additional perils—in a small craft—to bring him medical treatment. The end of the war had produced an emotional letdown. Dying now would be even more tragic than being killed in combat, a fate the crew of *Tate* had escaped. The war had provided focus, and the future was now perhaps more uncertain than before.[2]

As the convoy sailed toward Okinawa, events in Tokyo Bay formally ended the war on September 2. Upon sighting Okinawa, *Tate*'s column of ships peeled off from the convoy. With *Tate* in the lead, they sailed to Buckner Bay, where Transport Squadron 17 was anchored while awaiting its departure for Inchon, Korea, the next morning.[3]

Because of operational requirements, accidents, and battle damage, the composition of Transport Squadron 17 had frequently changed since its formation seven months earlier. The last ship to leave the squadron was the attack transport *LaGrange*. Just before sunset on August 13, 1945, *LaGrange* was resting at anchor in Buckner Bay. Relying on the picket ships for early warning, only a few of *LaGrange*'s guns were manned at the time. Most of its men were in the crew's mess watching the movie *The Flying Tigers*. Even though the film was showing for perhaps the tenth time, the crew was in high spirits as they anticipated the end of the war. As the Japanese aircraft were bombing and strafing the Flying Tigers' airfield on the movie screen, two sailors on watch on *LaGrange*'s signal bridge spotted a Japanese aircraft. They could even see the pilot, who was flying approximately 300 feet away, looking back at them. Extending their middle fingers, the sailors waved their hands at the pilot while yelling a warning to the nearby officer of the deck. The aircraft then quickly disappeared behind a nearby mountain on Okinawa.

Since the plane had made no hostile actions, the men wondered whether the war was indeed over. They then sighted the same plane heading directly for their ship. Before *LaGrange* could react, the Japanese aircraft climbed from wave-top level and dived into the deckhouse, exploding into the ship's communications compartment where men had gathered to listen for the news of the war's end. A second aircraft then attacked *LaGrange,* coming under fire from several neighboring ships. One of *LaGrange*'s 40-mm guns struck the kamikaze, sending it out of control and into the top of the ship's king post before it careened into the water and exploded. *LaGrange* lost 21 men, while another 89 were wounded and gained the unlucky distinction of being the last ship casualty of World War II.[4]

Arriving too late to sail with the squadron, *Tate* cruised around Okinawa to Hugushi with several other AKAs. There the ship loaded 917 tons of cargo, including 478 tons of vehicles from the signal corps, engineers, and quartermaster truck corps of the Tenth Army. Also taken on board were fifteen officers and 155 enlisted army personnel. Shortly after completing the loading on September 10, a sailor fell from the main deck into an LCM alongside. The unlucky seaman cracked several of his ribs but remained on board as an unpleasant reminder that even peacetime service at sea was dangerous. Early the next day *Tate* sailed with three other attack cargo ships and a single destroyer escort for Inchon, Korea. The small convoy was carrying part of the second echelon of troops and equipment for the occupation of Korea. Tasked with providing security in the void of the surrendering Japanese, the troops were in a hurry to arrive in order to dissuade the Soviets from making any further advances on the Korean peninsula.[5]

Before departing Okinawa, Ens. Lewis Crew posted a letter in which he happily wrote that "all censoring had stopped." He also said, "The Skipper authorized shorts for all hands so Crew has been sporting a very deep bronze color of late." The young officer also boasted about a smoker the officers had organized. The party included a wrestling tournament with the *Tate*'s captain taking on all comers. Several plucky enlisted men accepted the challenge, but none were able to defeat their large and powerful skipper. Rupert E. Lyon proved once again he was truly the master of *Tate*. Even with the temporary boost this social event gave his spirits, Ensign Crew still stated that he was "mighty sick of the Pacific."[6]

To their dismay, some of the sailors found army personnel asleep in their bunks. A sailor at sea does not have much to call his own, but his bed is definitely his private territory. The situation became contentious before the officers straightened it out. Their solution was to order the soldiers to stay out of the navy's berthing spaces. Even more disturbing was the news that *Tate* would have to pass through seven lines of moored mines while navigating off obsolete prewar charts. With the aid of a Japanese pilot and a Korean interpreter, the rest of the squadron, which had sailed without *Tate,* had successfully passed through this gauntlet a few days before. Vigilance was required, and extra lookouts were posted to keep an eye peeled for mines, as *Tate's* convoy passed through the minefield in daylight while the rough seas continued to build.[7]

In a heavy squall, *Tate's* convoy reached the approach to Inchon on the morning of September 13 and briefly anchored. Just five days earlier, the United States had landed its first ground forces in Korea at Inchon. The next day, the Japanese forces had formally surrendered all of Korea south of the 38th parallel, ending thirty-five years of Japanese rule in Korea. Soviet forces already controlled the northern portion of Korea. General MacArthur repeated the scenario five years later on September 15, 1950, during his daring high-stakes landing at Inchon.[8]

Following the destroyer escort *Nawman* (DE-416), *Tate* sailed down the channel to Inchon, where it anchored and immediately began discharging cargo. On the pier at Inchon were Japanese troops at attention, their rifles stacked, awaiting their formal surrender to the U.S. Army troops that were already ashore.[9]

Tropical Storm Ursula also arrived in Korea at the same time as *Tate,* but the bad weather was not the worst of the ship's problems. In an official report, Commander Lyon described the cooperation between the army and the navy as inadequate. "This ship and several others unloading by small boat were singularly dependent upon the state of the tide, whose range prevented certain discharging operations in the tidal basin at low tide. The Army unloading teams on the beach, without regard to these considerations, followed a routine meal schedule, without relief, with 1½ hours allowed for each meal. This greatly impeded operations." Lyon also expressed his displeasure that the landing ships mechanical (LSMs), which were required to offload his cargo of vehicles, were instead unloading low-priority merchant ships. *Tate* and the other ships in the task unit, however, had operational commitments requiring "a speedy return to Okinawa." Despite these difficulties, the ship was unloaded in thirty-six hours after finally getting a good twelve hours of service out of the LSMs.[10]

At noon on September 15 *Tate,* along with three other attack cargo ships, got under way and rendezvoused with two high-speed destroyer transports and two destroyer escorts. The attack cargo ships formed two columns with the other ships in a screening disposition.[11]

On the afternoon of September 16, advisories indicated that Typhoon Ida would pass close to the track of the convoy. Receiving orders by radio to ballast all available tank spaces, the ships in light draft began securing their boats and equipment for heavy seas. Conditions worsened as the typhoon passed north of Okinawa. Rolls of thirty-five degrees from the beam seas were endangering the landing craft, so the convoy slowed and changed course several times before finally heading northwest into the teeth of the building waves. The storm also caused a traffic problem as numerous ships cleared out of the anchorages west of Okinawa and crossed the sector northwest of the island. Several times during the night of September 17, the ships in *Tate's* convoy ran the risk of collision.[12]

With the fate of his ship and others at stake, *Tate's* captain, the officer in tactical command of the convoy, ordered the ships to disperse, fearing a collision if they stayed in formation. Commander Lyon took personal control of the situation, issuing frequent orders throughout the night, changing speeds, and guiding his ship over each monstrous wave. When the ship nosed into a wave too hard, its bow plunged downward, causing the propeller to come out of the water, dramatically spinning up the screw and sending an ominous shudder down the length of the ship. Lyon's continual presence, obvious experience, and confidence were a comfort to all who were on the bridge that long night.[13]

By dawn on September 18, conditions improved enough to allow the convoy to head for the Hagushi anchorage, where they arrived in mid-morning. Receiving orders via visual signals on September 21, *Tate* joined its old compatriot, the *Chilton,* and began loading cargo with its boats. While at Okinawa, Lt. Walter Hall relieved Lt. Cdr. Kells Boland as *Tate's* executive officer. Boland was the first of *Tate's* crew to get orders home, less than three weeks after the war officially ended. On the morning of September 24, *Tate* moved to the Nago Wan anchorage, where the ship finished loading the remainder of its 1,325 tons of cargo.[14]

On September 26, *Tate,* now at last with Transport Squadron 17, set sail for Taku, China, with five officers and 147 men of the 1st Marine Division. Known as the "Old Breed," the 1st Marine Division had fought in three of the most brutal campaigns of the war: Guadalcanal, Peleliu, and Okinawa. Similar to the U.S. Army troops that landed in Korea, the U.S. Marines were providing a 50,000-man vanguard in North China as part of a postwar move against the Communists in Asia. Nearly 500,000 Nationalist Chinese soldiers from southern China would join the marines in a personnel sealift that proved to be several times larger than the entire Okinawa campaign.[15]

As the convoy entered the Yellow Sea on September 26, it encountered at least eight floating mines. One passed alongside the port column with *Tate* in the rear. Eight ships fired on the mine in succession. *Tate* had the last crack at it and fired 160 rounds of 20-mm, 264 rounds of 40-mm, and one five-incher without effect. Keeping a sharp lookout for these explosive devices was a necessity. Many of the thousands of moored mines planted by U.S. B-29 bombers in the East China Sea and the Yellow Sea were now adrift, cut free by fishermen, mine-sweeping operations, and the typhoons that had ravaged the region.[16]

As the squadron pushed north into the Yellow Sea, the escorts spotted several Chinese junks and investigated them. The mission of the escorts was to land the marines in a volatile region containing large numbers of combatants from several distinct military entities. The Soviet Red Army, the defeated Japanese Imperial Army, Chinese Communists under Mao Tse-tung, Generalissimo Chiang Kai-shek's Nationalist forces, and opportunistic bands of roving thugs led by warlords were all poised to take advantage of the simmering postwar political chaos in Manchuria.[17]

On August 9 the Soviets launched a massive invasion into Manchuria. More than 1.5 million men participated in the campaign, which covered a front of more than 2,500 miles. Following the fall of Germany, the Red Army began shifting troops east across Asia from the battlefields of Europe. The Soviets made multiple thrusts from the coastline of the Sea of Japan to the wastelands of Inner Mongolia. This was the first time the Japanese had faced an attack on a continental scale. Using the tactics learned during their four years of war in Europe, the Red Army achieved decisive results, advancing from 300 to 570 miles into Manchuria in just nine days—before the cessation of hostilities.[18]

On the last day of September, *Tate*'s squadron anchored off Taku Bar at the mouth of the Hai Ho River in the Gulf of Chihli. Taku was thirty-six miles downstream from Tientsin, the cultural and intellectual center of northern China and a key industrial complex for textiles, chemicals, and iron and steel production. Tientsin's important rail junction was the gateway to China's ancient capital of Peiping. During the Boxer Rebellion of 1900, the strategic Taku-Tientsin-Peiping corridor was the focus of much of the fighting. In response, marines who were defending U.S. interests landed in Taku before advancing first to Tientsin and then to Peiping, another eighty miles inland. Now history was repeating itself, with the marines returning to Taku-Tientsin.

Tate remained at anchor until October 2, while ships with more important cargoes unloaded at the staging area in Taku. Using landing craft flying both the U.S. and Chinese Nationalist flags, the vessels transported their cargoes upriver to Tientsin.

As the marines came ashore, the local inhabitants cheered, hoping their presence would at last bring some stability to the area. Being greeted by friendly civilians was a new experience for the marines. Their previous contacts with noncombatants during the war had resulted either in mass suicides or bewildered submission. The marines' primary mission was to accept the surrender and supervise the repatriation of the Japanese forces in the region. This was an enormous undertaking since more than 630,000 armed Japanese were still in Manchuria. Complicating the job was a fermenting civil war between the Chinese Nationalists and the Communists. Some of the Japanese were even taking sides with their former Chinese adversaries. The discipline and military expertise of the Japanese were now attractive commodities to both the Nationalists and the Communists, who just a few weeks before had both fought against the Japanese.[19]

Tate spent five days unloading cargo, using its own boats as well as Chinese lighters. Finding himself with a chance to look around Taku, Electrician's Mate 2nd Class Theron W. Hokanson noticed a silver service for sale for fifteen U.S. dollars, but he did not have any cash. Returning the next day with his money, Hokanson found the price was now seventy dollars. When he asked about the price increase, a marine in the same shop chimed in: "Damn sailors come in and cause inflation." After their country's long occupation by the Japanese, the Chinese merchants understood American money surprisingly well.[20]

The commander of Transport Division 50 ordered *Tate* to pick up a battalion of Chinese troops from a village near the mouth of the Yellow River, a short cruise to the south of Taku. Expecting that the Chinese might have as many as forty mules, a work detail began constructing wooden stalls in the number one and number five cargo holds. After several days of waiting for the Chinese, marine 2nd Lt. Dewey Maltsberger went ashore to investigate. There he discovered that the designated embarkation point was nothing more than a village of mud huts. Maltsberger found corpses in the streets and realized that the sympathetic locals were too scared to remove them. Obviously, the rendezvous had gone awry, so *Tate* departed, leaving two LCMs behind for service in the Taku boat pool.

Coxswain Charles B. Hathaway was one of those remaining at Taku with his boat crew. The boat pool's assignment was to keep the river open for the small ships and boats supplying Tientsin. This involved using the LCMs as tugs to turn the ships in the narrow river and to remove obstructions the Communists had placed in the river. Sleeping on the deck of their LCM under a makeshift tent and eating off the good graces of a nearby patrol boat, the boat crew's duty was both arduous and mundane. Heading south away from its two forlorn LCM crews, *Tate*'s convoy was now under tactical control of the attack transport *Crescent City* (APA-21), bound for Manila Bay in the Philippines.[21]

On October 8 the convoy began heading into increasingly rough seas. Riding high without cargo, the ship's gasoline and ammunition spaces were flooded for ballasting, and later that night the ships reversed course to evade Typhoon Louise. The tropical cyclone was approaching from the south and packing winds of more than one hundred knots, with seas of 30–35 feet. Making a series of course changes during the night to minimize the storm's impact, the convoy eventually resumed a southerly course.[22]

Below decks, the situation was grim. Many of the men were seasick. After being violently tossed about in their beds, some of the sleepy men resorted to lashing themselves to their berths. Expecting the worst, many of them went to bed wearing life jackets. Seaman 1st Class "Forty" Salerno was ordered aloft to secure a wildly swinging cargo hook that was endangering the boats. After surviving that harrowing ordeal, he took refuge in his bed on the top tier of three bunks. Trying to prevent being thrown out of his bunk during the storm was bad enough, but a pessimistic sailor in a neighboring top-tier bunk kept repeating, "I'll never see my wife and son again." Fed up with his moaning, Salerno told the sailor, "I hope the ship goes over on the next roll so I won't have to listen to you any more!"[23]

There would be no rest for Chief Water Tender Henry Noga. Known as the Oil King, his job was one of most important ones on *Tate* during a storm. It was Chief Noga's duty to keep the ship ballasted by strategically pumping water and fuel oil in the ship's tanks. Under such conditions, pumping seawater into the fuel tanks was a matter of survival. Each tank had both a high and a low suction point for pumping out fluid from the top and bottom of the tank. Knowing the level of the burnable oil was the key issue. Lowering a sinker on a line down a sounding tube into each tank and getting accurate measurements was a difficult task as the ship rolled and pitched in the heavy seas.[24]

The storm was taking a toll not only on the crew but also on the ship as some key welds began failing. A crack that developed in a fuel tank threatened to spill oil into the engine room. After pumping out the damaged tank, welders made emergency repairs. Then another long, jagged tear opened up in the deck of the number one hold. During some of the heavier rolls, seawater blew down the smokestack, threatening to put out the ship's boilers. Chief Noga lamented, "[We] can't burn seawater," and then went back to his vital tasks. Watching the bulkheads bending and bulging below decks, Seaman 1st Class Zeblin V. Midgett decided that, if the ship was destined to sink, it should happen in the daylight since he "would rather drown during the day than at night" in total darkness.[25]

The flooding of the ammunition spaces was a mistake since they could be only partially flooded, and the moving water was adding momentum to the already dangerous rolls. Removing the water required lowering a submersible pump, along with a man on a tether, to handle a hose running up to the main deck. Pumping the spaces out was a risky job, but it was done without incident. Things were not any better in the radio shack, either, as the crew listened to the distress calls from floundering ships that had men in the water. There was nothing to do except hope that *Tate* would not share a similar fate.[26]

The ship continued taking thirty-eight-degree rolls, hesitating as it heeled over, making many men wonder whether it would capsize. From the low side of the ship during a heavy roll, green water towered above the bridge. A few of the more seaworthy members of the crew, such as Signalman 2nd Class Willard Whitcome, found playing basketball in the empty cargo hold as the ship tossed them about to be a real adventure.[27]

At 2055 on October 10, the ship took a sudden forty-two-degree roll. An LCM with an LCVP nested inside filled with water and broke loose from the top of the number four hatch. Securing the boats to pad eyes on the deck were one-inch chains from the bow and stern, as well as two ¾-inch steel cables cross-griped with turnbuckles over the gunwales. The pad eyes tore loose from the deck, and both boats passed over a cargo winch and into the sea, carrying away the guardrail. A warning followed from *Tate* over the TBS radio to "Beware of small boats in the sea." Fearing more than just boats had gone over the side, a muster was held below decks to account for all hands.[28]

The cooks secured the galley due to the violent weather. Chow was limited to finger food and sandwiches of bologna and cheese, more commonly referred to as horse cock and bung binder. Laboring in the boiler room along with Chief Noga, Water Tender 2nd Class W. T. Drake complained, "We only got spam and crackers to eat and, worst of all, no coffee!"[29]

The typhoon conditions persisted into the next day. By nightfall the weather had improved enough to increase speed to fourteen knots. Chief Nago had spent fifty-two hours on his feet fighting the storm. For many of the crew the storm was more frightening than the kamikazes off Okinawa. Riding out a typhoon in an area littered with floating mines was not how anyone had expected to spend his postwar service. The battered ship passed by the dark shores of the Bataan Peninsula and the barren, forlorn silhouette of the fortress of Corregidor, arriving in Manila Bay on the morning of October 13, where it finally dropped anchor, out of reach of the cruel sea at last.[30]

For three days *Tate* lay at anchor in the shallow waters of Manila Bay among a graveyard of sunken Japanese hulks. On October 16 the ship transferred its five remaining LCMs to neighboring ships. The following morning the ship made the short trip to Subic Bay to pick up eight LCMs and an LCVP before returning to anchor in Manila Bay for another four days. The cruise book of the attack transport *Mountrail* in *Tate*'s squadron describes the heavily damaged Manila, known as the "Paris of the Orient," as only "a caricature of a city, a Memorial to the destruction of modern war. Flame, steel and high explosives had gutted every structure of any size; the jagged skyline presented a pitiable and terrifying scene of destruction." It "looked like a scene from the seventh ring of hell as described in Dante's *Inferno*." Still, the war-torn capital of the Philippines offered many opportunities for recreation from its "numerous bars, bistros, and gaudy night clubs that the enterprising natives had built out of rubble and palm fronds." Concerned about the spread of cholera in the devastated city, the ship's medical officer gave everyone an immunization, leaving many of the crew "walking around a little heavy on the port side."[31]

The shrewd natives took advantage of the huge influx of servicemen in the Philippines. The souvenir business was in full swing, and rampant inflation made the prices exorbitant. Contraband liquor containing wood alcohol was a local indulgence of great concern to the navy. Warnings failed to dissuade some sailors, and several of *Tate*'s crew became ill from the bad booze.

One of the more wholesome entertainment opportunities on tap was an army versus navy football game played at "Rizal Coliseum, which had been spared from the destruction for some unknown reason. Both teams boasted pro ball players as well as college gridders." Ens. Lewis Crew attended the event and found it "an exciting game to watch, but the gang from [the] navy got dunked as over 50,000 swabbies and doughboys screamed their lungs sore. I kinda missed the characters with the bear skin coats and the pocket-sized pints, but that will come again. It didn't seem right without the bright plaid colors. Somehow the army drabs and the navy whites just can't paint the unforgettable picture of a typical Saturday afternoon collegiate clash."[32]

Tate's crew, including some sailors who were not granted shore leave, took full advantage of their liberty in Manila. Knowing they were on the wrong side of the rulebook, the errant sailors really celebrated. The shore patrol from the *Tate* eventually rounded them up and confined them in a muddy pen before putting them on a boat heading back to their ship. Between the mud and wading knee-deep through the black water in Manila Bay to board the boats, their dress white uniforms were now anything but white. Ensign Crew, the officer in charge of "playing nurse maid" to this wayward bunch of sailors, was called "every expression in the books for being inhuman." It was a minor miracle that they all made it back. Some of the drunken sailors were unloaded from the boat in a cargo net. As the crew hauled the men on board, arms and legs hung from the netting like the limbs of dead sheep. Since so many men were involved in the illegal liberty incident, no formal disciplinary actions were taken, and the men had only their hangovers as punishment.[33]

Before *Tate* set sail on October 23, the mail arrived. This was a pleasant surprise because a great deal of the mail had been lost when Typhoon Louise destroyed the fleet post office on Okinawa. One lonely officer described the incident quite dramatically: "Today was a day of days for we of the *Tate*—Mail Came!! We live once again."[34]

Nonetheless, the mail did not always bring good news. A sailor from Pennsylvania, who had already received a letter a few months earlier telling him that his brother, a marine, had been killed on Iwo Jima, got more bad news. His best friend had gotten the sailor's fiancée pregnant. Although his shipmates rallied around him to help lift his spirits, the despondent sailor was inconsolable. The thoughts of home that he had clung to in hard times were now darkened by the betrayal.[35]

It took only forty-eight hours for *Tate*'s squadron to cross the South China Sea to Hong Kong. That time was spent constructing wooden latrines and metal urinal troughs for the estimated one thousand Chinese soldiers they would be picking up. The ship's carpenter boasted that the "outdoor Boy Scout rice pot latrines were just like the officer's wardroom" and "would accommodate 45 at one sitting." For Shipfitter 2nd Class J. C. Bostic, who was in charge of general repairs, it was the biggest construction project undertaken during his service on the ship.[36]

On October 25 *Tate* anchored off Hong Kong. Arriving two days earlier, *Chilton* had paved the way for its squadron as the first U.S. flagship to visit Hong Kong and nearby Kowloon after the war. At the entrance to Victoria Bay, pirate gangs in dugout canoes and sampans, living off blackmail tolls collected from shipping, welcomed *Chilton*. Unimpressed, the flagship simply steamed past the rickety boats before receiving a formal military tribute from two British aircraft carriers and several smaller Royal Navy warships inside Victoria Bay. When it was *Tate*'s turn, the vessel sailed into Kowloon without a pilot or a tug. Coxswain Mike Larsen watched with amazement as *Tate* brushed a rotten wooden pier, moving it several feet before it rebounded. Several huge wharf rats were sent scurrying for safety.

Throughout the night, 986 troops from the 1st Battalion, 161st Regimental Headquarters, 54th Division, 13th Chinese National Army boarded *Tate*. No one was prepared for what they saw. The soldiers' condition was appalling. *Tate*'s medical officer, Lieutenant Heinan, stood at the gangway and inspected each man as he passed, looking for obvious signs of communicable disease. Men were excluded for a variety of infectious illnesses, including leprosy. After passing inspection, one of the soldiers leaned over the gangway to fill his canteen from the ship's graywater discharge.[37]

Even more disturbing than the general health of the soldiers was the way in which they carried their explosives on board. Ens. Alvin Joslyn described the situation in detail in a letter home:

> We have carried many different units since we came out here but this group is in a class by itself. The greatest number of troops we have ever had before was 250, we now have on board 1000. Where before we had the entire ship with cargo, all that they had went into the bottom of one of the holds of the ship. It consisted of rice, some small caliber guns, ammunition, hand grenades in burlap sacks, and some wooden crates. The army is equally interesting [as] they are well clothed in new thin cotton uniforms. Their arms are modern and look like our last war rifles with a few automatic rifles. The amazing part of the story is their age. There were boys who came aboard who were I am sure [no] more than 9 or 10 years of age. They were all rigged out in new uniforms. One chap had a half dozen grenades strapped to him and we had to hold him up for a while until the grenades could be stowed with the rest of the ammunition. Another one of the same age came up lugging a couple of mortar shells. There were a large number who came aboard that looked no more than 14 or 15 years toting rifles that were as long as they were tall. Fully 50% of them were under 20 years old. I got the full meaning of some writer who some time ago said that the only thing that the Chinese army had to put between the Japanese armored might and their country was their bodies and their spirits.[38]

The Chinese ammunition was stored in the bottom of the number three cargo hold and surrounded by stacks of rice bags to keep it from being disturbed and to absorb the shock of a possible accidental explosion. Disease and a lack of commonsense safety practices by the Chinese were threatening to accomplish what the Japanese had failed to do: inflict a single fatality on the lucky crew of *Tate*.[39]

The makeshift latrines, a source of so much labor and humor, proved unsatisfactory. The Chinese stated that, because toilet seats were unsanitary, they did not use them. They preferred to stand while defecating. Dismayed that their hard work was wasted, Shipfitter 2nd Class William Polikowski and others in the construction and repair division began modifying the toilets. The seats were removed, and boards were placed on either side of the holes. A horizontal stay was attached for the Chinese to hold on to while defecating. They had the appearance of a closet with a hole in the bottom, hanging over the sides of the ship. A Chinese lighter coming alongside of *Tate* clipped some of the stalls, damaging several of them enough to necessitate rebuilding. Providing the Chinese with toilets had become a major enterprise.[40]

On the morning of October 26, the convoy set sail for Dairen, Manchuria, under the command of the attack cargo ship *Aquarius* (AKA-16) in view of the fact that the squadron's flagship, *Chilton,* had already departed. *Aquarius,* manned by a coast guard crew, was a veteran of both the European and the Pacific theater and had an impressive eight battle stars to its credit. Once at sea, the Chinese troops began getting sick in large numbers. The new latrines were not being used, and the ship was becoming unsanitary by any standards. A Chinese laundry was set up on the fantail, and the men washed their clothes in the urinal troughs, which had salt water continually running through them. They would then hang their clothes off the 5"/38 mount. Some of the Chinese were urinating in the troughs, while others washed themselves in the same water. Human excrement was on the decks, and the doctor was overwhelmed with the number of men needing treatment.[41]

Doc Heinan was obtaining missionary-like status with the suffering Chinese. He set up shop on the bow in the morning and on the stern in the afternoon, treating as many soldiers as he could. The most frequent ailment was open sores, which were often as large as silver dollars. He painted the sores with a cotton swab dipped in the antiseptic Gentian Violet and then sprinkled on sulfa powder. The sores responded quickly to the treatment, thus making the doctor the most popular soul on the ship. A more serious matter was severe diarrhea, which was complicated by a poor diet and a tendency for those who were cooped up by their illness to develop seasickness. Heinan also diagnosed four cases of yellow fever, but there was no danger of transmission since there are no mosquitoes at sea.[42]

Tate was not alone in its unsavory experience with the Chinese. Large numbers of transports were moving troops up the Chinese coast to Manchuria. One of the ships that shared a similar fate was the attack transport *Clinton* (APA-144). In an effort to halt an epidemic of seasickness, *Clinton*'s captain required the Chinese commanding general to sign a notice that contained ten rules that would be posted throughout the ship in both Chinese and English:

2 November 1945
Officers and Men of the Chinese 52nd Army, attention:
Subject: American Sailors' Remedy for Seasickness
You may have wondered why American sailors aboard the USS *Clinton* do not get seasick. If you follow the prescribed rules below, it [sic] will help you avoid seasickness, like they do.

1. American sailors do not stay in their quarters all day. They come up on deck and breathe fresh air at least twice a day.
2. They air their bedding on deck once a day.
3. They do not eat garlic and salt fish.

Photo 11.1 Tate's medical officer Frederick C. Heinan was an obstetrician from Milwaukee, Wisconsin. Courtesy Carole Hanzel.

4. They do not cook in sleeping quarters or bring cooked food from the mess hall.
5. They bathe once a day.
6. They wash uniforms every day and dry their wet clothing on deck.
7. American sailors do not have bowel movements in the urinal trough. They defecate in the white enamel bowls for that purpose.
8. They scrub their compartment floors every day and rinse with clean sea water.
9. There is no need to store firecrackers or loaded weapons in your sleeping quarters. All evil spirits have been driven from the USS *Clinton* by qualified U.S. doctors with strong joss. American sailors store these items in the ship's armory.
10. The 52nd Army's regimental surgeon has agreed that, on this ship, all medical work is American doctor's rice bowl. While you are aboard, only U.S. navy doctors will treat you.[43]

The rules were as much about safety and the well-being of everyone on board as they were about seasickness. Although most of the Chinese were ignorant of even the most obvious facts of safety and sanitation, some of their officers were trying to make a difference. The commanding general and his interpreter, a recently liberated Canadian prisoner of war, toured the ship to address the Chinese. In an effort to improve the situation, they went from cargo hold to cargo hold, packed with soldiers, giving the same speech. After Commander Lyon joined the group, he asked what the general was saying. Lyon was informed that the general was appealing to his men's pride, which was keeping them from showing what they perceived as weakness in front of their American allies. Shortly after finishing his speech, the general turned away and vomited in front of Lyon. The condition of the Chinese was so pathetic it was almost humorous.[44]

On October 29, after three days at sea, Pvt. Tong De Shu died. *Tate*'s doctor determined that an intestinal infection was the cause of death. Rumors spread that Tong had fallen through a cargo hatch due to his weakened condition. With the health of more than thirteen hundred men at stake, Commander Lyon understood that the cause of death was not as important as disposing of the body. As *Tate*'s crew quickly prepared the man for burial, the Chinese general protested to Commander Lyon. He wanted the body kept on board until they arrived in port for burial according to Chinese customs. Lyon's response was terse and definitive: "He goes over the side, and we would do the same thing if he was one of our men." Ensign Joslyn wrote home that his captain was "at somewhat of a loss as to what kind of service should be held since you could not hold a regular navy service for a Chinese soldier. Consequently, it was very brief. The Chinese adjutant called the group to attention, a salute was held, and the flag lowered to half mast and then the body was committed to the sea." Not all of the Chinese mustered for the burial. Most remained below, and some, to the dismay of *Tate*'s crew, remained on their hands and knees not far away, gambling on the deck. They were either too focused on their game or too callous to care.[45]

Tensions were building with the Soviets, who were taking exception to so many troops moving in their direction. As the *Tate*'s squadron headed north to Dairen, these tensions caused several changes in the ship's orders before the final destination became Chinwangtao. Adding credence to these concerns, several Soviet aircraft buzzed the convoy, giving *Tate*'s squadron something to worry about other than floating mines for a change. The intentions of the aircraft were unknown, and the U.S. ships had no orders to engage Soviet forces. So, to discourage such aggressive behavior, the guns were manned and began tracking the aircraft as a warning to avoid the ships and their experienced anti-aircraft gunners. Chinwangtao was a strategic all-weather port connected by rail to the vital coal-mining area of Tangshan. The remaining Japanese puppet troops were still fighting the Communists in the hills outside the town, and the U.S. Marines had seen action in the area. *Tate* was heading for a bad neighborhood.[46]

During the transit to Chinwangtao, the senior officer present afloat (SOPA) on *Aquarius* frequently rebuked ships for being out of line or not maintaining the proper spacing. While his motive was surely to keep the ships in a tight formation to reduce their chances of hitting a mine, the perception on *Tate* was that the convoy needed continual management by the SOPA. As they approached their destination, the SOPA insisted that the ships anchor in the center of their assigned circular berths. All of the ships were instructed to observe *Aquarius* performing this task. Dropping two LCMs to nudge the *Aquarius* into place, the flagship eased into its designated position by taking navigational shots off landmarks. When the ship dropped anchor, it plunged straight through the bottom of one of the LCMs as its crew bailed out. When the anchor was hoisted, it snagged the LCM, pulling it partially through the hawse pipe, producing a horrible sound as its metal hull twisted and collapsed. No further chatter was heard from the SOPA.[47]

The embarrassment of the SOPA was especially amusing to *Tate*'s captain. At Okinawa, Commander Lyon was reprimanded for steaming around his flagship as it lingered at the entrance to the anchorage area, causing the ships behind it to stack up in a dangerous manner. Already having seen one flagship grounded in front of him at Leyte, Lyon was not about to put his ship at risk in blind obedience to rules contradicting his common sense. He was an extraordinary ship handler and demonstrated obvious confidence in maneuvering in tight spots. Unfortunately, some of his superiors viewed Lyon's ship-handling ability as a contemptuous exhibition of his skill. This was an example of the different leadership styles between the regular navy and the reserve officers who had considerable nonmilitary maritime experience.[48]

On November 1 *Tate* anchored briefly in Shallow Bay at Chinwangtao before moving to a pier to disembark troops. Unlike the unloading operations with U.S. troops carrying tons of equipment, the Chinese merely picked up what little they had and walked off. It was all over in a few hours, and the ship again anchored in Shallow Bay.[49]

In the first wave of postwar discharges, nineteen enlisted men left *Tate* for transfer to the continental United States. A points system determined who was eligible for discharge. Points were awarded for the number of months in service, the number of months overseas, combat decorations, participation in campaigns in which a battle star was awarded, being married, and each minor child up to a maximum of three. It was a promising sight to see your shipmates going home, but most of the remaining men only became more impatient for their own departure. One of the men heading home was Gunner's Mate 3rd Class Uel Smith. He later regretted his decision to leave the ship on his first opportunity. Transported first to the familiar and bleak Taku Bar, Smith spent nearly a month there under unfavorable conditions awaiting a ride home to the States.[50]

Chinwangtao was full of depravity and brutality resulting from years of war and occupation. For some of the more adventurous souls, there was limited liberty in town. One of those testing his luck was Chief Water Tender Noga. As he left *Tate,* he observed Chinese soldiers receiving tea and rice as they disembarked. When one of the young soldiers, not more than twelve, asked for seconds, he instead received a savage blow in the face from a rifle butt. After a few hours in town, Noga missed *Tate*'s last boat. Now with the tide out and the sounds of shooting nearby, he was sorry he had ever left the ship. Noga managed to hitch a ride on a small boat from a destroyer, arriving back on *Tate* feeling "ten years older."[51]

From the signal bridge, Ensign Joslyn peered through binoculars at the Great Wall of China, about ten miles away, twisting along the jagged peaks that rose abruptly from the cultivated coastal plain. "It appeared as if it were a giant snake winding its way down to the sea." To him, the wall was symbolic of China itself. "It had been built with the intent to keep out the Mongols and to provide a sense of security." To Joslyn, it seemed that "since the wall was built, China had gone to sleep for a thousand years. Now the country was undergoing a painful awakening from centuries of wishful thinking."[52]

On November 2 *Tate* transferred an LCM and an LCVP to the marines before departing. Again under the command of *Chilton* with various units of

Transport Squadron 17, the ships headed back to Kowloon for another load of Chinese. With the ship now empty, the crew was able to clean things up, hosing out the compartments so badly fouled by the Chinese.[53]

The ship's medical officer, Lieutenant Heinan, no longer had hundreds of Chinese to care for, but he did have one gravely ill sailor in sick bay. Signalman 3rd Class James L. Zupke was seriously sick with acute cerebrospinal meningitis. On the afternoon of November 4 Heinan consulted with other navy physicians over the radio and then arranged to transfer Zupke to a hospital ship. On the night of November 4 the young sailor succumbed to his disease, the first fatality of *Tate's* crew. It was a sobering event for a group of men who had so far defied the odds, living a charmed existence and coming through so many dangerous situations unharmed.[54]

The following morning the crew mustered in their dress blues. *Tate* veered out of formation, stopped, and lowered its flag to half-mast. To anyone in the squadron who saw this, the meaning was obvious. It was a scene that had been repeated all too often during the war. Four pallbearers stood on each side of the flag-draped body, which was placed on a wooden plank resting on a platform at the edge of the main deck. Seven sailors with rifles lined the rail. Calling the assembled men to attention, Commander Lyon read from the scriptures and followed with a short prayer. Then the assembled men held a hand salute for the reading of the committal. "Unto Almighty God we commend the soul of our shipmate departed, Signalman 3rd Class James L. Zupke, and we commit his body to the deep, in the sure and certain hope of the resurrection unto eternal life, when the sea shall give up its dead, and the life of the world to come." As a bugler played taps, the pallbearers tipped the board upward, and the body, encased in a canvas bag and weighted with a five-inch shell, slid into the sea with an abrupt splash. The men bowed their heads as the benediction was read and then came to attention to hold a final hand salute. Three volleys sounded over the foreboding sea, putting a dramatic punctuation on the sad event. The M-1 rifles automatically ejected their empty brass cartridges, which went tumbling through the air. The spent rifle cases skittered across the cold steel deck in a final reminder of the capricious absurdity of the crew's first death.[55]

The pallbearers folded the flag, and Commander Lyon dismissed the men. The officer of the deck, Lt. (j.g.) Leroy J. Carter, noted the exact time and position of the burial in the ship's deck log for formal notification of Zupke's unsuspecting family. A burial at sea is perhaps the briefest and most dramatic of military ceremonies. It was all over in a few minutes, and *Tate* quickly caught up with the convoy.[56]

The work routine changed significantly since nine officers and numerous enlisted men had left the ship. Assuming the duties of the departed personnel was keeping many men on their feet as much as when they were in combat.

Photo 11.2 The burial of James L. Zupke in the East China Sea. Courtesy Alvin L. Joslyn.

Mitigating the extra workload was a brutal efficiency gained from the hardships of almost a year of service on the seas.

On November 9 the Commander Lyon took over as the officer in tactical command for elements of the squadron not going directly into Kowloon. The ships under his control refueled at sea, anchoring briefly off Hong Kong before sailing to Kowloon to embark troops from the Chinese Eighth Army. Knowing what to expect on this second visit, *Chilton* advised the ships in its squadron to take extra precautions against the locals. A crewmember from *Chilton* recalled this situation years later. "Great care was taken to protect the crews of the squadron's ships from roving gangs of criminals, money-hungry restaurant, hotel, and pub owners, as well as the ever-present 'ladies' who even tried to come aboard our ships in the harbor. What you couldn't buy for a five-cent Hershey bar!"[57]

In Kowloon the same pathetic situation appeared as before, and the crew watched the Chinese pass by the ship's doctor for medical inspection. Before boarding, one of *Tate's* sailors sprayed the Chinese with insecticide in an attempt to prevent lice infestation of the ship. Meanwhile, Signalman 2nd Class Whitcome's friends were having some fun at his expense. Spotting one of the locals on the pier wearing a denim shirt pulled from the trash bearing Whitcome's stenciled name, his shipmates mercilessly ribbed him about having

a Chinese brother. The loading went quickly, and *Tate* bade farewell to Kowloon and Whitcome's pseudobrother. On the morning of November 12 *Tate*
made its way single file with the other transports into the South China Sea,
where they formed a convoy and headed north for Tsingtao.[58]

Tate's crew was warned to keep their distance from the Chinese and ordered
not to interfere with their discipline. The arrogant brutality of the Chinese
officers was revolting. They frequently kicked, beat, and pistol-whipped their
men for what appeared to be minor or contradictory reasons. To Storekeeper
2nd Class Norman Nisen, theirs was a caste system at its very worst. The Chinese officers were spick and span, decked out with full leather accoutrements,
while the enlisted men groveled for the extra bits of rice littering the decks.[59]

Tate's mess cooks prepared the rice brought on board by the Chinese and
then carried the it throughout the ship in GI cans and dished it out into helmets, outstretched handkerchiefs, or open hands. To the delight of the Chinese, pieces of foul-smelling beef known as Guam goat and considered inedible
by *Tate*'s crew were mixed into the rice.[60]

On the morning of November 14 a fire started in the number five cargo
hold when a Chinese soldier discarded a cigarette onto a stowed cargo net. Less
than two minutes after the fire alarm sounded, the first stream of water was on
the flames. Gunner's Mate 1st Class Hubert Six's fire station was on the control
wheel for flooding the aft ammunition magazine on the other side of the bulkhead from the fire. Six never got an order to flood the magazine, and the fire
was quickly extinguished. After securing from his station, Six went to examine
the damage. He found the paint blistered on the inside of the magazine's bulkhead. It had been a narrow escape.[61]

A couple of hours after the fire, floating mines were sighted by the high-
speed destroyer transport *Weber* (APD-75), which quickly exploded three of
them as the convoy made emergency evasive maneuvers. *Tate* then sighted and
destroyed a final mine on its own, bringing the busy morning to an end.[62]

The following day the squadron arrived at Tsingtao, and the Chinese troops
disembarked in just sixty minutes. Two of the Chinese were too sick to walk.
In a letter home, recently promoted Lieutenant (j.g.) Joslyn described the disembarkation: "None of them died on this trip, but we lowered two over the
side who I expect were cold and stiff this morning. With little or no medical
care and their condition, they could not possibly live for any length of time.
Life is cheap out here, and the law of survival of the fittest is amply demonstrated in many ways."[63]

After the unloading, *Tate* anchored in the harbor for the next seven days.
During this time the two LCM crews that had been left behind at Taku rejoined their ship after transportation to Tsingtao on a heavy cruiser. Liberty in

Photo 11.3 Hubert J. Six Sr. had this portrait made amid the ruins of Manila. He signed it "With all my love" and then mailed it to his wife, Lillian. Courtesy Hubert J. Six Jr.

Tsingtao offered many of the men a chance to reflect on the hardships that they hoped would now be ending. The scuttlebutt was that their transport squadron would be broken up and that *Tate* would return to the States.[64]

An odd mix of European and Asian influences, Tsingtao had an unusual flavor. One of *Tate's* saltier chiefs, who had visited the port before the war, recommended a Russian steak house. Several of the officers piled into rickshaws and went there for a meal. The steaks came with an egg on top, and for Lt. (j.g.) David Waller this was a treat worth repeating. As his friends waited for Waller's second steak to arrive, they listened to music from a hand-cranked Victrola.[65]

Many of the town's streets and establishments had American names such as Golden Gate, American Bar, and New York. Oddly, armed Japanese troops still roamed the town, and Communist troops were just outside the city. Peddlers and beggars were on every street corner. Dire poverty, hunger, and looks of hopelessness were rampant reminders of the legacy of the Japanese occupation.[66]

Dominating the skyline in the heart of Tsingtao was Saint Michael's Catholic Cathedral, which was nearly three hundred feet tall. Many of *Tate's* crew met or posed for photographs in front of the landmark. From *Tate's* bridge, the sight of Saint Michael's twin spires looming above Tsingtao reminded newly promoted Lt. (j.g.) Lewis Crew that he was long overdue for a church call. Crew found Saint Michael's exterior handsome yet modest for a cathedral. Upon entering the church, he discovered its atmosphere was austere and somber, with the only light filtering through vivid stained-glass windows.

Seated on the church's few pews were about a dozen elderly women, deep in prayer. Crew, who had studied music before the war, walked cautiously toward the front of the sanctuary. From an alcove at the top of a tall spiral staircase, a practicing organist cut loose with the powerful opening strains of Bach's *Toccata and Fugue in D Minor.* Crew froze in his tracks, overwhelmed with the emotional impact of the gigantic pipe organ, which was suddenly filling the stone building with familiar music. He had an epiphany. For the first time he acknowledged to himself that the war was truly over and he had survived it unscathed. The organist followed with an equally stirring rendition of Massenet's "Meditation" from *Thaïs,* a personal favorite of the music-student-turned-naval-officer.[67]

Thursday, November 22, was a Thanksgiving Day the crew of *Tate* would long remember. Before departing Tsingtao, the ship took on board thirty-nine servicemen for transportation to the United States. Now officially detached from the amphibious forces, the ship was heading for Seattle after a stop at Okinawa. However, *Tate's* busy schedule caused the postponement of the holiday celebration until the next day. Nevertheless, the crew enjoyed a traditional meal of "roast turkey, dressing, mashed potatoes, peas, cranberry sauce, pickles, olives, bread and butter, mince pie and coffee." After his meal, Lieutenant (j.g.) Joslyn wrote home that he "had more to be thankful for today than ever before. The war has ended and if it had not we would be in the middle of the invasion of Japan proper. I have come through with my skin intact and my health good. I have a family that I love dearly who are waiting for me back home, whose loyalty has been a source of inspiration that has built up my spirits when they have lagged. And last of all, but in no way the least; I am on my way back home, this time I think to stay. I know no one who has more to be thankful for than I."[68]

MAGIC CARPET

Now He's Waiting for Me

AS *TATE'S* CONVOY STEAMED SOUTH on the morning of November 23, 1945, the crew hoped it was the last time they would transit the unfriendly waters of the Yellow Sea. As a reminder of what they were leaving behind, the ship went to general quarters after sighting floating mines. In a now routine manner, the gun crews ran to their battle stations. Shoes scurried across steel plate as bodies twisted and turned through hatches and around the boats and equipment that cluttered the decks. With an ease born of necessity, the ship's forward 40-mm mounts went into action, sinking a mine with some "good straight shooting." A short time later, the crew destroyed another mine that the ships forward of *Tate* had passed unseen. Later that afternoon, another floating object sent the ship to general quarters, but it turned out to be only a barnacle-encrusted box. During eight transits through the Yellow Sea, *Tate* and its accompanying ships destroyed approximately twenty mines. That evening, finally clear of the mine area, the belated Thanksgiving program began. Coming a day late, the celebration was worth the wait. A double quartet sang "Prayer of Thanksgiving," "This Is My Country," and "When Day Is Done." A community sing followed the performance, and there was much to be thankful for with the war over and everyone heading home, hopefully for Christmas.[1]

On November 25 the ship entered Okinawa's Buckner Bay and began embarking navy and marine personnel for transportation to Seattle. To these war-weary and homesick servicemen, *Tate* was the ship they often dreamed about. Of all the passengers the ship carried, this was its happiest load. The transportation of servicemen home to the United States was called Operation Magic Carpet, evoking the fabled storybook ride to a life lived happily ever after.[2]

Tate sailed independently on November 26 for what promised to be a cold trip across the North Pacific. With the AKA now officially one year old, a special edition of the *Hot Tater* celebrated the ship's first anniversary. In one year the ship steamed more than sixty thousand miles, while transporting more than sixteen thousand tons of cargo. For all those on board since the commissioning in Charleston, it had been a very long year indeed.[3]

Out of sight of land for more than two weeks, the ship headed steadily homeward at fifteen knots. No longer on board were two of the ship's three pets: a parrot and Josephine the monkey. Both animals had been a source of much amusement, as well as aggravation. The squawking parrot often turned up in officer's country at night, where its vocalizations kept the officers awake. Moving the offending bird to the enlisted spaces only invited its return to the officers' spaces. The saga of the tropical bird ended in the chief's mess. After it perched in front of a ventilation fan, the chiefs joked that the parrot would soon misjudge the fan and meet its end. The remarks were prophetic, as soon afterward a grotesque noise and a cloud of brightly colored feathers interrupted their breakfast.[4]

Josephine's fate was less accidental. The female monkey seemed inclined to antagonize everyone, including the ship's dog, Penny. The two animals often slept together under the gun deck of the forward 40-mm. The monkey would pet and groom the dog for hours before pulling her tail or biting her ear. Then it was off to the races, as the barking dog chased the monkey across the deck. When the marines were on board, they had a monkey of their own, Pablo, a male. The results were predictable, and the anticipated blessed event between the two animals was the source of great humor.[5]

Josephine's bad habits included frequent biting and climbing the masts to defecate in her hand, then throwing it at anyone who happened to be below her. Since the officers were often the brunt of these attacks, the crew put up with her indiscretions. Josephine's habit of stealing items such as cigarettes and keys and throwing them over the side went too far when she tossed one of the cook's shoes overboard. Knowing the monkey's habits, the cook rubbed grease on a rail on the main deck, where she liked to perch. The next time Josephine jumped to the rail, she went over the side.[6]

The long transit allowed *Tate*'s officers and crew to work on the duties they assumed from their discharged shipmates. Some of the men found they were now holding jobs for which they had minimal training. As the ship neared its anticipated landfall, visibility was poor due to heavy fog. Commander Lyon checked with his radar officer, who had only recently transferred to that position. He was told the set was clear and showed no radar returns. A few minutes later, Lyon returned, led the officer out onto the bridge wing, pointed to the mountains of the Olympic peninsula poking up through the fog, and asked, "What do you think that is?" Lyon, the old-time mariner, was reluctant to depend on the new technology of radar for navigation. Once again, his instincts were vindicated since the radar set had apparently been dysfunctional for the entire trip across the Pacific.[7]

The ship made its way through the Straits of Juan de Fuca, taking frequent navigational shots off landmarks. With the crew anxious to shake off their sea legs, *Tate* docked in Seattle on December 10, disembarking its 235 Magic Carpet passengers and discharging several crew members.[8]

After moving to an anchorage off Manchester, Washington, the ship used its boats to offload its considerable stores of antiaircraft and small-arms ammunition. The work routines remained light, and the signs looked promising for an impending end to *Tate*'s service. Two-week periods of leave began on a rotational basis. However, for most of the men, their leave did not begin until after Christmas. With the hope of spending the holidays with their families fading, they remained on board the idle ship and awaited orders.[9]

Slated to head home, boat group commander Lt. Joseph Neblett turned over his duties to Lt. (j.g.) Charles E. Gerber. Over the past year the two officers had frequently played cribbage for a penny a point. Deciding to square up any debt, they tallied up their pile of score chits and amusingly found the outstanding debt was only a nickel.[10]

A few days before Christmas, Commander Lyon received a letter addressed to the ship's chaplain from Jeanne Martin, a cadet nurse in Detroit, Michigan. She was "the girl back home" to Signalman 3rd Class Zupke, the sailor who had been buried at sea. Martin had written the letter on December 12, three days after the Zupke family learned of James's death. Despondent, she was looking for information and described how she had believed they would be together after the war. "Funny, isn't it? I promised to wait for him—now he's waiting for me."[11]

Since *Tate* had no chaplain, Commander Lyon passed the letter to Lt. (j.g.) Alvin Joslyn, who was also from the Detroit area. Joslyn had already written to his wife, Erma, about Zupke: "It was ironical that we should go through all that we have gone through and lose a man at this time. It does not seem right. Deaths of this type seem harder than those suffered in combat because you expect it and know that it is your silent companion at all times."[12]

On Christmas Eve, Joslyn answered Martin's letter. He expressed his regrets and assured her the ship's doctor had provided Zupke with every possible medical attention. Joslyn said that he had known "Jimmy as well as any officer knows an enlisted man" and that, in the close quarters of life on the *Tate,* the elements of his character were evident. Jimmy was conscientious, sincere, and well liked. He lived a Christian life and regularly attended church services when boats carrying a chaplain went to other ships. "During the trying days we had at Okinawa he was devoted to his duty and willingly accepted the risks

Photo 12.1 Alvin L. Joslyn. His wartime letters to his wife, Erma, poignantly captured the human impact of war. Courtesy Alvin L. Joslyn.

which were involved in the amphibious operations." Joslyn offered to meet Martin when he took his leave to Michigan in early January. The gesture was a gift of healing and compassion given to a mourning woman that would bring the two strangers together.[13]

Christmas passed, and *Tate* continued discharging men and unloading supplies, including five hundred pounds of TNT demolition blocks, fuses, and blasting caps. On New Year's Eve, Commander Lyon threw a party in his stateroom. A large metal urn full of spiked punch helped ring in 1946, a year that promised peace and, for most, a return to civilian life.[14]

Every ship has its cliques and subcultures, and *Tate* was no different. These social divisions are usually based on rank, experience, or often just coincidence and proximity to men of similar ilk. One group was based strictly on discrimination. The African American stewards kept to themselves, eating and bunking separately from the other enlisted men. Their duties of serving and cleaning for the white officers further solidified the cultural castes that society projected into the military. However, the stewards had one important thing in common with their white shipmates: They wanted to fight. After arguing for a battle station where they could participate in combat, the stewards got their wish and were assigned to man a 20-mm mount. Through a lack of either training or direction, the stewards' gun nearly hit an aircraft that was towing a target sleeve. The pilot radioed his displeasure and refused to make another pass. This near mishap resulted in the stewards' removal from the gun, and they never got another opportunity to fight.[15]

One of the exceptions to the navy's policy of limiting African Americans to nontechnical billets was Samuel O. Braxton. Braxton joined *Tate* in San Francisco in July 1945 as an Electrician's Mate 1st Class and was soon promoted to chief. A native of Virginia, Braxton was articulate and educated. Projecting confidence, patience, and professionalism, he earned the respect of the men with whom he worked in the engineering department.[16]

Throughout the navy, African Americans felt bitter about not being allowed to fight, and many whites resented the fact that African Americans were given less hazardous assignments. Braxton was part of an experiment to address this problem. In April 1942 the navy began accepting African Americans for general service. Relegated to segregated units, many of these men served as laborers in construction battalions. Approximately thirty-one percent of the African American navy recruits qualified for additional training in an occupational specialty, but they too remained in segregated units. In August 1944 the navy began assigning a limited number of African Americans to sea duty in general service billets on large auxiliaries. The Chief of Naval Operations, Admiral King, insisted on "equal treatment in matters of training, promotion, and duty assignments." The commanding officers determined berthing.[17]

Of the men selected for this pilot program, none ranked higher in the beginning than a third-class petty officer. Braxton was an excellent choice for the racial experiment. He quickly proved his merit, moving up through the ranks to chief petty officer. Commander Lyon saw to it that Braxton berthed and ate with his white counterparts, taking full advantage of the navy's integration trial, even if the stewards on his ship remained segregated by regulation.[18]

On January 8, 1946, *Tate* transferred eight LCMs and ten LCVPs to the Manchester boat pool. It would be another ten dull days before the ship got under way for Everett, Washington, after more than five weeks of waiting at anchor. Using the captain's cabin as a honeymoon suite for the short cruise were the newlyweds, Mr. and Mrs. Norval Righter. Engaged for more than two years, the couple had waited for an opportunity to marry. They finally got their chance when Righter went home to Maryland on leave, returning the next week with his bride. Once again, Commander Lyon showed his soft touch for his enlisted men. Offering his room to the couple was a violation of the navy's policy prohibiting women on board a warship.[19]

Catherine Righter was not the only woman on board for the short cruise. Lt. (j.g.) Albert Dorsey's wife, Daisy, also accepted an invitation from Commander Lyon for the ride to Everett. Lyon promised Dorsey, who had enough service points to qualify for a discharge, a promotion if he would stay with the ship, but he declined the offer. After visiting her husband six months earlier, Mrs. Dorsey had conveniently remained in the Seattle, where she found employment with Boeing, making aircraft as a Rosie the Riveter. When Dorsey left the ship, he was delighted to read in his formal orders that he was now officially in the custody of his wife, Daisy.[20]

The ship anchored at Port Gardner for three days before going into dry dock at the Everett Pacific Shipyards. Scraped and repainted, the affectionate and temporary name "Queen of the Seas" adorned *Tate*'s bow. Shifting from the dry dock, the ship moored outboard of a commercial ship, and repairs continued on *Tate*. The bearings on the propeller shaft required replacement due to the stress of riding out two typhoons. The ship's systems were inspected, repaired, and upgraded when needed. The extensive maintenance signaled that there was no longer any hope of decommissioning the ship in the near future.[21]

Frequent liberty, combined with the boredom of waiting for several weeks to again sail off into the Pacific, resulted in an increase in disciplinary problems. Returning to the ship late, six enlisted men landed in the brig for five days and received twenty days of extra police duty. Another enlisted man, returning from leave three days late, got five days in the brig in solitary confinement on bread and water.[22]

Being back in the States, *Tate*'s crew had opportunities to enjoy some additional freedom. Eating off the local economy was one such pleasure. Yet, the conditions of living at sea, which they had long been accustomed to, caused them to practice some peculiar habits in public. While eating in a local restaurant, Signalman 1st Class Blaine Lakes and some of his shipmates routinely held slices of bread up to the light for examination. When queried about the behavior, Lakes explained that roaches were not uncommon in his ship's flour supply, and the men were accustomed to picking insect parts out of their bread.[23]

The letters home often focused on the details of an impending discharge. The points needed for discharge favored family men over bachelors. Carpenter's Mate 3rd Class James Anthony affectionately addressed a letter home to his wife in North Carolina as "My Dear Ten Points." To help assist his crew with their impending return to civilian life, Commander Lyon reassigned Lt. Ben Propek from his job as the head of the 2nd Division to the newly created position of Education and Civil Readjustment Officer. Propek, a schoolteacher from Peoria, Illinois, encouraged his departing shipmates to pursue educational opportunities upon their release from the navy. Combining any specialized skills they had acquired in the navy with additional training or education would increase their chances of obtaining gainful employment in what promised to be a highly competitive postwar economy.[24]

One of those heading home was Motor Machinist's Mate 2nd Class Ivo Cecil. Riding on an eastbound train, Cecil sat next to a Roman Catholic priest who was a navy veteran of the Spanish American War. The two veterans from different wars struck up a conversation, and Cecil listened to the man's tales of fighting in the Philippines. After watching two brawling sailors put off the train, the old priest remarked, "The navy must have changed. In my day the other sailors would not have let them be thrown off the train." Cecil, who would one day become a priest himself, agreed, "The navy *has* changed. They indeed *needed* to be thrown off."[25]

Like his shipmate Cecil, Gunner's Mate 3rd Class Raymond M. Comstock was on a train heading home for Kentucky when it became snowbound in Montana for three days. After the tracks were finally cleared, the cattle trains got first priority. It was ironic to fight and win a war and then, on the way home, to see cows heading for the slaughterhouse get preferential treatment. However, the small Montana town where Comstock waited was unlike anything he had ever seen in the United States. It seemed like a throwback to the 1800s, and the locals were reluctant to accept paper money, preferring to deal instead in silver coinage. Comstock's delay in Montana was his final adventure in the navy before returning to Louisville, where his hard-earned paper money was readily accepted.[26]

On February 20 *Tate* got under way for a few hours of speed trials in Puget Sound. Returning that night to a pier in Everett, the ship waited three more

days before shifting to Seattle for provisioning. On February 25 the ship again
anchored off Manchester but this time only briefly before getting under way
for Oakland, California, where it would load cargo for yet another voyage
across the Pacific.[27]

Commander Lyon was reluctant to wait for a pilot who would probably
be less competent than he to enter the familiar waters of San Francisco Bay.
Without hesitating, he conned his ship under the Golden Gate Bridge, then
ran into a dense fog bank. Utilizing a set of sound-powered phones, a lookout
posted on the bow reported several times that they were approaching other
ships. Fireman 1st Class Linwood Tudor, on duty in the boiler room, was
puzzled with the numerous "all back full" commands ringing up on the engine
room telegraph. The ship repeatedly shuddered to a halt, backed up, and then
eased ahead again. When the lookout reported "There's a pier dead ahead!"
he was surprised to hear the bridge ask, "What pier number is it?" Trying to
find his way through the fog, Commander Lyon needed a geographical reference point. Stopping his ship just short of the San Francisco waterfront, Lyon
then backed up and anchored. After a short time, the visibility improved, and
the ship sailed under the Oakland Bay Bridge before anchoring again. *Tate*
remained there for four days before mooring in Oakland.

The ship continued to discharge men while receiving fewer replacements.
On March 13 one replacement that reported on board was Cdr. Andrew
Morthland, *Tate*'s new commanding officer. Lyon's more than five years of
active-duty service, four battle stars, a citation for valor at Guadalcanal, and
family easily qualified him with enough points for discharge. With his duty
done, he took advantage of *Tate*'s arrival in Oakland to depart for his nearby
home in San Francisco.[28]

Lyon's departure caused him to pause for reflection on his tenure as captain
of *Tate*. The *Hot Tater* printed his thoughts, which were characteristic of the
colorful style his crew had come to love:

> In glancing through the ship's War Log I see that we are aboard a
> mighty proud and fortunate ship. I say fortunate because she is that in
> this respect, having a fine hard working crew without which no ship
> can function properly.
>
> Talking to some of the old salts who have been aboard the *Tate* since
> her commissioning one gets the feeling that he is aboard a ship whose
> life is charmed. She took part in the famed Ie Shima invasion in which
> we lost one of our most beloved war correspondents, Ernie Pyle. To
> add to her other list of exploits, the *Tate* remained in Okinawan waters
> for twenty-eight days under threat of Japanese aerial attacks. She took
> all they could throw at her and came out fighting without a scratch.

So men take heed, this trusty craft on which we rest out humble carcasses is not a cargo carrier but a fighting ship as well. So with all due credit I think that she, a ship among ships, has earned her campaign stars.[29]

Commander Lyon's considerable communication skills were nonetheless inadequate to express the respect and affection he felt for his officers. As a final gesture, he threw a party for them at his home in one of San Francisco's finer neighborhoods.[30]

Lt. (j.g.) David Waller was impressed with Lyon's beautiful home and intrigued as to what clues it might offer about the man who had led him safely through the war. Curious about the rabbits he saw outside in cages, he asked Mrs. Lyon about them. She confided that the rabbits were for use on the table but that her husband was too sensitive to kill them. They paid a neighbor girl to kill and clean the rabbits when needed. It was a remarkable revelation that the man who had led them in battle had such a soft side. Yet, after two world wars, Rupert Lyon had certainly earned whatever peace he could find.[31]

As the party wound down and the recreational lubrication began making its full effect known, the officers gathered on the Lyons' terraced front lawn. There they sang familiar songs, slices of Americana, in a final tribute to their wartime skipper.[32]

On March 15 Commander Morthland assumed command of Tate from Commander Lyon. In a short but formal ceremony Morthland uttered the traditional words, "I relieve you, sir," and Tate had a new captain. Lyon said his good-byes and was piped off the ship. The veterans who had served under him in combat and relied on his leadership, strength, and compassion lost a man to whom they would always be indebted. The extent of their indebtedness would take the wisdom of many years for them to fully appreciate.

Andrew Morthland was a native of Los Angeles, California. His navy career began with three years of enlisted service from 1930 to 1933. He reentered the navy in 1941 with a reserve officer's commission from Harvard and began the war on the coast guard cutter Itaska. Later he served on Celeno, the same ship Rupert Lyon helped save off Guadalcanal. Most recently, he had been the captain of the destroyer minesweeper Stansbury (DMS-8). With four campaign stars on his breast, he had certainly not spent the war on the sidelines.[33]

Within a few hours of taking command, Morthland had Tate sailing independently west across the Pacific for the Marshall Islands. After an uneventful trip, the ship arrived at Eniwetok on March 28 and disembarked six naval officers and sixty-four army personnel. For the next three days, the ship unloaded cargo. Fireman 1st Class Linwood Tudor noticed that many of the wooden cargo crates going ashore were marked with "Crossroads X" in stenciled black letters. The ship's scuttlebutt was that the cargo was part of an atomic bomb test. The ship then sailed on to nearby Kwajalein. On the evening of April 2 Kwajalein's port director ordered the *Tate* immediately out of the atoll to avoid a possible tsunami. A major earthquake in the Aleutian Islands had generated a tidal wave that had already killed more than two hundred people in Alaska and Hawaii. With *Tate* safely at sea, the tidal wave caused the sea level to rise only about three feet in the Marshall Islands. The ship returned to Kwajalein the next morning to offload the remainder of its cargo and pick up passengers.[34]

On April 5 the ship was again conducting Magic Carpet service, taking on board thirty navy personnel and seven enlisted marines at Kwajalein for transport to Norfolk, Virginia. Upon reaching Norfolk, the ship would be decommissioned and the crew discharged. It was the news *Tate*'s crew had awaited since the war ended.[35]

Sailing alone, *Tate* reached the Naval Operating Base, Balboa, Panama Canal Zone, on April 23 and waited for orders. On May 6, to the disillusionment of the crew, they went to work chipping and painting the ship. Getting *Tate* ready for a formal inspection was the last thing anyone wanted, and the sailors could not understand the purpose since the ship was due to go out of service.[36]

The reason the ship needed squaring away was obvious when Rear Adm. John R. Beardall, commandant, Fifteenth Naval District, and commander, Panama Sea Frontier, came on board with his chief of staff, Capt. D. A. Spencer, and his aide, Lieutenant Commander Sedgewick. On his return from hunting in the jungle, Beardall presented a wild boar to Morthland. A fierce-looking beast, it was roasted and served up with an apple in its mouth, to the delight of the crew, who thought it tasted like lamb.[37]

While inspecting the crew, Beardall stopped in front of Seaman 1st Class Zeblin Midgett. He asked, "Sailor, why don't your shoes shine?" Midgett replied, "It's the salt water, sir." He got a stern glance from Beardall, who moved on. Having an admiral on board did not impress the homesick sailors, who felt he was responsible for delaying their arrival in Norfolk.[38]

Unknown to the crew, Beardall was President Roosevelt's naval aide at the beginning of the war before becoming the superintendent of the U.S. Naval Academy. He was present at some of the most significant meetings of the era, including the Atlantic Conference, where Roosevelt and Churchill had mapped out the basic goals for the war.[39]

On May 10 *Tate* set sail for the Galapagos Islands, Ecuador. As the ship crossed the equator, King Neptune appeared, along with his trusty shellbacks. Together they whipped about forty uninitiated pollywogs into shape. Shortly after the ship dropped anchor in the Galapagos off Baltra Island, a sailor who had hidden to avoid the equator initiation met a humorous fate. While men with rifles pretended to be lookouts for sharks, the traumatized and reluctant pollywog was forced to walk the plank. The salty veterans of Okinawa showed the squeamish sailor no mercy.[40]

The Galapagos presented a bizarre and intriguing landscape made famous by Charles Darwin and the expedition of the HMS *Beagle* in 1831. Darwin's trip to these islands played an important role in the publication of his revolutionary work, *The Origin of the Species*. Here, in a pristine environment and unclouded by the selfish impacts of the human race, the clues of evolution revealed themselves to Darwin. For *Tate*'s crew, the abundance of unusual animals was intriguing, and the timeless, undisturbed coastlines were a stark contrast to the troubled beaches they had known. To Lt. (j.g.) Paul Leahy the seals and walruses resting on the rocky shoreline seemed as puzzled by the presence of humans as the humans were by them.[41]

Tate's official mission in the Galapagos was to transport army personnel from the 29th Bombardment Squadron to Panama. Since 1942, the squadron had patrolled off the western approaches to the Panama Canal in their B-24 bombers and seen nothing but the empty backwaters of the war. After spending three boring but safe years on the remote islands, the U.S. Army Air Forces personnel now anxiously awaited their Magic Carpet ride home.

President Roosevelt had traveled to the Galapagos on a fishing trip in 1938 as part of a presidential trip on the heavy cruiser *Houston* (CA-30). Beardall knew of Roosevelt's experience in the Galapagos from his time on the president's staff. While *Tate* lay at anchor, the admiral fished off the LCP-L. The fishing was excellent, and Electrician's Mate 2nd Class Theron Hokanson overheard the supply officer ask Machinist's Mate 2nd Class Arthur O. Pigadis to increase the ship's ice production to preserve the admiral's catch. To Hokanson's amusement, Pigadis told the officer, "Sir, the ice makers are running at full capacity, and I can't shit ice." The officer just walked away, and the enlisted men had a good laugh.[42]

For three days, the admiral and his staff fished before departing for Panama by aircraft. Lieutenant (j.g.) David Waller and James R. Ewing also did well in the seafood department with just their bare hands. The young officers swam ashore through the brisk waters to Baltra Island and waded through the shallows, picking up rock lobsters. When they returned to the ship, they each handed a gunnysack full of the spiny crustaceans to the cook. It was a meal to remember, and they boastfully claimed they had caught enough lobsters for the enlisted men to get a taste.[43]

On May 18 the ship got under way for Panama with twenty army passengers from the 687th Air Warning Company. Since the U.S. base in the Galapagos was closing, the diversion of an attack cargo ship to pick up a small number of men and no cargo was nothing more than a ruse for what was ostensibly a flag-level fishing trip.[44]

Skipper Andrew Morthland was far different from Rupert Lyon. Lyon's brand of leadership was a de facto standard for the crew. Morthland was reserved and detached, unlike the colorful and gregarious Lyon. He was more in the mold of a traditional commanding officer: Play by the rules, delegate responsibility, and put your faith in the system. Lyon was an interventionist. Any time his ship was involved in other than routine operations, he was on the bridge. While Lyon gave the enlisted men a good deal of latitude in their behavior, if they took advantage of his tolerance, he came down hard on them. Although Morthland strictly enforced the rules, his punishments were less severe for the same infractions. Morthland handed out extra duties or removed privileges for the same violations that had previously landed sailors in Lyon's brig on bread and water.[45]

On May 20 *Tate* moored at the Naval Operating Base in Balboa for three days before entering the Panama Canal. During the canal transit, the ship energized its degaussing coils while passing through the Galliard Cut degaussing range. This process helped to minimize the ship's magnetic signature and reduce its vulnerability to mines. Exiting the canal, the ship headed for Norfolk, Virginia.[46]

After arriving at the Norfolk Naval Operating Base, *Tate*'s crew spent the next month getting their ship ready for decommissioning. All of the ammunition and stores were off-loaded, and the crew began processing off the ship. Lieutenant (j.g.) Waller was inventorying equipment and could locate only 35 of the 250 pairs of binoculars that had been issued to the ship. Confronted by the inspectors, Waller was chewed out and lectured on how each piece of equipment was to be signed out before use and then turned back in. The reality of the inspectors' world was unlike his own navy experience. Being accused of being a German spy, jailed, rescued, and vindicated—only to go into combat against a suicidal enemy—was his reality. Signing out chits on equipment under combat conditions seemed petty. The inspectors might as well blame the Emperor of Japan for the missing equipment.[47]

On June 24 the ship moved to Craney Island for defueling, then sailed to the Portsmouth Naval Shipyard. On July 1 a fire broke out on the fantail from a broken acetylene hose. It was quickly extinguished, and the damage was negligible. After the decommission on July 10, 1946, the last fire in the ship's engine room was allowed to die out. With it went the last impulse of life in a warship not yet two years old. Nine days later, the USS *Tate* was struck from the Navy List.[48]

EPILOGUE

You May Never Know

SEAMAN 1ST CLASS JOHN J. TOOMBS'S TRAIN pulled into his hometown of Gulfport, Mississippi, late at night. Throwing his seabag over his shoulder, he walked to his home, which was just a few blocks from the station. On his uniform Toombs wore the five service decorations *Tate* had earned: the World War II Victory ribbon, the American Campaign ribbon, the China Service ribbon, the Philippine Liberation ribbon with a bronze star, and the Asiatic Pacific Area Campaign ribbon with a bronze star. Toombs's son, Jon, three and a half years old, was too young to remember his father. When the boy awoke in the morning, he walked into his parents' bedroom. There he sat quietly, waiting for his father to wake up, thinking, "So, that's my daddy." [1]

Gunners Mate 3rd Class Clinton Alexander wrote to his wife that he was heading home soon but was uncertain as to what day he would arrive. Alexander detrained onto the same platform in Charlotte, North Carolina, where he had thrown his sailor's hat with a note inside to his wife, fearing he would suffer a fate similar to that of his brother, who had been killed in Italy. When Alexander arrived home, he found no one there, but there was a note from his wife informing him that, if he came home, she was at his mother's house and that his dinner was in the refrigerator. Alexander's war began and ended with two simple handwritten notes, the first based on fear, and the second on hope. [2]

Like Toombs and Alexander, most of those serving on *Tate* returned to their civilian lives, which had been interrupted by the war. Promises of promotion did not dissuade most of them from leaving the service. In many cases, the officers making the offers were planning their own departure from the navy. Those who had left jobs to go to war were entitled to return to them for one year after their honorable discharge, but many of the men had no such opportunity. They had entered the service directly out of school and had yet to test their wings in the commercial workplace. Many of them felt a gnawing anxiety concerning their peacetime future.

The family men had more complicated readjustment issues. Not only did they have to rebuild a livelihood to support their families, but they also needed to reestablish ties with their children, who in many cases were virtual strangers. The wives they left behind had become independent heads of their households or moved in with relatives. Now they too were in transition, shifting to a more traditional family lifestyle while assessing the impact of the war on their husbands and marriages.

For the more than sixteen million uniformed Americans who served in World War II, their wartime experiences, the need to adapt, to meet hardship head-on, and to function in an authoritative culture proved beneficial to their readjustment. With their broadened perspectives from extensive travel, a sudden maturity, and in some cases specialized training, the veterans were honed into shape unlike any other American generation. With the introduction of the GI Bill, education and home ownership became more affordable, and the American Dream, which had lost its way during the Depression, was now within reach. The baby boom was on, and the next generation was growing up on the stories of what their fathers did in the war.

The war forever marked a dividing point in the lives of the veterans. Their existence was broken into the years before and the years after the war. The war's threat of a sudden violent death caused a compression of time and space that affected some men's minds in ways that would later cause them to question their experiences. The intensity of the experiences tested the limits of cognition and remembrance of the most complex of all war machines, the human mind. How a man's mind behaved in battle could leave him feeling like a stranger to himself.

Accounts of the April 2, 1945, kamikaze battle, *Tate*'s most dramatic action, contain a common visual theme: the face of the enemy. When aircraft pressed close during their attacks, the veterans consistently recalled the same details: "I could see the pilot's face, his white scarf, and his flying helmet." It was the face of an enemy who was resolved to die in battle and take his enemy with him. The Japanese believed their highest destiny lay in dying for their emperor. The Americans they were trying to kill received no such conditioning. While their enemies were undergoing their morbid indoctrination, the Americans had spent their youths on the playing fields of the United States, learning to hit, catch, and throw. Judging the speed and distance of a baseball or a football became their childhood training for estimating the speed, range, and altitude of plunging aircraft. For William Polikowski, the memory of the Japanese pilot's face as his plane crashed into the sea lingered through the years, like the silent partner Alvin Joslyn so poignantly described who accompanies all men who go into battle.[3]

Through a combination of good fortune and good shooting, *Tate* missed the worst of the war's horrors. Witnesses to the tragedy of Okinawa, the ship's crew members were impacted by the war in ways not easily understood. Byron Larsen stated, "The events at Okinawa are burned into my memory. Yet I do not think much about the war, but the effects of it are there." Whether recognized or not, the war's influence continues to cast lengthening shadows across the boundaries of the passing generation that lived through it. Those shadows reveal themselves in more than the veterans' stories. They compose the very fabric of American culture, which is waiting for discovery by those who are willing to explore and acknowledge their heritage and to become a custodian of these memories before they fade from existence.[4]

The only tangible item of remembrance for many *Tate* veterans was the *War-Time Log of the U.S.S.* Tate *AKA-70,* which was published two years after the ship returned to Seattle in December 1945. This hardback book is predominantly a photo album with a brief history of the ship. Yet, no physical item could replace the wartime comradeship shared by the shipmates. The veterans' efforts to stay in touch took a variety of forms. A cluster of veterans from western North Carolina got together for an occasional card game. Other meetings were coincidental, as when John Borenski from Ohio passed a car on a Michigan highway and recognized Lyle R. Boyd at the wheel. Borenski flagged Boyd down, and the two shipmates shared a few beers at Boyd's nearby home. Another accidental meeting occurred when Albert Dorsey was teaching at an agricultural camp in Kentucky. He overheard another teacher talking about a kamikaze crashing into the water just behind his hospital ship. He ended by saying, "I always wanted to meet the man who shot that plane down." Dorsey stepped forward and asked, "Was your ship the *Rixey?*" When the man answered, "Yes," Dorsey stuck out his hand and replied, "Lieutenant (j.g.) Albert Dorsey, gun captain, number one, 40-mm mount, USS *Tate.* I shot that plane down!" Both men were stunned by the coincidence of how their paths had crossed in both war and peace.[5]

After the war, William Newton returned to Arkansas and found himself face to face with Winthrop Rockefeller, who was campaigning for governor. As Rockefeller reached out to shake his hand, Newton told him, "We have something in common. I was on a ship behind your ship, *Henrico,* when it was kamikazied. I saw the whole thing. I also read in the newspapers that your opponent says you were not really wounded and only had your mustache singed off."

Rockefeller, who had spent time recovering from burns in a Guam hospital, bristled and replied, "I had a lot worse, but I am not going to get into that." Newton voted faithfully for Rockefeller during his political career and then for his son, who became the lieutenant governor of Arkansas. The bond stretched into the twenty-first century.[6]

James Baker left *Tate* in March 1945 after his father suffered a heart attack and needed help running the family dairy farm in Iowa. One of the men his father later hired to work on the farm was a survivor of the *Dickerson* tragedy. Years later Baker met a fellow employee at work who was one of the construction battalion stevedores driven from his ship in Guam. Baker also worked with a man in the 77th Infantry Division whom *Tate*'s transport squadron had carried into battle. Even in small-town America, veterans found themselves bound together by unusual circumstances.[7]

Although these encounters seem unlikely, the United States was flooded with millions of combat veterans with stories to tell. In many cases, only other veterans could appreciate those experiences. Drawn to each other by the fraternity of shared danger, the veterans naturally gravitated toward each other. In so doing, the likelihood of crossing paths with someone with a common experience greatly increased. Stretching from every corner of the United States, an invisible web of circumstance bound the veterans together. Yet, more times than not, they would encounter each other without ever realizing their common bonds.

As *Tate*'s veterans aged, their maturity allowed them to look back at the war with a greater perception than was possible earlier. Their sense of community, which focused around their service to their ship, was an almost universal feeling. Many proud veterans felt that *Tate* was the best ship in the navy and manned by one big happy family. Moreover, some of the men also realized the influence that Rupert Lyon's leadership had had on their lives. During times of turmoil or stress, they fell back on the wisdom and self-confidence their wartime skipper had instilled in them. Lyon was not the kind of man the navy would pick as a commanding officer in normal times, but 1944 was not a normal year. In the prewar regular navy, he would have been an outcast. His unconventional leadership style came from the heart; consequently, he earned the uncompromising loyalty of both his officers and his crew.

Lyon understood the limitations of rigidly applying regulations to a mostly mobilized civilian crew. He frequently left the rulebook on the shelf when established navy standards called for its use. This fostered even more cohesion and hard work from his men. He was a skipper whose goal was to create a happy and productive crew. Yet, even with a nearly perfect war record, he eventually ran afoul of the regular navy. Any hopes of remaining in the navy after the war probably ended at Okinawa, when his hesitant-to-maneuver division commander perceived Lyon's ship-handling actions as intentionally contemptuous. Regardless, with a glut of naval officers in a rapidly shrinking postwar navy, career advancement prospects for reserve officers such as Lyon were not favorable. Retiring to San Diego, Lyon kept in touch with his officers through annual letters every Christmas until his death in 1984.[8]

The subsequent wars in Korea and Vietnam had ambiguous results and controversial endings. As historians worked to define the impact of those conflicts, the World War II veterans, who delivered a total victory, patiently waited. Born in an era in which hard work, self-denial, and humility were common traits, they quietly began dying off. For millions of veterans, their most noble recognition lay in their own hearts, where they knew they had performed the duties that had befallen them to the best of their abilities. Coming long after the veterans of later wars received their national monuments, the World War II Monument, erected in Washington, D.C., was not dedicated until 2004. Sadly, it came too late for most of those it honors, now commonly referred to as the Greatest Generation, as defined by Tom Brokaw's best-selling book of the same name.

Alvin Joslyn, sensing what he felt was a growing lack of knowledge of and compassion for the Greatest Generation, wrote to his local newspaper. Appearing on Memorial Day of 2001, the letter points out that the veterans themselves finally started the World War II national monument project because no one else would take up the cause:

> [The monument is] properly placed on the mall and it will not be a "Kitschy" memorial to themselves but one placed there to remind future generations of the price that was paid to ensure the freedoms that we enjoy in the greatest country in the world. We are now revealing some of the horror, anguish, fright, and suffering that we went through and grieving the loss of comrades in arms and those found in veterans' hospitals throughout this land of ours. With this we remind Americans that the greatness of America does not rest in Tinsel Town and its attempts to reproduce what was experienced, but in our brain, heart and soul which we tried to bury [for] so long a time. We are getting old and we think we should let you in on a little of what took place 50-plus years ago. We are in our 70s and 80s and are dying at a rate of 1,000 a day. If the story is not told now, you may never know.[9]

While a series of World War II fiftieth anniversary events focused on the historical significance of the war in Europe, men like Alvin Joslyn continued struggling to gain the recognition and respect they felt was overdue. One of the most influential advocates for World War II veterans was historian Stephen E. Ambrose. His efforts helped create a new genre of World War II historical literature and motion pictures as well as the National D-Day Museum in New Orleans. After becoming terminally ill in 2002, Ambrose wrote *To America,* a broad-scoped final tribute to the nation he loved, in which he stated that "the ferocity and rage that defined the war in the Pacific" made it "the worst war there ever was." The bloodiest of the Pacific War's battles was Okinawa, where massive artillery and troop concentrations, along a relatively static front, turned the island into a tortured landscape hauntingly similar to a World War I battlefield and where more deaths occurred than from the combined atomic bombings of Hiroshima and Nagasaki. With arguably the worst experience of the Pacific War occurring on Okinawa, the casualties the navy absorbed off-shore from the kamikazes were equally appalling. While living in a relatively sterile and orderly environment at sea, the navy suffered more fatalities than either the army or the marines.[10]

The tranquility of present-day Okinawa and the rest of the Ryukyu Islands is in stark contrast to the events of 1945. Kerama Retto is now a Japanese national park known for its excellent scuba-diving opportunities. Tourists ferry over from Okinawa to the villages of Tokashiki and Zamami. They come seeking the beauty of nature, where the sea dramatically meets land in a complicated maze of shoals, reefs, and cliffs that were once scouted and mapped by the underwater demolition teams. Okinawa, where more than two hundred thousand Japanese lost their lives, is the home of permanently stationed U.S. military forces that consist primarily of marine units who built their reputations fighting the Japanese. On Ie Shima, the Veterans of Foreign Wars periodically holds commemorative services at Ernie Pyle's monument, where U.S. and Japanese flags routinely fly, a testimonial to reconciliation with a country that is now one of the United States' most important allies and a vital economic partner.

The National Memorial Cemetery of the Pacific is located in Oahu's Punchbowl in an extinct volcanic crater not far from Pearl Harbor. The cemetery became the final resting place for many of those initially buried on islands across the Pacific. Ernie Pyle's body was one of those transferred there from Ie Shima in 1949, along with the 77th Infantry Division's Private 1st Class Martin O. May, the sole Medal of Honor recipient from the battle of Ie Shima. The cemetery's central avenue runs to the base of a broad staircase, flanked by eight "courts of the missing." The white stone walls of the court contain the names of 18,094 service members who went missing in action or were buried at sea. At the foot of the staircase is a simple stone monument with this inscription: "In These Gardens Are Recorded the Names of Americans Who Gave Their Lives in the Service of Their Country and Whose Earthly Resting Place Is Known Only to God." One of the names etched in the garden of stone is that of Signalman 3rd Class James L. Zupke of Michigan, *Tate*'s lone fatality. At the top of the staircase is a gallery of colorful inlaid ceramic maps representing the campaigns of the Pacific, Korean, and Vietnam wars. Inside the gallery is a small memorial chapel, whose reverent nature beckons respectful visitors to cast their thoughts across the Pacific Ocean to a time when courage and self-sacrifice were common virtues.[11]

Ernie Pyle's grave is adjacent to the cemetery's central avenue. Flanking him are graves marked only as "Unknown." His other closest neighbor's headstone carries the inscription "Unknown Pearl Harbor December 7, 1941." Ernie Taylor Pyle's simple, military-style headstone lists his rank as Seaman 3rd Class, from his brief service in the naval reserves in World War I. His inscription also recognizes the Purple Heart he earned on Ie Shima. As an embedded reporter, Pyle repeatedly shared the life and dangers of the anonymous frontline soldiers and sailors. Although Pyle was technically a civilian, his final burial as a member of the military in a national cemetery, surrounded by three unknown servicemen, is a fitting tribute.

World War II historical literature has constantly acknowledged the fighting prowess of the Germans. However, a comparison by the surgeon general of the army has shown that, in the Pacific, casualties per day per thousand men in a protracted campaign were more than three times greater than in Europe. Had Ernie Pyle lived, he would likely have changed his opinion about the Pacific being a secondary theater of the war.[12]

Decades after the war, *Tate* veterans Norval Righter and Willard Whitcome each made pilgrimages to the Punchbowl cemetery, and both men made a point of visiting Ernie Pyle's grave. It was a sad visit for Righter, who shook Pyle's hand and wished him luck the day before his death on Ie Shima. Those who met the sensitive little man found comfort in the hope that he might preserve the story of their war experience. Meeting Ernie Pyle was a good omen in an otherwise dismal ordeal. Being one of the last men to see him alive became a curse on a memory that had started out so fondly. In *Here Is Your War,* Pyle fatalistically wrote, "I guess it doesn't make any difference, once a man has gone. Medals and speeches and victories are nothing to them any more. They died and others lived and nobody knows why it is so. They died and thereby the rest of us can go on and on." In Pyle's case, it made a great difference. Those who were still searching for the meaning of what they endured would miss the voice that could express the human side of World War II unlike any other.[13]

If, as Ernie Pyle implied, survival and perseverance provide the real meaning to war, he would have been gratified to see two *Tate* veterans who had not seen each other in fifty-seven years boarding the same flight heading for Raleigh, North Carolina, on September 12, 2003. Both men wore navy blue hats with the gold lettering "USS Tate (AKA-70)." Anxious and waiting to see what the trip would reveal, they chose not to seek each other out. Upon arriving in North Carolina, the two men suddenly felt the distance of six decades melt. Walking side by side through the airport concourse, "Forty" Salerno and Mike Larsen headed for their first-ever ship's reunion.

Other shipmates were gathering at a nearby hotel. Gerald J. Keniry checked out of a hospital in New York and drove alone to North Carolina. He arrived two days early because he wanted to take no chances on missing anything. Sons and daughters nurtured on the stories of what their fathers did in the war also attended to offer their assistance and to seek the truth from a passing generation.

Throughout the day, twenty-one *Tate* veterans renewed their friendships. One of the last to arrive was David Waller from Washington State. Pausing in the entrance to the room that held his socializing shipmates, he took in the scene and said, "If I went home now, it would have been worth the trip." When it came time to eat, few of the veterans could be bothered. One man stated, "We have been eating for the last fifty-seven years but have not had the company of each other. I think we can do without the food."

The next morning, the veterans attended a formal reunion program. They began by singing their national anthem while facing a flag flown over the U.S. capitol in their honor. A touching invocation written by their shipmate Father Ivo Cecil followed, along with the playing of the "Navy Hymn." As many aging eyes began to water, the master of ceremonies read three congratulatory letters. The first was from Rear Adm. W. C. Marsh, commander, Amphibious Group Three, acknowledging *Tate*'s legacy in the amphibious forces of the modern Pacific Fleet. The second letter, from Tom Brokaw, recognized *Tate* veterans as part of the Greatest Generation, who deserved all of the recognition and thanks they could get. The final letter, from Pres. George W. Bush, acknowledged the veterans' stature as role models for courage and devotion to duty.[14]

All of the veterans got a chance to speak. They described their postwar lives and then recounted their most memorable wartime experience. Alvin Maw was the oldest man in attendance. When his turn came, he slowly rose, stretching out his tall, aging frame. With a sparkle in his eye, he spoke of the kamikazes who dived at his ship through a wall of antiaircraft fire: "When we started shooting, it was with everything we had, 20-mm and 40-mm just blazing away. You could see the planes being hit and pieces flying off, but still they came, and we poured it on." Then the eighty-nine-year-old gunner's mate raised his hand and pointed upward: "When a five-incher let loose, well, I am here to tell you, a direct hit is a wonderful thing."

Some of the last words written by Ernie Pyle dealt with wartime comradeship, which he felt became "part of one's soul." Reunited after fifty-seven years, the veterans proved Pyle was right, as they discovered that the bonds of brotherhood they had forged in combat were undiminished by the long postwar lives they had fought for and dreamed of during World War II.[15]

The most commonly asked question at the reunion was "What happened to *Tate* after the war?" The inquisitive veterans fondly spoke of the ship as if it were a long-lost, beloved relative. A strong emotional need existed to know the fate of the ship that had carried them into battle and safely home again. The answer to the question they had carried within themselves for so long was fitting for a ship they felt Providence had blessed.

Tate was a product of the mobilized wartime shipyards that in five years produced more tonnage in the United States than was previously built in the history of the world. As a result, the postwar era saw an unprecedented availability of commercial shipping. One of the most capable types of ships available was *Tate*'s class of *Tolland* AKAs. In 1947 the Luckenbach Shipping Lines bought the *Tate* and renamed it *Julia Luckenbach*. J. Lewis Luckenbach, who ran his family's shipping lines, was the president of the American Bureau of Shipping, a member of the U.S. Maritime Commission, and an important contributor to the design of attack cargo ships. It was the third time that name was used. The first *Julia Luckenbach,* a coastal freighter built in 1882, sank within two minutes from a collision in Chesapeake Bay in 1913, with a loss of fifteen lives. The second *Julia Luckenbach,* a freighter built in 1917, served as a World War I troop ship. Like its namesake, the freighter sank as the result of a collision in 1943 in the South Atlantic, with the loss of one life.[16]

The third *Julia Luckenbach* continued to carry the good fortune *Tate* enjoyed during the war. The lucky ship transported the cargoes of peace that Chief Gilmore had hopefully prophesied during the ship's first visit to San Francisco. Sold in 1960 to the States Marine Lines, the ship was renamed *Bay State.* The ship made its final voyage in 1970, after becoming obsolete due to the introduction of containerized cargo. Its destination was Kaohsiung, Taiwan, on the island of Formosa, where so many kamikaze attacks originated against the ships off Okinawa. The ship died an obscure and natural death at the age of twenty-six. At the time the cutting torches broke the ship into pieces, it was older than most of the crew had been when they walked its decks and stood at its rails, contemplating their fates during some of the darkest days of the twentieth century.[17]

One of the historical hallmarks of World War II is joint amphibious operations. It is impossible to look back at the world's worst war without remembering the images of allied troops storming hostile beaches. Yet, while most classes of World War II ships are preserved as floating museums, none of the nearly 350 frontline APA or AKA amphibious transports has been so honored. Only a handful of these ships remain, with just one, the attack transport *Gage* (APA-168), in a condition suitable for preservation. Resting faithfully as part of the James River Reserve Fleet near Fort Eustis, Virginia, *Gage* awaits its fate—to either join the other transports in oblivion or to represent an entire generation of amphibious warriors who helped save the world from tyranny.

APPENDIX A

USS Tate *(AKA-70) Organization*

Commanding officer (CO): senior officer responsible for all of the actions of the ship, boats, and crew

Executive officer (XO): second in command and responsible for executing the CO's orders

Officer of the deck (OOD): represents the commanding officer for a four-hour watch interval and is superior to all other officers except the executive officer

Administration (yeoman): performs administrative and personnel functions; reports directly to the XO

Transport quartermaster (TQM): manages cargo and passengers; reports directly to the XO

Deck department: headed by the 1st lieutenant and divided into three divisions. This group was responsible for the ship's weather (exterior) decks, guns, boat davits, and cargo-handling equipment. The 1st Division was responsible for the forward section of the ship, the 2nd Division for the deckhouse, and the 3rd Division for the aft section of the ship. A 1st class gunner's mate (GM), assisted by other GMs, maintained each division's guns under the direction of the gunnery officer. *Tate* had no chief gunner's mate.

Medical department: The medical officer ran the hospital, or "H" division, and was in charge of the pharmacist's mates, sick bay, and casualty treatment stations.

Boat group: Subdivided into seven sections (L-1 through L-7), the landing, or "L" division, maintained and operated all of the ship's boats. While on board, it assisted the deck department as needed. Since the boat group might be in their boats during general quarters, their shipboard battle station duties were predominately to provide additional manpower for ammunition handling and damage control.

USS *Tate* (AKA-70)
Organization

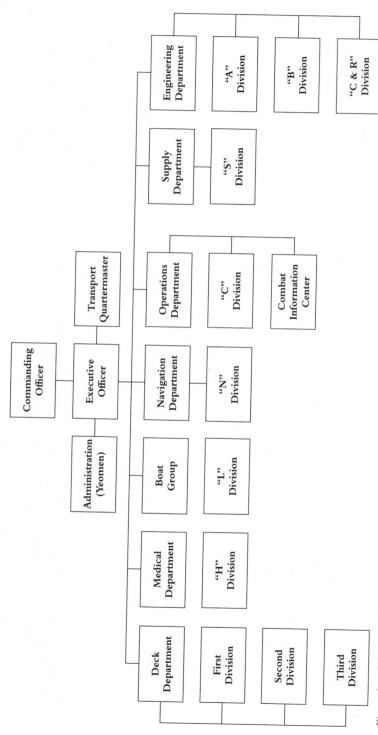

Figure A.1. USS Tate *(AKA-70) organization.*

Navigation department: The navigator ran the "N" division and was aided
by an assistant navigator and a team of quartermasters. He was responsible
for the safe navigation of the ship, the continuous determination of the
ship's position, maintenance of all navigation equipment, and the chart and
navigational publications library.

Operations department: The "C" or communications division consisted
mostly of radio operators and signalmen and managed the ship's visual
and electronic communications, including the coding and decoding of
messages. The combat information center (CIC) was responsible for the
operation and maintenance of the radars and for the flow of tactical information during combat and battle exercises. The communications officer
ran the entire department.

Supply department: The "S" division supervised the procurement and stor-
age of all general stores. It operated the galley and bakery and served and
disposed of all foodstuffs. It cleaned the messing areas and the officers'
staterooms. It also disbursed the ship's funds, including its payroll. Store-
keepers and stewards made up the bulk of the personnel.

Engineering department: operated and maintained the propulsion systems
and the various mechanical and electrical systems throughout the ship.
The "A" or auxiliary division managed the ship's nonpropulsion mechanical systems and machinery, including the boat engines. The "B" or boiler
division maintained the ship's fire room, main propulsion machinery,
generators, and electrical systems. The construction and repair (C&R)
division maintained watertight integrity and handled damage control, hull
maintenance, welding, carpentry, general repairs, and construction duties.
On most warships, the C&R division was known as the "R," or repair,
division.

Each division head was assisted by at least one other officer in leading a team
of enlisted specialists. The departments were also responsible for the upkeep of
their own work spaces. Many ships had a separate "E" or electrical division.
The consolidation of these duties with the "B" division helped simplify the
Tate's engineering department.

In late 1945, after *Tate* lost a considerable number of officers and crew to
postwar discharges, the navigation and operations departments merged into a
single "N" division under the navigation department in order to consolidate all
of the activities in the command spaces.

APPENDIX B

Josephine Goes to Sea on the USS Tate

My story is really not important; in fact, I'm not at all important myself, but I'm well acquainted with lots of people who are, and I'd like to tell you about these people, all men with whom I have been associated, sometimes intimately.

I was born in the Philippine Islands. I won't tell you when. I'm sure some would think me very young, while some would think me ancient. After all, being female, I reserve the right to conceal my age.

The Japanese killed many of my friends. They cared for none of them—neither male nor female. My memories of the Japanese are not pleasant, but for some reason Providence spared me, and I managed to escape them. Then one day it happened; for months there was great speculation about the return of the Americans, our liberators. They came, they fought, and they conquered our arrogant tormentors. We were free again. That is when my life really began. I was rescued by the brave men of the 77th Division of the U.S. Tenth Army. All of my memories of these men are wonderful ones, for they protected me from all kinds of evil. They showered their affection upon me. I was their inspiration, so to speak. I adored them, and they named me Josephine.

When the Tenth Army was scheduled for a new task, farther up on the road to Tokyo, I begged them to take me along. I pleaded with them and even rolled my big brown eyes demurely, so how could they refuse? Then came the day to board the ship that was to take us to Okinawa, Ie Shima, and Kerama Retto.

In March 1945 we boarded the USS *Tate* (AKA-70), commanded by Lt. Cdr. R. E. Lyon, a veteran of the sea. The *Tate* was and still is a beautiful ship. This was my first voyage, so I was very excited, and the sailors—God bless them—were all clamoring for my attention and affection. I became their off-duty entertainer. The trip from the Philippines to the Ryukyus was a long one, and during that time I became very attached to Chief Electrician C. E. De Baun from Texas. He pampered me as though I were his one and only. So, when the 77th Division debarked at Ie Shima, I was allowed to decide whether to stay on board *Tate* or go with the army. This was a delicate decision; I hardly knew which way to turn. Finally, the soldier to whom I owe my life when he rescued me near Leyte told Chief De Baun that it would be pretty tough on a girl of my type to go along on an initial invasion of enemy territory. He gave Chief De Baun full permission, with my consent, to care for me and take me home with him to the United States of America. So I remained on board *Tate*.

Things happened in the Ryukyus. Our sister ships were maimed by the Japanese suicide planes, the kamikaze. We had some close calls ourselves. Some of our landing craft division were in on the beach several hours prior to "H" hour. Things that can't be helped, or things that weren't planned, always happened during the most efficiently designed operations; this was no exception.

Night after night we were at general quarters (the navy's term for "man your battle stations"). One of our electrician's mates 2nd class, A. F. Herndon from Indiana, rigged up a speaker in the engine room so the watch-weary engineers could have music to break the terrible monotony of the fatiguing watches during these operations. I was probably the most frightened one of all until I got used to the excitement, which then actually became routine until we left that area.

Many of the brave men who left *Tate* on those operations fell during battle. They spilled their blood on enemy ground to save their loved ones at home and the millions of freedom-loving people throughout the world. Ernie Pyle gave his life there with the men he loved and about whom he wrote. General Buckner, the gallant, intelligent leader of the Tenth Army also lost his life there; he was loved by the navy and the marines, as well as by his own men.

We left that area in the latter part of April 1945 and made some shuttle trips from Saipan to Guadalcanal and Guam. Then, one day, my good friend De Baun was transferred. He went to the United States for honorable discharge from naval service. He left me with the ship.

In June 1945 we received orders to go to San Francisco, California. We were loaded and lying in Guam. They gave us docking space, and the CBs started unloading us. They were so slow that our incomparable Captain Lyon asked the crew to help. Therein lies a story, along with a tale of unloading *Tate* in Guam.

Prior to our arrival on the West Coast, our orders were changed from San Francisco to Seattle. Chief Electrician's Mate D. P. Cross and the whole engineering force were seeing to my personal effects and care. Chief Machinist A. T. Robinson from Norfolk, Virginia, vied for my affections, and sometimes I would fall asleep in his arms as he caressed me. He gave me chewing gum and cookies and showered me with the little attentions a girl enjoys. He even bathed me at times, especially if Electrician's Mate 2nd class H. L. Childress from Georgia and Electrician's Mate 1st Class F. A. Westerman from Maryland weren't around.

Everyone in the whole ship's company teased and played games with me. My favorite trick was to disrupt the privacy of Lieutenant (j.g.) Schonfeld from New York and Lieutenant (j.g.) Propeck from Illinois. Sometimes I visited all of the officers' staterooms.

Once the crew put on a smoker, and I was the guest of the captain and the executive officer, Lieutenant Commander Boland from Melrose, Massachusetts. Lieutenant (j.g.) Hoerske, Ensign Blunk, and Lieutenant (j.g.) Schonfeld made a motion picture of the show. It was lots of fun and very exciting. Ensign Crew had his glee club perform for us, along with Ensign Ewing and his band, a very talented bunch of fellows.

On June 27 we arrived in Seattle, and when leave commenced on June 28, two ten-day leave periods were granted to all hands. Everyone enjoyed the brief respite from war. I visited the towns of Everett and Seattle.

We left Seattle on July 19 and stopped in San Francisco for three days, then headed back to the South Pacific and Guam. On our way to Guam, we heard the news of our enemy's cracking under the terrific pounding of our ships and planes. Then the world was rocked with the concussion of the atomic bomb, and Japan surrendered. The war was over, and the world was free again.

We loaded in Okinawa for the occupation of Korea (this was the latter part of August and the first part of September 1945, five months after my first voyage). Upon our return trip to the Ryukyus, these are the thoughts that struck us:

> It's quiet now on Okinawa's shores.
> The ships ride at anchor with lights aglow.
> They're targets for the kamikazes no more,
> And at night their crews watch a topside show.
> The ground is hallowed here,
> As on the neighboring isles,
> With brave men who gave their lives
> Alongside their friend, Ernie Pyle.
> From the Solomons, the Gilberts,
> The Marshalls, New Britain,
> The Philippines, the Ryukyus,
> The enemy has been beaten.
> Pray the ones who died gave not in vain
> Their lives for freedom's sake.
> Let's keep the peace they gave to us
> And never repeat a grave mistake.
> So sleep, brave men, and rest in peace

With your Maker and buddies in arms.
We're still united and free men. We'll stand,
Watch over your loved ones, and keep them safe
from harm.

Now we have the 1st Division of the U.S. Marines on board for the occupation and policing of the part of China the Japanese had controlled. In the that
division, I have found a real lover; he and I are made for each other. His name
is Chico; what else doesn't matter. I'm deeply enamored of him, and I'm sure
that he loves me. Some times when we're in a very thrilling episode, we have
a few witnesses, but then Chico ruffles his mane and bares his fangs and chases
them away. You can't blame him 'cause I'm sure if you were in an intimate
mood with your lover, you wouldn't want a bunch of monkeys from the jungle
watching you—now would you?

So ends this little tale of my life so far. Even though I am a little monkey, I
think that people have more fun than anybody.[1]

APPENDIX C

Index of World War II Attack Cargo Ships (AKA)

Table C.1. World War II Attack Cargo Ships (AKA)

Ship	Class	Builder	Commissioned	Battle Stars
Arcturus (AKA–1)	*Arcturus*	Sun Shipbuilding & Dry Dock	10/26/40	5
Procyon (AKA–2)	*Arcturus*	Tampa Shipbuilding	8/8/41	5
Bellatrix (AKA–3)	*Arcturus*	Tampa Shipbuilding	6/14/41	5
Electra (AKA–4)	*Arcturus*	Tampa Shipbuilding	3/17/42	6
Fomalhaut (AKA–5)	*Fomalhaut*	Pennsylvania Shipyards	3/2/42	5
Alchiba (AKA–6)	*Arcturus*	Sun Shipbuilding & Dry Dock	6/15/41	3 + PUC[1]
Alcyone (AKA–7)	*Arcturus*	Sun Shipbuilding & Dry Dock	6/15/41	8
Algorab (AKA–8)	*Arcturus*	Sun Shipbuilding & Dry Dock	6/15/41	4
Alhena (AKA–9)	*Alhena*	Bethlehem Steel	6/15/41	5
Almaak (AKA–10)	*Almaak*	Bethlehem Steel	6/15/41	6
Betelgeuse (AKA–11)	*Arcturus*	Sun Shipbuilding & Dry Dock	6/14/41	6
Libra (AKA–12)	*Arcturus*	Federal Shipbuilding & Dry Dock	5/13/42	9
Titania (AKA–13)	*Arcturus*	Federal Shipbuilding & Dry Dock	5/27/42	7
Oberon (AKA–14)	*Arcturus*	Federal Shipbuilding & Dry Dock	6/15/42	6
Andromeda (AKA–15)	*Andromeda*	Federal Shipbuilding & Dry Dock	4/2/43	5

Ship	Class	Builder	Commissioned	Battle Stars
Aquarius (AKA-16)	*Andromeda*	Federal Shipbuilding & Dry Dock	8/21/43	8
Centaurus (AKA-17)	*Andromeda*	Federal Shipbuilding & Dry Dock	10/21/43	6
Cepheus (AKA-18)	*Andromeda*	Federal Shipbuilding & Dry Dock	12/16/43	2
Thuban (AKA-19)	*Andromeda*	Federal Shipbuilding & Dry Dock	6/10/43	7
Virgo (AKA-20)	*Andromeda*	Federal Shipbuilding & Dry Dock	7/16/43	7
Artemis (AKA-21)	*Artemis*	Walsh-Kaiser	8/28/44	1
Athene (AKA-22)	*Artemis*	Walsh-Kaiser	9/29/44	2
Aurelia (AKA-23)	*Artemis*	Walsh-Kaiser	10/14/44	1
Birgit (AKA-24)	*Artemis*	Walsh-Kaiser	10/28/44	0
Circe (AKA-25)	*Artemis*	Walsh-Kaiser	11/10/44	1
Corvus (AKA-26)	*Artemis*	Walsh-Kaiser	11/20/44	1
Devosa (AKA-27)	*Artemis*	Walsh-Kaiser	11/30/44	1
Hydrus (AKA-28)	*Artemis*	Walsh-Kaiser	12/9/44	1
Lacerta (AKA-29)	*Artemis*	Walsh-Kaiser	12/19/44	1
Lumen (AKA-30)	*Artemis*	Walsh-Kaiser	12/29/44	1
Medea (AKA-31)	*Artemis*	Walsh-Kaiser	1/10/45	1
Mellana (AKA-32)	*Artemis*	Walsh-Kaiser	1/20/45	0
Ostara (AKA-33)	*Artemis*	Walsh-Kaiser	1/31/45	0
Pamina (AKA-34)	*Artemis*	Walsh-Kaiser	2/10/45	1
Pollana (AKA-35)	*Artemis*	Walsh-Kaiser	2/21/45	0
Renate (AKA-36)	*Artemis*	Walsh-Kaiser	2/28/45	★
Roxane (AKA-37)	*Artemis*	Walsh-Kaiser	3/12/45	0
Sappho (AKA-38)	*Artemis*	Walsh-Kaiser	4/24/45	0
Sarita (AKA-39)	*Artemis*	Walsh-Kaiser	3/22/45	0
Scania (AKA-40)	*Artemis*	Walsh-Kaiser	4/16/45	0
Selinur (AKA-41)	*Artemis*	Walsh-Kaiser	4/21/45	0
Sidonia (AKA-42)	*Artemis*	Walsh-Kaiser	4/30/45	0
Sirona (AKA-43)	*Artemis*	Walsh-Kaiser	5/10/45	0
Sylvania (AKA-44)	*Artemis*	Walsh-Kaiser	5/19/45	0
Tabora (AKA-45)	*Artemis*	Walsh-Kaiser	5/29/45	0

(Continued)

Table C.1. Continued

Ship	Class	Builder	Commissioned	Battle Stars
Troilus (AKA-46)	*Artemis*	Walsh-Kaiser	6/8/45	0
Turandot (AKA-47)	*Artemis*	Walsh-Kaiser	6/18/45	0
Valeria (AKA-48)	*Artemis*	Walsh-Kaiser	6/28/45	0
Vanadis (AKA-49)	*Artemis*	Walsh-Kaiser	7/9/45	★
Veritus (AKA-50)	*Artemis*	Walsh-Kaiser	7/19/45	0
Xania (AKA-51)	*Artemis*	Walsh-Kaiser	7/28/45	0
Zenobia (AKA-52)	*Artemis*	Walsh-Kaiser	8/6/45	0
Achernar (AKA-53)	*Andromeda*	Federal Shipbuilding & Dry Dock	1/31/44	3
Algol (AKA-54)	*Andromeda*	Moore Dry Dock	7/21/44	2
Alshain (AKA-55)	*Andromeda*	Federal Shipbuilding & Dry Dock	4/1/44	5
Arneb (AKA-56)	*Andromeda*	Moore Dry Dock	11/16/43	4
Capricornus (AKA-57))	*Andromeda*	Moore Dry Dock	5/31/44	4
Chara (AKA-58)	*Andromeda*	Federal Shipbuilding & Dry Dock	6/14/44	4
Diphda (AKA-59)	*Andromeda*	Federal Shipbuilding & Dry Dock	7/8/44	1
Leo (AKA-60)	*Andromeda*	Federal Shipbuilding & Dry Dock	8/30/44	2
Muliphen (AKA-61)	*Andromeda*	Federal Shipbuilding & Dry Dock	10/23/44	2
Sheliak (AKA-62)	*Andromeda*	Federal Shipbuilding & Dry Dock	12/1/44	1
Theemin (AKA-63)	*Andromeda*	Federal Shipbuilding & Dry Dock	12/22/44	1
Tolland (AKA-64)	*Tolland*	North Carolina Shipbuilding	9/4/44	2
Shoshone (AKA-65)	*Tolland*	North Carolina Shipbuilding	9/24/44	2
Southhampton (AKA-66)	*Tolland*	North Carolina Shipbuilding	10/8/44	2
Starr (AKA-67)	*Tolland*	North Carolina Shipbuilding	10/21/44	2
Stokes (AKA-68)	*Tolland*	North Carolina Shipbuilding	11/4/44	2

Ship	Class	Builder	Commissioned	Battle Stars
Suffolk (AKA-69)	*Tolland*	North Carolina Shipbuilding	11/14/44	1
Tate (AKA-70)	*Tolland*	North Carolina Shipbuilding	11/25/44	1
Todd (AKA-71)	*Tolland*	North Carolina Shipbuilding	11/30/44	0
Caswell (AKA-72)	*Tolland*	North Carolina Shipbuilding	12/13/44	1
New Hanover (AKA-73)	*Tolland*	North Carolina Shipbuilding	12/22/44	0
Lenoir (AKA-74)	*Tolland*	North Carolina Shipbuilding	12/31/44	1
Alamance (AKA-75)	*Tolland*	North Carolina Shipbuilding	1/9/45	0
Torrance (AKA-76)	*Tolland*	North Carolina Shipbuilding	11/18/44	1
Towner (AKA-77)	*Tolland*	North Carolina Shipbuilding	12/1/44	0
Trego (AKA-78)	*Tolland*	North Carolina Shipbuilding	12/21/44	1
Trousdale (AKA-79)	*Tolland*	North Carolina Shipbuilding	12/21/44	1
Tyrrell (AKA-80)	*Tolland*	North Carolina Shipbuilding	12/4/44	1
Valencia (AKA-81)	*Tolland*	North Carolina Shipbuilding	1/9/45	1
Venango (AKA-82)	*Tolland*	North Carolina Shipbuilding	1/2/45	1
Vinton (AKA-83)	*Tolland*	North Carolina Shipbuilding	2/23/45	0
Waukesha (AKA-84)	*Tolland*	North Carolina Shipbuilding	9/20/44	0
Wheatland (AKA-85)	*Tolland*	North Carolina Shipbuilding	4/3/45	0
Woodford (AKA-86)	*Tolland*	North Carolina Shipbuilding	3/3/45	0
Duplin (AKA-87)	*Tolland*	North Carolina Shipbuilding	5/15/45	0

(Continued)

Table C.1. Continued

Ship	Class	Builder	Commissioned	Battle Stars
Uvalde (AKA-88)	*Andromeda*	Moore Dry Dock	8/18/44	1
Warrick (AKA-89)	*Andromeda*	Moore Dry Dock	8/30/44	2
Whiteside (AKA-90)	*Andromeda*	Moore Dry Dock	9/11/44	2
Whitley (AKA-91)	*Andromeda*	Moore Dry Dock	9/21/44	1
Wyandot (AKA-92)	*Andromeda*	Moore Dry Dock	9/30/44	1
Yancey (AKA-93)	*Andromeda*	Moore Dry Dock	10/11/44	2
Winston (AKA-94)	*Andromeda*	Federal Shipbuilding & Dry Dock	1/19/45	0
Marquette (AKA-95)	*Andromeda*	Federal Shipbuilding & Dry Dock	6/20/45	0
Mathews (AKA-96)	*Andromeda*	Federal Shipbuilding & Dry Dock	3/5/45	0
Merrick (AKA-97)	*Andromeda*	Federal Shipbuilding & Dry Dock	3/31/45	0
Montaque (AKA-98)	*Andromeda*	Federal Shipbuilding & Dry Dock	4/13/45	0
Rolette (AKA-99)	*Andromeda*	Federal Shipbuilding & Dry Dock	4/28/45	0
Oglethorpe (AKA-100)	*Andromeda*	Federal Shipbuilding & Dry Dock	6/6/45	0
Ottawa (AKA-101)	*Tolland*	North Carolina Shipbuilding	2/8/45	0
Prentiss (AKA-102)	*Tolland*	North Carolina Shipbuilding	2/11/45	1
Rankin (AKA-103)	*Tolland*	North Carolina Shipbuilding	2/25/45	1
Seminole (AKA-104)	*Tolland*	North Carolina Shipbuilding	3/8/45	0
Skagit (AKA-105)	*Tolland*	North Carolina Shipbuilding	5/2/45	0
Union (AKA-106)	*Tolland*	North Carolina Shipbuilding	4/25/45	0
Vermillion (AKA-107)	*Tolland*	North Carolina Shipbuilding	6/23/45	0
Washburn (AKA-108)	*Tolland*	North Carolina Shipbuilding	5/7/45	0

1. PUC = presidential unit citation

- Only World War II battle stars are listed. Subsequent awards from other wars are not included.
- *Alchiba* received a presidential unit citation for service at Guadalcanal, as well as three battle stars for her World War II service.
- According to the *Dictionary of American Naval Fighting Ships, Tate* received only one battle star for Okinawa, but her crew was also authorized to wear the Philippine Liberation ribbon with a bronze star for being in the designated area for more than thirty days.
- An asterisk (★) designates a ship that was commissioned but not used as an AKA.

By the end of World War II, 108 AKAs from seven different design classes were commissioned. Fourteen auxiliary cargo ships (KAs), already in service, were redesignated as attack cargo ships on February 1, 1943. Still classified as auxiliaries, the AKAs officially became frontline combatants. These 14 included all of the ships from the first four design classes and saw heavy service that earned them eighty battle stars. Eleven of these 14 AKAs were *Arcturus* class ships, with one each from the *Fomalhaut, Alheana,* and *Almaak* classes. Beginning in 1943, the shipbuilding program for the construction of AKAs produced 94 ships of three design classes. The Walsh-Kaiser Company built 32 *Artemis* class ships. The Federal Shipbuilding and Dry Dock Company and the Moore Dry Dock Company combined to build the 30 *Andromeda* class ships. The North Carolina Shipbuilding Company built the remaining 32 ships, all of the *Tolland* class.

Approximately forty percent of the AKAs never earned a battle star, and, of those that did, each earned at least one in the Pacific theater of operations (PTO). Only 14 AKAs saw combat outside the Pacific in the European theater, the North Atlantic, or the Caribbean, and all of these ships went on to fight in the PTO. The low percentage of AKAs fighting in the European theater is partly attributable to the timing of the AKA shipbuilding program, which did

Table C.2. AKA Shipbuilders

Shipbuilder	Location
Sun Shipbuilding & Dry Dock Company	Chester, Pennsylvania
Tampa Shipbuilding Company	Tampa, Florida
Pennsylvania Shipyards Incorporated	Beaumont, Texas
Bethlehem Steel Company (AKA-9)	Sparrows Point, Maryland
Bethlehem Steel Company (AKA-10)	Quincy, Massachusetts
Walsh-Kaiser Company	Providence, Rhode Island
Moore Dry Dock Company	Oakland, California
North Carolina Shipbuilding Company	Wilmington, North Carolina

not reach its full capacity until after the last major amphibious assaults in Europe. Even though the Pacific War lasted another three months after V-E Day, 43 of the 92 AKAs never saw combat. Miraculously, although several AKAs were badly damaged, not one was lost.

World War II AKA shipbuilding was dwarfed by nonamphibious cargo ship construction. When compared to the AKAs, more than 25 times as many Liberty ships and nearly 5 times as many Victory ships were built. Yet, while the Liberty's cargo capacity was comparable to that of an AKA, its reciprocating steam engines could produce a maximum speed of only 11 knots. In 1944, steam turbine production reached sufficient capacity to support the construction of large numbers of Victory ships that were similar to the AKAs in design, speed (15 knots), and cargo space. Although the Liberty and Victory ships were armed, they did not have the hit-the-beach capability of the AKAs, which had a full complement of landing craft.

NOTES

Chapter 1

1. Milton J. Buswell, telephone interview, Elyria, Ohio; Robert Browning Jr., *U.S. Merchant Vessel War Casualties of World War II*, 271. The salvage rights for *Ballot* went to the Soviet Union. Buswell and several other shipmates remained on board the wrecked freighter until the negotiations for its transfer were completed. *Greylock* had been torpedoed previously while en route from New York to Murmansk on May 8, 1942, but managed to limp into Halifax with part of its stern blown off. After being torpedoed a second time, *Greylock* was abandoned and sunk by gunfire from a British escort. Browning's book credits the escort trawler HMS *Lady Madeleine* (FY-283) with saving *Greylock*'s crew. Buswell stated that, after his rescue by HMS *Oxlip* (K-123), "you never forget the hull number of a ship that pulls you out of the Arctic Ocean."

2. National Archives Branch Depository, College Park (NABD-CP), Attack Plan for Capture of Ie Shima, A406-45, from COM PHIB Group 4, Ser 00215, of 12 Apr 1945.

3. Buswell, interview; Howard C. Colley, telephone interview, Memphis, Tenn.

4. U.S. troops assaulted beaches in Europe, North Africa, Asia, and North America during the Aleutian Islands campaign.

5. Buswell, interview.

6. The attribution of the "awaken a sleeping giant" quote to Yamamoto is largely due to its use in the motion picture *Tora, Tora, Tora*. There is no evidence that the admiral ever made this comment. Still, the quote accurately summarizes Yamamoto's views about going to war with the United States.

7. Smithsonian Institution, National Museum of American History, Maritime Administrative Collection of Ship Plans (1939–1970), U.S. Maritime Commission, C2-S-AJ1, ship plans; North Carolina Shipbuilding Company, *Five Years of North Carolina Shipbuilding*, 7–14; James L. Mooney, ed., *Dictionary of American Naval Fighting Ships*, vol. 7, 52. Hereafter referred to as DANFS, the dictionary was published in nine volumes between 1959 and 1991. *Tate*'s cargo-handling gear consisted of two cargo derricks, one 20-ton cargo boom, four 25-ton booms, and a 35-ton boom forward of the number three hold. Tate County's remoteness had not helped it escape the war. Off the East Coast, a U-boat torpedoed, shelled, and sunk the tanker *India Arrow* on Feb. 4, 1942. Twenty-six men were lost in the cold water of the Atlantic, including Seaman James Samuel Kerr, making Mrs. Bina Presley of the small town of Arkabutla, Mississippi, the first of Tate County's twenty-eight Gold Star Mothers. Hull numbers are used with ship names in italics only on their first citation: *Henrico* (APA-45), for example. In subsequent uses, the ship name is given in italics without the hull number.

8. *Wilmington Morning Star,* Sept. 26, 1944, North Carolina Collection, Joyner Library, East Carolina University Library, Greenville, N.C.

9. DANFS, vol. 7, 52; NABD-CP, USS *Tate* (AKA-70) war diaries, 25 Nov 1944–31 Oct 1945 (hereafter referred to as TWD); NABD-CP, USS *Tate* (AKA-70) deck logs, Nov. 20, 1944, to July 1, 1946 (hereafter referred to as TDL).

10. John F. Borenski, telephone interview, Punta Gorda, Fla.; Colley, interview; James K. Baker, telephone interview, Mount Pleasant, Iowa. The circumstances of each veteran's entrance into the service were established early in each oral history interview.

11. Lewis Kampel, email interview. All of Kampel's family in Poland died in the Holocaust. A wrenching account of their impending fate is conveyed in their letters.

12. Leroy W. Kemske, telephone interview, Frostproof, Fla.

13. Charles H. Gries, telephone interview, Boca Raton, Fla.; Cam Munro, telephone interview, Valparaiso, Ind.

14. Tim Alexander, telephone interview, Charlotte, N.C. Alexander provided the quotation used from the original note, which his family preserved.

15. David M. Waller, telephone interview, Copalis Beach, Wash.; Alvin L. Joslyn, telephone interview, Ypsilanti, Mich.

16. Defense Intelligence Agency, *Characteristics of U.S. Vessels, Vehicles, and Equipment for Amphibious Operations,* 8, 15, 28; U.S. Navy training film, *Amphibious Warfare: The LCM-3;* Lewis A. Crew, interview, Pontiac, Mich. The LCP-L, while similar to the LCVP, was slightly faster due to its streamlined bow. Gray marine diesel engines powered all of the boats. Placed on movable nesting frames, the LCMs were stowed on top of the cargo hatches on the main deck, with an LCVP placed inside each of their well decks. Davits on both sides of the deckhouse each held two LVCPs. The remaining boats were stowed on the main deck in various locations.

17. Albert H. H. Dorsey, telephone interview, Columbia, S.C.; Byron W. Larsen, interview. Larsen was posted at Fort Pierce for more than a year before joining *Tate.*

18. Crew, interview; G. V. Marshall, letter to his wife, Nov. 13, 1944.

19. Crew, interview; Buswell, interview.

Chapter 2

1. TWD, Nov. 25, 1944; Joslyn, interview.

2. Mary Boland, telephone interview, Bethesda, Md.; National Personnel Records Center at St. Louis (NPRC-SL), Military Personnel Records, William Jordan; DANFS, vol. 2, 252–53.

3. TWD, Dec. 1–15, 1944; degaussing was a countermeasure against magnetic mines.

4. Anti-aircraft Training Center, U.S. Naval Operating Base, Guantanamo Bay, Cuba, *Anti-aircraft Gunnery,* 6–7; Hubert J. Six Sr., telephone interview, Wheelersburg, Ohio.

5. *Anti-aircraft Gunnery,* 9–11.

6. Ibid.

7. Waller, interview; Joslyn, interview. After Jordan left *Tate,* the deck logs were changed to show that Waller was never arrested.

8. Waller, interview; Joslyn, interview; Norval W. Righter, telephone interview, Hyattsville, Md.

9. Waller, interview; Joslyn, interview; Dorsey, interview; TDL, Dec. 10–11, 1944; John W. Worthington, telephone interview, Opelika, Ala. Jordan's military records show that *Tate* was his last assignment, but he remained in active service until Sept. 30, 1945. Military medical records are not obtainable under the Freedom of Information Act, so the exact details of Jordan's breakdown remain unknown.

10. NPRC–SL, Military Personnel Records, Rupert E. Lyon; DANFS, vol. 1, 106; vol. 2, 30, 61; vol. 6, 470.

11. Paul R. Leahy, telephone interview, Boston. Leahy provided the most precise and credible information of any of the veterans. After nearly sixty years, he remembered exact dates and even approximate times with astounding accuracy. The officer of the deck represents the commanding officer for a four-hour watch and is superior to all other officers except the executive officer.

12. Alfred S. Coslett, telephone interview, Milmont Park, Penn. Regular and reserve officer designations are not used. All of the officers on *Tate,* with the exception of Glenn S. Parker Jr., were reserve officers (USNR). All other army and navy officers mentioned by name are regulars (USA or USN).

13. Six, interview. Six also kept a wartime diary, and although it does not include all of the events related in his interview, those it does mention coincide with what he told me.

14. Crew, interview; Morris A. Larsen, telephone interview, Whippany, N.J.

15. TWD, Dec. 21, 1944; Leahy, interview.

16. Joslyn, interview. His periodic reading of the more than 800 pages of his personal wartime letters helped keep Joslyn's memory sharp.

17. Uel Smith, telephone interview, Vancouver, Wash.

18. TWD, Dec. 30, 1944.

19. Ibid., Jan. 4, 1945; Leahy, interview. All times and dates are local and based on those given in the official records and logs. All of the times are in twenty-four-hour military notation.

20. TWD, Jan. 5, 1945; Worthington, interview.

21. Joslyn, interview; TWD, Jan 7, 1945.

22. Hubert J. Six Sr., private wartime diary, Hubert J. Six Sr., Personal Collection.

23. Donald L. Patrie, telephone interview, Niskayuna, N.Y. Earl W. Buss, telephone interview, Hot Springs National Park, Ark. Buss's account of the lazy, argumentative chief in the sick bay is unverifiable. However, on all other issues Buss was a credible source.

24. TWD, Jan. 17, 1945.

25. Smith, interview.

26. Colley, interview. Several other accounts exist about the possession of a stolen jeep, but no one besides Colley ties it to Pearl Harbor.

27. Joslyn, interview; Dorsey interview. The ship's company consisted of everyone but the landing division, which was also called the boat group.

28. TWD, Jan. 28, 1945; William G. Newton, telephone interview, Hope, Ark.

29. TWD, Feb. 3, 1945; Henry C. Noga, telephone interview, Charlemont, Mass.

30. Lyon, Military Personnel Records; DANFS, vol. 2, 61. For his meritorious actions under fire on *Celeno,* Lyon received the Navy Commendation Medal with a bronze "V" service device for valor.

Chapter 3

1. TWD, Feb. 7, 1945; *War-Time Log of USS* Tate, *AKA-70, 25 November 1944 to 12 December 1945* (hereafter referred to as the *Tate* cruise book).

2. TDL, Feb 8, 1945; Dewey Maltese, telephone interview, Ramona, Calif. After the war Maltsberger changed his name to Maltese. A retired career marine, he provided precise and credible information in his interviews when it could be checked against other sources. His perspective as *Tate's* TQM was critical to this project.

3. TDL, Feb 10, 1945; Maltese, interview; Buswell, interview; Waller, interview.

4. Waller, interview, Buswell, interview.

5. TWD, Feb. 12, 1945; Righter, interview.

6. TWD, Feb. 12–15, 1945.

7. TWD, Feb. 22, 1945; Buswell, interview; Lyon, Military Personnel Records.

8. TWD, Mar. 3, 1945; Charles B. Hathaway, telephone interview, Lake Mary, Fla.

9. TWD, Mar. 5, 1945; NABD-CP, USS *Tate* (AKA-70), "Kerama Retto Action 26 March–3 April 1945, Action Report of 10 April 1945" (hereafter referred to as TAR, Kerama Retto).

10. Joseph H. Alexander, *Storm Landings: Epic Amphibious Battles in the Central Pacific,* 78.

11. See 77th Infantry Division Association, *Ours to Hold It High: The History of the 77th Infantry Division in World War II,* (hereafter referred to as OTHIH), 430.

12. Joslyn, interview; Arthur Lee Norman, telephone interview, Bethesda, Md.

13. Buswell, interview; Buss, interview.

14. Buswell, interview. It is assumed that the woman's underwear was brought on board as part of a gag and ended up in the rag locker, where cleaning rags are kept.

15. Six, interview; Six, diary.

16. TWD, Mar. 13, 1945; J. C. Bostic, telephone interview, Greensboro, N.C.

17. TWD, Mar. 14, 1945. U.S. Infantry unit designations are cited in simple alphanumeric format, with the company, followed by battalion, followed by regiment. Example: Company A, 1st Battalion, 305th Infantry Regiment is rendered as A/1/305.

18. Leahy, interview.

19. TWD, Mar. 16, 1945; Charles S. Nichols and Henry I. Shaw, *Okinawa: Victory in the Pacific,* 34.

20. TWD, Mar. 16, 1945; Thomas J. Donnelly, *"Hey, Padre": The Saga of a Regimental Chaplain in World War II,* 104–105; Ivo Cecil, telephone interview, Elizabethtown, Ky. "Boots" refers to soldiers who are fresh from boot camp and therefore have minimal experience.

21. Donnelly, *Hey, Padre,* 105–106. Donnelly does not mention *Tate* by name, but it was the only cargo ship (AKA) in Transport Division 50 assigned to carry the 305th Infantry.

22. Samuel Eliot Morison, *Victory in the Pacific,* 119; Joslyn, interview; Lida Mayo, *The Ordnance Department: On Beachhead and Battlefront,* 454.

Chapter 4

1. George C. Dyer, *The Amphibians Came to Conquer: The Story of Admiral Richmond Kelly Turner II,* vol. 2, 1071, 1075–76; Worrall Reed Carter, *Beans, Bullets, and Black Oil:*

The Story of Fleet Logistics Afloat in the Pacific during World War II, 331–33. Effective carrier strikes in the months before Operation Iceberg destroyed most of the Japanese aircraft based on Okinawa. The threat of land-based air attacks from Okinawa against the invasion of Kerama Retto never materialized. While Kerama Retto, Okinawa, and their surrounding islands were technically part of Japan due to their annexation in 1879, their residents were ethnically different from the residents of Japan's main islands and did not consider themselves to be Japanese.

2. Morison, *Victory in the Pacific,* 88.

3. Ibid., 122; TWD, Mar. 25, 1945.

4. Patrie, interview; Anthony, interview; Maltese, interview.

5. TAR, Kerama Retto; Patrie, interview; Six, diary; DANFS, vol. 3, 645–46; Theodore Roscoe, *United States Destroyer Operations in World War II,* 467–68.

6. Morison, *Victory in the Pacific,* 120; Walter Karig, Russell L. Harris, and Frank A. Manson, *Battle Report: Victory in the Pacific,* 364–65; cruise book of the USS *Mountrail* (APA-213).

7. Morison, *Victory in the Pacific,* 120–21.

8. Warren C. Thompson, telephone interview, Monterey, Calif.; Warren C. Thompson, "History of Wave Forecasting for the Western Pacific Invasions of Peleliu, Leyte, Lingayen, Iwo Jima, and Okinawa."

9. Joslyn, interview; Dorsey, interview.

10. TAR, Kerama Retto; Gerald Astor, *Operation Iceberg: The Invasion and Conquest of Okinawa in World War II,* 60; Morison, *Victory in the Pacific,* 122; U.S. Navy training film, *Amphibious Warfare: The LST.*

11. Alvin Joslyn, letter to his wife, May 20, 1945, Alvin Joslyn Personal Collection.

12. TAR, Kerama Retto; Dorsey, interview; Norman, interview. Dorsey's letters were delivered to the *Tate* after he transferred to an LST at Leyte.

13. Francis T. Miller, *The Complete History of World War II,* 923–24; Patrie, interview; Cecil, interview.

14. OTHIH, 223, 235, 238; DANFS, vol. 6, 608. Joslyn, interview; Gordon L. Rottman, "Japanese Suicide Boats at Okinawa, 1945," 51–57. Roy E. Appleman et al., *Okinawa: The Last Battle,* 60.

15. TAR, Kerama Retto; Cecil, interview.

16. Cecil, interview.

17. OTHIH, 231.

18. Ibid., 231–32.

19. TAR, Kerama Retto; Joslyn, interview; Charles O. West et al., *Second to None! The Story of the 305th Infantry In World War II,* 149–50.

20. TAR, Kerama Retto; James W. Anthony, telephone interview, Drexel, N.C.

21. OTHIH, 233–35.

22. Ibid.; Astor, *Operation Iceberg,* 61–62.

23. OTHIH, 235.

24. Joslyn, letter to his wife, May 20, 1945; Joslyn, interview.

25. OTHIH, 236–37.

26. Joslyn, interview.

27. TAR, Kerama Retto; Buswell, interview; Joslyn, interview.

28. TWD, May 28, 1945; Coslett, interview; Buswell, interview; Patrie, interview; Worthington, interview.

29. TAR, Kerama Retto; Maltese, interview; Six, interview; Colley, interview.

30. DANFS, vol. 8, 487–88; TWD, May 29, 1945; Six, interview; Hathaway, interview. The fluorescence of *Tate*'s wake was due to the presence of plankton that release bioluminescent light when disturbed. Under the right conditions, the light makes an easy trail for aircraft to follow.

31. DANFS, vol. 8, 487–88; Mayo, *Ordnance Department,* 454; Six, interview; Victor E. Weaver, *The 233d Engineer Combat Battalion, 1943–1945,* 95. Sergeant Dunham received the Bronze Star for his efforts in saving *Wyandot.*

32. TAR, Kerama Retto; Six, diary.

33. OTHIH, 237–38; Appleman et al., *Okinawa,* 56; Hiromichi Yahara, *The Battle for Okinawa,* 38–39, 206.

34. NABD-CP, USS *Bowditch* (AGS-4) war diary, 1 Mar–30 Jun 1945; Morison, *Victory in the Pacific,* 127; Stewart B. Nelson, *Oceanographic Ships Fore and Aft,* 112.

35. TWD, Mar. 30–31, 1945; Gordon Rottman, *Okinawa 1945: The Last Battle,* 54.

36. Mark I. Johnson, interview with author, telephone, Frankfort, N.Y.

37. OTHIH, 239.

Chapter 5

1. Michael Evans, *Amphibious Operations: The Projection of Power Ashore,* 28. The numbers of naval combat ships supporting the invasion of Okinawa were similar to those present for the Normandy invasion. The total number of ships present at Normandy was larger than that at Okinawa. A vast number of smaller ships, ancillary craft, and merchant vessels supported the invasion of Normandy.

2. Rikihei Inoguchi, Tadashi Nakajima, and Roger Pineau, *The Divine Wind: Japan's Kamikaze Force in World War II,* 93, 225. Statistical Japanese war records have proven problematic due to omissions. While it is possible that additional aircraft made sorties to the waters around Okinawa on Apr. 2, 1945, *Divine Wind* provides an adequate understanding of the tempo of the operations.

3. John A. Lorelli, *To Foreign Shores: U.S. Amphibious Operations in World War II,* 297.

4. TAR, Kerama Retto; NABD-CP, USS *Rixey* (APH-3), "Action Report on Occupation of Kerama Retto and Ie Shima, Okinawa Gunto, Nansei Shoto, Covers Landing Units of 307th RCT 77th Infantry, 26 March–22 April 1945, in Task Unit 51.1.1"; Alvin F. Maw, interview, Raleigh, N.C. The aircraft Maw saw crash was likely hit by 20-mm fire from a ship forward of *Tate.* The Japanese pilot's use of the cockpit light was probably either to assess wounds and damage or to assist him in an attempt to bail out. If *Tate* hit this aircraft, it was only after it began its plunge into the sea.

5. TAR, Kerama Retto.

6. Ibid.; NABD-CP, USS *Harry F. Bauer* (DM-26), "Report of Capture of Okinawa Gunto, Phases I and II, 25 March to 11 June 1945. Covers Minesweeping, Fire Support, and Screening Activities for Iceberg Operation in Task Unit 52.6.4"; NABD-CP USS *Mountrail* (APA-213), "Covers Suicide Attack on Night Retirement Group Southwest of Okinawa, in Task Unit 51.1.5"; DANFS, vol. 3, 142–43; Joslyn, interview.

7. TAR, Kerama Retto; NABD-CP, USS *Henrico* (APA-45), "Battle Damage Report, 2 April 1945, Summary of. Covers Damage Sustained as a Result of Attack by Japanese Suicide

Bomber and Resulting Explosions, while Under Way in Night Retirement Course West of
Kerama Retto, Okinawa." *Henrico*'s action report mentions a flash blue condition issued by
the OTC on *Chilton*. *Chilton*'s action report, however, does not mention a flash blue condition. *Dickerson*'s action report states that the ship was under an all-clear, flash white condition when the attacks began. Whatever the readiness condition of the ships, the attack was
certainly a surprise since only ready gunners were in position to counter the initial wave of
aircraft that began attacking at 1841.

8. Joslyn, interview; Buss, interview; Newton, interview.

9. TAR, Kerama Retto; John S. Carpenter and John H. Donald Jr., "Any Time, Any
Beach: Being a History of the USS *Chilton*, APA-38," 13; NABD-CP, USS *Chilton*, "Ac-
tion Report of Capture of Okinawa Gunto, Phases I and II, Covers Activities during Kerama
Retto and Ie Shima Landings, Had Aboard Personnel of 77th Division Headquarters Staff
with Special Troops and Cargo, Period 26 March thru 30 April 1945, in Task Unit 51.1.3";
OTHIH, 254. A squawk box is an intercom speaker.

10. Joslyn, interview; *Henrico*, action report; NABD-CP, USS *Suffolk* (AKA-69), "Antiaircraft Action by Surface Vessel."

11. Joslyn, interview; *Henrico*, action report; *Suffolk*, action report; Astor, *Operation Iceberg*, 184, 186. On board *Chilton* was another future governor, Herman Talmidge of Georgia.

12. Astor, *Operation Iceberg*, 184; Joslyn interview; Newton, interview; Waller, interview.

13. *Rixey*, action report; *Harry F. Bauer*, action report; NABD-CP, USS *Natrona* (APA-
214), "Action Report of Capture of Okinawa Gunto, Covers Landing Miscellaneous Units
in Kerama Retto and Okinawa from 26 March–17 May 1945, in Task Unit 51.1.4."

14. Buss, interview; William M. Polikowski, telephone interview, Whitesboro, N.Y.

15. *Mountrail*, action report; NABD-CP, USS *Eastland* (APA-163), "Revised Form for
Reporting A. A. Action by Surface Ships"; NABD-CP, USS *Telfair* (APA-210), "Covers
Damage from Suicide Plane Attack while on Night Retirement Course West of Kerama
Retto in Task Unit 51.1.5"; NABD-CP, USS *Montrose* (APA-212), "Covers Varied Activities
during Okinawa Operation from 26 March to 26 April 1945."

16. *Chilton*, action report; *Rixey*, action report.

17. NABD-CP, USS *Dickerson* (APD-21), "Loss of *Dickerson*, 2–4 April 1945, Report of
Circumstances surrounding Loss of *Dickerson* as a Result of Bombing and Kamikaze Attack
on 2 April 1945. In Mine Squadron 7, Screen for Task Unit 51.1.1 SW of Kerama Retto. On
4 April 1945, Ship Was Towed Out and Sunk by Salvage Crew"; Joslyn, interview; Borenski, interview; Crew, interview; David L. Hibbs Sr., "USS *Bunch* DE-694/APD-79." There
are conflicting accounts of the attack on *Dickerson* that suggest either that a second kamikaze
crashed into its forecastle soon after the first plane struck or that a bomb was dropped by
another aircraft almost simultaneously to the crash, hitting the area of the 3" gun. These
accounts appear to be attempts to justify the amount of damage done to *Dickerson* and are
not supported by action reports of the surrounding ships or by eyewitness accounts. A single
aircraft likely caused all of the damage. Either its bombs were dropped just before impact
(similar to the *Henrico* attack), or they penetrated during the plane's impact forward through
the bridge and struck near the forward 3" mount. The delay between the crash and the
explosion suggests a fused delay from armor-piercing ordnance that also set off the 3" ready
ammunition. A single twin-engine aircraft carrying bombs could certainly have caused the
damage suffered by *Dickerson*, a thin-skinned converted World War I destroyer.

18. NABD-CP, USS *Goodhue* (APA-107), "AA Action Report, Forward without Com-

ment, AA Form Report covering Action on 2 April 1945 while 35 Miles South of Kerama Retto in Task Unit 51.1.5"; DANFS, vol. 3, 119; Morison, *Victory in the Pacific*, 390.

19. TAR, Kerama Retto; Buswell, interview; Bostic, interview; Borenski, interview; Crew, interview; Robert F. Olkosky, telephone interview, Olean, N.Y.; Ray A. McCaffrey, telephone interview, Daphne, Ala. During the action the squadron made several course changes, all of which were 45- or 90-degree emergency turns. Most of the ships' records do not specify course changes. Some mention a series of turns without giving specific courses. Some courses that were reported are obviously wrong and contain errors of 180 degrees, where north and south appear to have been confused. For the same actions, timing errors of several minutes exist between ships. Resolving these contradictions to reconstruct a navigation track is problematic. It is likely that the critical 5"/38 shell fired by *Tate* at the Val did not detonate due to its close range. The fuse setting may not have allowed sufficient time for centrifugal motion to arm the shell. This may also have played into Parker's decision to hold his fire if the closing aircraft was already inside the range of the shell's fuse setting when it was acquired by the gun sighter. In this case only a direct hit would have been effective.

20. Leahy, interview; Anthony, interview.

21. Joslyn interview; *Montrose,* action report; *Mountrail,* action report; *Eastland,* action report; NABD-CP, USS *Torrance* (AKA-76), "Covers Action on 2 April 1945, against Enemy Aircraft during Retiring Operation from Kerama Retto in Task Unit 51.1.3."

22. TAR, Kerama Retto; *Rixey,* action report; Dorsey, interview; Anthony, interview; Harold R. Russell, telephone interview, Chincoteague Island, Va.

23. TAR, Kerama Retto; Bostic, interview.

24. TAR, Kerama Retto; Bostic, interview.

25. *Harry F. Bauer,* action report; *Henrico,* action report; Kemske, interview.

26. *Dickerson,* action report; Arikara 50s Association, "Story of the Seagoing Tug USS *Arikara* (ATF-98)"; Hibbs, "USS *Bunch* DE-694/APD-79."

27. Astor, *Operation Iceberg,* 185–86; *Suffolk,* action report; Cecil, interview.

Chapter 6

1. Crew, interview.

2. Fortunate G. Salerno, telephone interview, Fanwood, N.J. While Salerno's account is unverifiable, he made no claims other than being too busy to notice the air battle about him.

3. Six, diary.

4. *Telfair,* action report.

5. Edward P. Stafford, *Little Ship, Big War: The Saga of DE343,* 236–38.

6. *Henrico,* action report.

7. *Dickerson,* action report; Arikara 50s Association, "Story of the Seagoing Tug USS *Akikara* (ATF-98)."

8. *Chilton,* action report; USS *Goodhue* (APA-107) cruise book.

9. TAR, Kerama Retto; *Chilton,* action report; Leahy, interview; Russell, interview; USS *Tazewell, Two-O-Nine: A Ship's Biography,* 21.

10. Waller, interview; Crew, interview; Wilmer J. Bosarge, telephone interview, Irvington, Ala.; Colley, interview.

11. Kenneth Dodson, *Away All Boats: A Novel,* 36.

12. Astor, *Operation Iceberg,* 204–205.

13. Morison, *Victory in the Pacific,* 189; Dyer, *The Amphibians Came to Conquer,* 1101.

14. TWD, Apr. 3–13, 1945.

15. E. P. Forrestal, *Admiral Raymond A. Spruance, USN: A Study in Command,* 203.

16. Ibid., 205.

17. Henry D. López, *From Jackson to Japan: The History of Company C, 307th Infantry, 77th Division in World War II,* 59.

18. Weaver, *233d Engineer Combat Battalion,* 98.

19. Six, diary.

20. Dyer, *The Amphibians Came to Conquer,* 1100; Joslyn, interview.

21. *DANFS,* vol. 2, 77–78; vol. 6, 608.

22. Leahy, interview; Norman M. Nisen, telephone interview, Little Neck, N.Y. Roosevelt died on the evening of Apr. 12, 1945, which was Apr. 13, 1945, in Okinawa.

23. TDL, Apr. 14, 1945; Newton, interview.

24. Patrie, interview.

25. Smith, interview. As a dedicated research assistant, Uel Smith worked very hard to ensure the authenticity of this project. In my estimation, his willingness to pursue every lead and double-check every fact gives his account the highest level of credibility.

26. Cecil, interview. While Cecil's account is unverifiable, it is representative of the emotional human-interest stories that have an unquestionable tone of credibility.

27. Dyer, *The Amphibians Came to Conquer,* 1064.

28. TDL, Apr. 14, 1945.

29. Blaine Lakes, telephone interview, Cincinnati; Byron W. Larsen, telephone interview, Ormond Beach, Fla. *Tate* did not have radio variable-time (VT) proximity-fuse capability. VT-fused shells are detonated by the increasing strength of the reflected radar signal as they approach the target.

30. Joslyn, letter to his wife, May 20, 1945.

Chapter 7

1. TDL, Apr. 16, 1945.

2. Nichols and Shaw, *Okinawa,* 28. In TransRon 17's case, for the Okinawa campaign, the tractor flotilla carried a portion of the assault forces and some of their cargo, decreasing the need for the full doctrinal complement of APAs and AKAs.

3. G. V. Corbett, "Operation Iceberg: Campaigning in the Ryukyus," 41; Maltese, interview.

4. Philip A. Crowl and Edmund G. Love, *The War in the Pacific: Seizure of the Gilberts and Marshalls,* 49; López, *From Jackson to Japan,* 67.

5. Maltese, interview.

6. Attack plan for capture of Ie Shima.

7. Appleman et al., *Okinawa,* 154.

8. Douglas F. Fane and Dan Moore, *The Naked Warriors,* 206–207.

9. Ibid.; Appleman et al., *Okinawa,* 156; Bruce F. Meyers, *Swift, Silent, and Deadly: Marine Amphibious Reconnaissance in the Pacific, 1942–1945,* 122.

10. Nichols and Shaw, *Okinawa,* 112; attack plan for capture of Ie Shima.

11. Nichols and Shaw, *Okinawa,* 112; OTHIH, 255.

12. James Belate and William Belate, *Typhoon of Steel: The Battle for Okinawa,* 193; Astor, *Operation Iceberg,* 258; Victor J. Croizat, *Across the Reef: Amphibious Tracked Vehicles at War,* 171.

13. OTHIH, 255–56.

14. Ibid.

15. Attack plan for capture of Ie Shima.

16. Nichols and Shaw, *Okinawa,* 114.

17. Attack plan for capture of Ie Shima.

18. Nichols and Shaw, *Okinawa,* 114; Appleman et al., *Okinawa,* 157.

19. Attack plan for capture of Ie Shima.

20. U.S. Navy training film, *Small Boat Landing Tactics and Supply.*

21. Ibid.; attack plan for capture of Ie Shima; Appleman et al., *Okinawa,* 157.

22. Joslyn, letter to his wife, May 20, 1945.

23. Astor, *Operation Iceberg,* 260; OTHIH, 256.

Chapter 8

1. TDL, Apr. 16, 1945.

2. DANFS, vol. 4, 17–19; Morison, *Victory in the Pacific,* 235–37; Karig, *Battle Report,* 406–408.

3. Morison, *Victory in the Pacific,* 235–38, 391; Karig, *Battle Report,* 410.

4. ANFS, vol. 3, 446–50.

5. TDL, Apr. 16, 1945; Nichols and Shaw, *Okinawa,* 114.

6. Nichols and Shaw, *Okinawa,* 114; Joslyn, interview.

7. Appleman et al., *Okinawa,* 157, 159.

8. Ibid.

9. Ibid.

10. *Princeton Union-Eagle,* "WWII Veteran Injured in South Pacific Battle."

11. OTHIH, 258.

12. TDL, Apr. 16, 1945.

13. Appleman et al., *Okinawa,* 159–60.

14. Dorsey, interview; Carpenter and Donald, "Any Time, Any Beach." Ernie Pyle appears in a photo with the command staff on board the *Chilton.*

15. Dorsey, interview; Carpenter and Donald, "Any Time, Any Beach"; B. Larsen, interview; Norman, interview; Righter, interview.

16. Dorsey, interview; Righter, interview; Baker, interview; Russell, interview.

17. Nichols and Shaw, *Okinawa,* 116; OTHIH, 260–61.

18. Nicholas and Shaw, *Okinawa,* 116; Appleman et al., *Okinawa,* 160, 162; Joslyn, letter to his wife, May 20, 1945.

19. Anthony, interview. This story is consistent with the documented level of minor resistance that opposed the landings.

20. Edwin H. Randle, *Ernie Pyle Comes Ashore and Other Stories,* 1–2; Lee G. Miller, *An*

Ernie Pyle Album: Indiana to Ie Shima, 148; Morison, 241; Karig, *Battle Report*, 418; Kenneth H. Goldman, *USS* Charles Carroll, *APA 28: An Amphibious History of World War II*, 199.

21. Randle, *Ernie Pyle Comes Ashore*, 3–5.

22. Ibid.

23. Nichols and Shaw, *Okinawa*, 116; Appleman et al., *Okinawa*, 161–62; OTHIH, 261.

24. Nichols and Shaw, *Okinawa*, 116; Appleman et al., *Okinawa*, 160, 163; Weaver, *The 233d Engineer Combat Battalion*, 99.

25. Attack plan for capture of Ie Shima; Miller, *An Ernie Pyle Album*, 148; James Tobin, *Ernie Pyle's War: America's Eyewitness to World War II*, 240; Newton, interview. The M-8 Howitzer motor carriage consisted of a 75-mm pack howitzer mounted on the M-5 tank carriage. The M-18 Hellcat tank destroyer was the fastest turreted tracked vehicle in the war.

26. Buswell, interview; Patrie, interview.

27. Ira T. Sanders, "Hydrographic Surveys for Amphibious Wartime Operation."

28. Newton, interview.

29. Ibid.

30. Marjorie Waidner, letter to author, May 19, 2004, containing a 1943 newspaper clipping about CSM Waidner from the *South Bend Tribune. Ancon's* original hull number was AP-66. After the North African campaign, the ship was converted to the amphibious command ship AGC-4. During the Italian campaign, *Ancon* served as the flagship of the commander of the amphibious forces of the Atlantic Fleet.

31. Bosarge, interview; Johnson, interview; Kemske, interview.

32. Attack plan for the capture of Ie Shima; Willard D. Whitcome, telephone interview, Fort Dodge, Iowa.

33. OTHIH, 261; Astor, *Operation Iceberg*, 277.

34. West, *Second to None!* 165.

35. Nichols and Shaw, *Okinawa*, 166–67; Appleman et al., *Okinawa*, 164, 167; OTHIH, 262–63.

36. Appleman et al., *Okinawa*, 172–73.

37. Tobin, *Ernie Pyle's War*, 240; Randle, *Ernie Pyle Comes Ashore*, 7–8; Bosarge, interview; Johnson, interview; Colley, interview; Worthington, interview; Hathaway, interview. Pyle's placement on Red Beach T-4 on the morning of Apr. 18, 1945, stems from multiple accounts of seeing him on and near an LST. Only Red Beach T-4 was accessible to LSTs. Accounts by the men who spent the night of Apr. 17–18 on an LCM tied up to an LST before seeing Pyle on the beach that morning include descriptions of Iegusugu Yama just inland from where they spent the night.

38. Tobin, *Ernie Pyle's War*, 240; Randle, *Ernie Pyle Comes Ashore*, 7–9; OTHIH, 265; Miller, *An Ernie Pyle Album*, 150.

39. TDL, Apr. 18, 1945; Waller, interview.

40. Waller, interview; Appleman et al., *Okinawa*, 170.

41. Appleman et al., *Okinawa*, 170.

42. TAR, Kerama Retto; TWD, Apr. 19, 1945; Cecil, interview; Johnson, interview.

43. Astor, *Operation Iceberg*, 271; Appleman et al., *Okinawa*, 170; Joslyn, letter to his wife, May 20, 1945; Wayne C. MacGregor Jr., *Through These Portals: A Pacific War Saga*, 135.

44. Nichols and Shaw, *Okinawa*, 114; Appleman et al., *Okinawa*, 156; John D. Fleming, Ie Shima diary, 24 January–2 September 1945; Colley, interview.

45. Nichols and Shaw, *Okinawa*, 117; Appleman et al., *Okinawa*, 173; López, *From Jackson to Japan*, 142–43.

46. Appleman et al., *Okinawa*, 175; Nichols and Shaw, *Okinawa*, 177–78; Fleming, Ie Shima diary.

47. Astor, *Operation Iceberg*, 283.

48. Appleman et al., *Okinawa*, 176–77.

49. Ibid.

50. TWD, Apr. 20, 1945; Patrie, interview; Buswell, interview.

51. Appleman et al., *Okinawa*, 178; OTHIH, 273–74.

52. Appleman et al., *Okinawa*, 178.

53. Ibid., 180–81; MacGregor, *Through These Portals*, 137–38. All six of the men who took part in placing the first U.S. flag on Iegusugu Yama received the Silver Star.

54. OTHIH, 279.

55. American War Library, *WW2 Famous Quotations;* OTHIH, 281; Appleman et al., *Okinawa*, 182; Astor, *Operation Iceberg*, 286.

56. OTHIH, 265; Karig, *Battle Report*, 419; Miller, *An Ernie Pyle Album*, 153–54; Astor, *Operation Iceberg*, 273; Fleming, Ie Shima diary.

57. Miller, *An Ernie Pyle Album*, 40; Astor, *Operation Iceberg*, 273.

Chapter 9

1. TWD, Apr. 21, 1945; Astor, *Operation Iceberg*, 287.

2. *Hot Tater*, Apr. 25, 1945; Hubert Six, personal collection.

3. Dorsey, interview. Dorsey provided a great deal of credible information, much of which was not used in this story. One of the first things he said during his interview was that his hearing had been damaged in the war and he hoped it would not interfere with our conversation.

4. TWD, Apr. 22, 1945; Julian F. Becton and Joseph Morschauser III, *The Ship That Would Not Die*, 295–96.

5. TWD, Apr. 23, 1945.

6. Ibid.; Becton and Morschauser, *The Ship That Would Not Die*, 296.

7. TWD, Apr. 27, 1945; Baker, interview; Six, diary.

8. Lewis Crew, letter to Alice Bueschlen, Apr. 27, 1945, Lewis Crew Personal Collection.

9. Ibid.

10. TWD, May 2, 1945.

11. Crew, letter to Bueschlen, Apr. 27, 1945.

12. *Tate* cruise book.

13. Joslyn, interview; Kampel, interview; *Tate* cruise book.

14. Crew, letter to Alice Bueschlen, May 14, 1945, Lewis Crew Personal Collection.

15. TWD, May 12, 1945; Six, diary.

16. Crew, letter to Bueschlen, May 14, 1945; *Time*, May 7, 1945.

17. Dodson, *Away All Boats*, 166.

18. TWD, May 18, 1945; DANFS, vol. 5, 134–35.

19. TWD, May 18, 1945; Borenski, interview.

20. Crew, letter to Bueschlen, May 14, 1945.

21. Joslyn, interview.

22. TWD, May 22, 1945.

23. Ibid.

24. Ibid., June 8, 1945; Cecil, interview; Linda O'Neil Milbourn, telephone interview with author, University Park, Md.

25. Buswell, interview; Cecil, interview; Theron W. Hokanson, telephone interview, Green Valley, Ariz.

26. TWD, June 12, 1945; B. Larsen, interview.

Chapter 10

1. TWD, June 18, 1945; Dorsey, interview.

2. TWD, June 19, 1945.

3. John C. Raynor, telephone interview with author, Camus, Wash. Leahy died several months before the Raynor interview, so this story could not be verified. Raynor had a reverential respect for Leahy, whom he credited with putting him on a professional career track.

4. Six, diary.

5. TWD, June 16, 1945.

6. Lewis Crew, letter to Alice Bueschlen, June 29, 1945, Lewis Crew Personal Collection.

7. Smith, interview.

8. Borenski, interview.

9. Gries, interview. Gries had no motive for inaccurately relating a story that he knew would represent his violation of navy regulations.

10. TWD, July 18, 1945; Maltese, interview.

11. Lewis Crew, letter to Alice Bueschlen, July 20, 1945, Lewis Crew Personal collection; Destroyer Escort Sailors Association, *Destroyer Escorts of World War Two*, 6.

12. TWD, June 19, 1945.

13. Leahy, interview.

14. Buswell, interview.

15. Polikowski, interview.

16. *Hot Tater,* "A Virgin Visits Frisco, USS *Tate*"; Fortunate Salerno, Personal Collection.

17. Lewis Crew, letter to Alice Bueschlen, July 27, 1945, Lewis Crew Personal Collection; Colley, interview.

18. Lewis Crew, "*Tate* Marching Song," Lewis Crew Personal Collection.

19. Ibid.

20. TWD, Aug. 6, 1945.

21. Ibid.; B. Larsen, interview; Coslett, interview; Milbourn, interview. No knowledge of radioactive fallout existed among the ship's crew when they first received the news of the atomic bombing of Hiroshima.

22. Crew, interview; B. Larsen, interview. CINCPACFLT moved from Pearl Harbor to Guam after the Marianas campaign was completed. In Guam, the news of the cease-fire was available shortly before it was made known in other areas. The Japanese Domei News Agency broadcast on Aug. 14, 1945, that Japan had accepted the Allied terms of surrender before the United States made the formal announcement. This may have been the source of the news *Tate*'s radioman intercepted.

23. Joslyn interview; Leahy, interview.

24. Borenski, interview.

25. J. C. Bostic, interview.

26. Patrie, interview; Norman, interview. Almost every veteran had a story about the friction between Boland and the other members of the crew. With the exception of this account, they have all been excluded as being beyond the scope of this project.

27. Joslyn, interview; Milbourn, interview.

28. Smith, interview; TWD, Aug. 15, 1945.

29. Naval Historical Center, "Japan Capitulates: Arrangements" (no date); *Hot Tater*, Aug. 15, 1945; Fortunate Salerno Personal Collection.

30. Naval Historical Center, "Japan Capitulates: Arrangements."

31. Fleming, Ie Shima diary. Fleming's diary contains transcripts of the messages exchanged between MacArthur and the Japanese. The Japanese delays were due to the lack of availability of the type of aircraft MacArthur had specified. Clearly impatient with the delay, MacArthur left the aircraft selection up to the Japanese and adamantly restated their need for immediate compliance in dispatching their delegation. Fleming's diary also contains the names of 15 of the delegation's 17 members: Lt. Gen. Torashiro Kawabe, head of the delegation; Morio Yukawa, Foreign Office; Katsuo Okazaki, chief of the research division, Foreign Office; Maj. Gen. Morikazu Amano, army general staff; Col. Arata Yamoto, army general staff; Lt. Col. Kiyoshi Minami, army department; Lt. Col Masao Matsuda, army department; Lt. Sadao Ohtake, army general staff; RADM Ichiro Yokoyama, naval general staff; Capt. Toshichi Omayo, naval general staff; Capt. Hidemi Yoshida, navy department; Cdr. Yoshimasa Torai, naval general staff; Kazuma Sugita, secretary to the navy minister; Shuichi Mizta, civilian secretary to the navy minister; and Lieutenant Fujiwara, paymaster.

32. Ibid.

33. TWD, Aug. 26, 1945.

Chapter 11

1. TWD, Aug. 28, 1945.

2. Ibid., Aug. 30, 1945. *Raymond* fought in the epic battle of Samar on Oct. 25, 1944, during the Leyte Gulf campaign, when destroyer types (DDs and DEs), plus six escort carriers, took on a Japanese task force of battleships, cruisers, and destroyers. In part due to the audacity of the U.S. attacks, the Japanese turned back, thus missing an opportunity to disrupt the ongoing invasion of Leyte. This was perhaps the most dramatic surface action in the history of the U.S. Navy.

3. Ibid., Sept. 2, 1945.

4. Gerald M. Yankee and the USS *LaGrange* (APA-124), "My Crew and I: The Story of

the Last Navy Ship Casualty of World War II," 119–20, 128. Yankee's book uses the ship as a first-person narrator, which is why he includes the ship as the coauthor.

5. TDL, Sept. 10, 1945; NABD-CP, USS *Tate,* "Covers Occupation Landing Second-echelon Troops and Cargo of XXIV Corps, Tenth Army, at Jinsen, Korea, in Task Unit 78.17.1."

6. Lewis Crew, letter to Alice Bueschlen, Sept. 9, 1945, Lewis Crew Personal Collection. Smoker parties included food, entertainment, and athletic activities such as wrestling and boxing.

7. B. Larsen, interview; Carpenter and Donald, "Any Time, Any Beach," 26.

8. TDL, Sept. 13, 1945. Since the United States was navigating with Japanese charts, the ships' logs and action reports refer to the Korean port of Inchon by its Japanese name, Jinsen.

9. TWD, Sept. 13, 1945; Colley, interview.

10. TAR, Korean Occupation.

11. TWD, Sept. 15, 1945.

12. TDL, Sept. 16, 1945.

13. Leahy, interview.

14. TDL, Sept. 18–21, 1945.

15. TWD, Sept. 26, 1945; Nisen, interview.

16. TWD, Sept. 26, 1945; Naval Analysis Division, *The Offensive Mine-laying Campaign against Japan,* 14, 49, 50.

17. Ibid.

18. David M. Glantz, *August Storm: The Soviet 1945 Strategic Offensive in Manchuria, 1945,* xvii–xviii; Bosarge, interview.

19. TWD, Sept. 30–Oct. 2, 1945; Henry I. Shaw Jr., *The United States Marines in North China, 1945–1949,* 2–3; E. B. Sledge, *China Marine: An Infantryman's Life after World War II,* 15.

20. TWD, Oct. 1–6, 1945; Hokanson, interview; Raymond M. Comstock, telephone interview, Louisville, Ky.

21. TDL, Oct. 6, 1945; Maltese, interview; Bosarge, interview; Hathaway, interview; Worthington, interview.

22. TDL, Oct. 8, 1945.

23. Salerno, interview.

24. Nago, interview.

25. Ibid.; Zeblin V. Midgett, telephone interview, Kill Devil Hills, N.C.; Waller, interview.

26. Joslyn, interview.

27. TDL, Oct. 10, 1945; Whitcome, interview.

28. Joslyn, interview; M. Larsen, interview; TDL, Oct. 10, 1945.

29. Crew, interview; W. T. Drake, interview by letter.

30. Nago, interview; TDL, Oct. 13, 1945.

31. Lewis Crew, letter to Alice Bueschlen, Oct. 21, 1945, Lewis Crew Personal Collection; *Mountrail* cruise book.

32. Lewis Crew, letter to Alice Bueschlen, Oct. 21, 1945, Lewis Crew Personal Collection.

33. Ibid.; Comstock, interview; Kemske, interview.

34. Lewis Crew, letter to Alice Bueschlen, Oct. 21, 1945. Typhoon Louise came to be known as the Great October Typhoon.

35. Cecil, interview.

36. Lewis Crew, letter to Alice Bueschlen, Oct. 19, 1945, Lewis Crew Personal Collection; Bostic, interview.

37. TDL, Oct. 25, 1945; Nago, interview; Smith, interview; Crew, interview; Carpenter and Donald, "Any Time, Any Beach," 29.

38. Alvin Joslyn, letter to his wife, Oct. 26, 1945, Alvin Joslyn Personal Collection.

39. Joslyn, interview; M. Larsen, interview.

40. Leahy, interview; Polikowski, interview.

41. TDL, Oct. 26, 1945; Joslyn, interview; Crew, interview.

42. Crew, interview; Joslyn, letter, Oct. 26, 1945.

43. Author's collection, "USS *Clinton* (APA 144), Posts Their Top Ten Commandments," Nov. 2, 1945. A *joss* is a Chinese idol.

44. Crew, interview; Patrie, interview.

45. TDL, Oct. 29, 1945; Alvin Joslyn, letter to his wife, Oct. 30, 1945, Alvin Joslyn, Personal Collection; Midgett, interview.

46. Joslyn, interview; Carpenter and Donald, "Any Time, Any Beach," 26.

47. Waller, interview. While this account is unverified, Waller provided many other credible stories.

48. Leahy, interview.

49. TDL, Nov. 1, 1945.

50. Ibid.; Smith, interview.

51. Nago, interview; Joslyn, interview.

52. Alvin Joslyn, letter to his wife, Nov. 3, 1945, Alvin Joslyn Personal Collection.

53. TDL, Nov. 2, 1945.

54. Ibid.; Alvin Joslyn, letter to Jeanne Martin, Dec. 24, 1945, Alvin Joslyn Personal Collection.

55. TDL, Nov. 4, 1945; Leahy, interview; Joslyn, interview. Representative text is used since the exact wording of the burial at sea commitment is unknown.

56. TDL, Nov. 5, 1945.

57. Ibid., Nov. 9, 1945; Carpenter and Donald, "Any Time, Any Beach," 29.

58. TDL, Nov. 12, 1945; Whitcome, interview.

59. Leahy, interview; Nisen, interview.

60. Crew, interview; Joslyn, interview.

61. TDL, Nov. 16, 1945; Six, interview.

62. TDL, Nov. 16, 1945.

63. TDL, Nov. 17, 1945; Alvin Joslyn, letter to his wife, Nov. 16, 1945, Alvin Joslyn Personal Collection.

64. TDL, Nov. 18–22, 1945; Bosarge, interview.

65. Joslyn, interview; Waller, interview.

66. Alvin Joslyn, letter to his wife, Nov. 16, 1945.

67. Ibid.; Crew, interview.

68. TDL, Nov. 22, 1945; Alvin Joslyn, letter to his wife, Nov. 22, 1945, Alvin Joslyn Personal Collection.

Chapter 12

1. Alvin Joslyn, letter to his wife, Nov. 24, 1945, Alvin Joslyn Personal Collection; TWD, Nov. 23, 1945.

2. TDL, Nov. 25, 1945.

3. Ibid., Nov. 26, 1945; USS *Tate* (AKA-70), *Hot Tater,* Nov. 26, 1945, Fortunate Salerno, Personal Collection.

4. Smith, interview; Buss, interview.

5. Milton J. Buswell, letter to author, Dec. 12, 2002; Joslyn, interview.

6. Borenski, interview; Smith, interview; Joslyn, interview.

7. Joslyn, interview.

8. TDL, Dec. 10, 1945.

9. Ibid., Dec. 18, 1945.

10. Joslyn, interview.

11. Jeanne Martin, letter to chaplain, USS *Tate,* Dec. 12, 1945, Alvin Joslyn Personal Collection.

12. Alvin Joslyn, letter to his wife, Nov. 5, 1945, Alvin Joslyn Personal Collection.

13. Ibid., letter to Jeanne Martin, Dec. 24, 1945; Joslyn, interview.

14. TDL, Dec. 26, 1945; Joslyn, interview.

15. B. Larsen, interview; Smith, interview; Joslyn, interview.

16. B. Larsen, interview. The deck logs show Braxton's promotion to chief, and the ship's cruise book has a group photo of the engineering department with Braxton in a CPO uniform.

17. Morris J. MacGregor Jr., *Integration of the Armed Forces,* 59–68.

18. Ibid.; Raynor, interview.

19. TDL, Jan. 8, 1946; Righter, interview.

20. Dorsey, interview. Both Dorsey and his wife attended *Tate's* reunion and spoke about this same event.

21. TDL, Jan. 23, 1946; Joslyn, interview.

22. TDL, Feb. 8, 1946.

23. Lakes, interview.

24. TDL, Jan 1, 1946; Anthony, interview; Crew, interview.

25. Cecil, interview.

26. Comstock, interview.

27. TDL, Feb. 20–25, 1946.

28. Ibid., Mar. 5–13, 1946; Linwood Tudor, telephone interview, Covington, Ga.; Colley, interview.

29. USS *Tate, Hot Tater,* Hubert J. Six, Personal Collection.

30. Waller, interview; Crew, interview.

31. Waller, interview.

32. Crew, interview.

33. NPRC-SL, Military Personnel Records, Andrew Morthland.

34. TDL, Mar. 28–Apr. 2, 1946; Fredrick Witte, telephone interview, Comstock Park, Mich.; Tudor, interview; Leahy, interview. The Aleutian earthquake occurred on Apr. 1,

1946, but the Marshall Islands are a day ahead of Alaska as they lie west of the International Date Line.

35. TDL, Apr. 5, 1946.

36. Ibid., Apr. 23–May 6, 1946; Crew, interview.

37. TDL, May 9, 1946; Leahy, interview.

38. Midgett, interview.

39. TDL, May 9, 1946.

40. Ibid., May 10, 1946; Midgett, interview; Hokanson, interview.

41. Leahy, interview.

42. Ibid.; Borenski, interview; Hokanson, interview; DANFS, vol. 3, 374–75.

43. Crew, interview; Waller, interview.

44. TDL, May 18, 1946.

45. Ibid.; Leahy, interview; Crew, interview.

46. TDL, May 20–23, 1946.

47. Ibid.; Waller, interview.

48. TDL, June 24–July 10, 1946; DANFS, vol. 7, 52.

Epilogue

1. Jon Toombs, telephone interview, Gulfport, Miss. A memorial pavilion near the site of Gulfport's old train station contains the names of all of the city's World War II veterans, including John J. Toombs.

2. Alexander, interview.

3. Polikowski, interview; Crew, interview; Borenski, interview.

4. B. Larsen, interview.

5. Borenski, interview; Dorsey, interview.

6. Newton, interview.

7. Baker, interview.

8. Lyon, Military Personnel Records.

9. "Story of Greatest Generation Deserves to Be Told Well," *Ann Arbor Press,* May 28, 2001. The article was submitted by *Tate* veteran Alvin L. Joslyn.

10. Stephen E. Ambrose, *To America,* 101.

11. The names on the Punchbowl cemetery's courts of the missing do not include those who went missing as the result of the sinking of the battleship *Arizona* on Dec. 7, 1941; those men are remembered on the USS *Arizona* Memorial.

12. Richard B. Frank, *Downfall: The End of the Imperial Japanese Empire,* 136. Casualty figures included losses to disease, which were higher in the Pacific; Appleman et al., *Okinawa,* 489. The numbers of those killed from Apr. 1 to June 30, 1945, during the Okinawa campaign are as follows: army, 4,582; marines, 2,792; and navy, 4,907. The Japanese used more than 4,600 kamikazes.

13. Ernie Pyle, *Last Chapter,* 144; Righter, interview; Whitcome, interview.

14. W. C. Marsh, rear admiral commander, Amphibious Group Three, letter to "Crew members of the USS *Tate* (AKA-70)"; Tom Brokaw, letter to "World War II veterans who served on the USS *Tate*"; Pres. George W. Bush, letter to "Those gathered for the first reunion of the USS *Tate*."

15. David Nichols, *Ernie's War: The Best of Ernie Pyle's World War II Dispatches*, 419.

16. DANFS, vol. 7, 52; *Empires of American Industry: Victory at Sea, Mass-producing Liberty;* North Carolina Shipbuilding Company, *Five Years of North Carolina Shipbuilding,* 7–14;

17. L. A. Sawyer and W. H. Mitchell, *From America to the United States: The History of the Long-range Merchant Shipbuilding Programme of the United States Maritime Commission (1937–1952),* vol. 2, 514. The name *Bay State* is used by the Massachusetts Maritime Academy (MMA) for its training ships. In this case, there is no connection to MMA.

Appendix B

1. Alvin Joslyn, personal collection.

BIBLIOGRAPHY

Unpublished Material

Manuscript Collections and Letters

Brokaw, Tom. Letter to "World War II veterans who served on the USS *Tate* (AKA-70)," June 11, 2003.

Bush, George W. Letter to "Those gathered for the first reunion of the USS *Tate*," Sept. 3, 2003.

Carpenter, John S., and John H. Donald Jr. "Any Time, Any Beach: Being a History of the USS *Chilton*, APA-38." Self-published, 2000.

Corbett, G. V. "Operation Iceberg: Campaigning in the Ryukyus." Master's thesis, Naval War College, Newport, R.I., 1994.

Crew, Lewis A. Personal Collection. Sylvan Lake, Michigan.

Crew, Thomas E. Personal Collection. Long Beach, Mississippi.

Fleming, John D. Diary. U.S. Army Military History Institute, Carlisle Barracks, Pennsylvania.

Joslyn, Alvin L. Personal Collection. Ypsilanti, Michigan.

Kampel, Lewis. Personal Collection. Scotch Plains, New Jersey.

Marsh, W. C. Letter to "Crew members of the USS *Tate* (AKA-70)," July 12, 2003.

Marshall, G. V. Letter to wife, November 13, 1944. Author's collection.

Salerno, Fortunate G. Personal Collection. Fanwood, New Jersey.

Sanders, Ira T. "Hydrographic Surveys for Amphibious Wartime Operation." Author's collection. (undated).

Six, Hubert J., Sr. Personal Collection. Wheelersburg, Ohio.

Thompson, Warren C. "History of Wave Forecasting for the Western Pacific Invasions of Peleliu, Leyte, Lingayen, Iwo Jima, and Okinawa." Matthew Fontaine Maury Oceanographic Library, Naval Oceanographic Office, Stennis Space Center, Mississippi, 1948.

Waidner, Marjorie. Personal Collection. Morrow, Ohio.

Yankee, Gerald M., and the USS *LaGrange* (APA-124). "My Crew and I: The Story of the Last Navy Ship Casualty of World War II." Undated memoir.

National Archives and Records Administration,
Branch Depository, College Park, Maryland.

RECORD GROUP 38, MODERN MILITARY RECORDS, ACTION REPORTS

Stack 370/44/4/4, Box 1003: USS *Goodhue* (APA-107). "AA Action Report, Forward without Comment, AA Form Report covering Action on 2 April 1945 while 35 Miles South of Kerama Retto in Task Unit 51.1.5," 14 Apr 1945.

Stack 370/45/2/5, Box 912: USS *Chilton* (APA-38). "Action Reports, Report of Capture of Okinawa Gunto: Phases I and II, Covers Activities during Kerama Retto and Ie Shima Landings, Had Aboard Personnel of 77th Division Headquarters Staff with Special Troops and Cargo, Period 26 March thru 30 April 1945, in Task Unit 51.1.3," 3 May 1945.

Stack 370/45/3/1, Box 1254: USS *Mountrail* (APA-213). "Covers Suicide Attack on Night Retirement Group Southwest of Okinawa in Task Unit 51.1.5," 28 Apr 1945.

Stack 370/45/3/3, Box 950: USS *Dickerson* (APD-21). "Loss of *Dickerson,* 2–4 April 1945, Report of Circumstances surrounding Loss of *Dickerson* as a Result of Bombing and Kamikaze Attack on 2 April in Mine Squadron 7, Screen for Task Unit 51.1.1 SW of Kerama Retto. On 4 April 1945, Ship Was Towed Out and Sunk by Salvage Crew," 10 Apr 1945.

Stack 370/45/3/4, Box 957: USS *Eastland* (APA-163). "Revised Form for Reporting A.A. Action by Surface Ships," 13 Apr 1945.

Stack 370/45/3/6, Box 1463: USS *Tate* (AKA-70), Serial 001. "Kerama Retto Action, 26 March–3 April 1945," Action Report, 10 Apr 1945.

Ibid. "Covers Occupation Landing Second-echelon Troops and Cargo, XXIV Corps, Tenth Army, at Jinsen, Korea, in Task Unit 78.17.1," Action Report, Korean Occupation, 24 Sept 1945.

Stack 370/45/4/7, Box 1027: USS *Henrico* (APA-45). "Battle Damage Report, 2 April 1945, Summary of. Covers Damage Sustained as a Result of Attack by Japanese Suicide Bomber and Resulting Explosions, while Under Way in Night Retirement Course West of Kerama Retto, Okinawa," 10 Apr 1945.

Stack 370/45/9/4, Box 1252: USS *Montrose.* "Covers Varied Activities during Okinawa Operation, from 26 March to 26 April 1945," Action Report, 30 Apr 1945.

Stack 370/45/9/6, Box 1267: USS *Natrona* (APA-214). "Action Report of Capture of Okinawa Gunto, Covers Landing Miscellaneous Units in Kerama Retto and Okinawa from 26 March to 17 May 1945 in Task Unit 51.1.4," 19 May 1945.

Stack 370/45/12/1, Box 1376: USS *Rixey* (APH-3). "Action Report on Occupation of Kerama Retto and Ie Shima, Okinawa Gunto, Nansei Shoto,
Covers Landing Units of 307th RCT 77th Infantry, 26 March–22 April
1945, in Task Unit 51.1.4," 1 May 1945.

Stack 370/45/13/4, Box 1455: USS *Suffolk* (AKA-69). "Anti-aircraft Action
by Surface Vessel," 17 Apr 1945.

Stack 370/45/13/7, Box 1465: USS *Tazewell* (APA-209). "Report of Anti-aircraft Action on 2 and 3 April 1945, Covers Two Heavy Air Attacks while
west of Kerama Retto-Okinawa Gunto," 6 Apr 1945.

Stack 37045/13/7, Box 1466: USS *Telfair* (APA-210). "Covers Damage from
Suicide Plane Attack while on Night Retirement Course West of Kerama
Retto in Task Unit 51.1.5," Action Report, 14 Apr 1945.

Stack 370/45/14/2, Box 1479: USS *Torrance* (AKA-76). "Covers Action on
2 April 1945 against Enemy Aircraft during Retiring Operation from
Kerama Retto in Task Unit 51.1.3," Action Report, 5 Apr 1945.

Stack 370/46/4/6, Box 1022: USS *Harry Bauer* (DM-26). "Report of Capture
of Okinawa Gunto, Phases I and II, 25 March to 11 June 1945. Covers
Minesweeping, Fire Support, and Screening Activities for Iceberg Operation in Task Unit 52.6.4," 12 Jun 1945.

RECORD GROUP 38: MODERN MILITARY RECORDS, WAR DIARIES

Stack 370/46/15/4, Box 1502: USS *Tate* (AKA-70). War Diary, 25 Nov
1944–31 Oct 1945.

USS *Bowditch* (AGS-4). War Diary, 1 Mar–30 Jun 1945.

RECORD GROUP 38: MODERN MILITARY RECORDS, OPERATIONAL PLANS

Stack 370/46/23/2, Box 206: Attack Plan for Capture of Ie Shima, A406–45,
from COM PHIB Group 4, Ser 00215, of 12 Apr 1945.

RECORD GROUP 24: MODERN MILITARY RECORDS, DECK LOGS

Stack 470/46: USS *Tate* (AKA-70). Deck Logs, 20 Nov 1944–1 Jul 1946.

National Personnel Records Center

MILITARY PERSONNEL RECORDS
Jordan, William, SN 92431
Lyon, Rupert E., SN 1823373
Morthland, Andrew, SN 87470

Smithsonian Institution

SMITHSONIAN INSTITUTION, NATIONAL MUSEUM OF AMERICAN HISTORY,
MARITIME ADMINISTRATION COLLECTION OF SHIP PLANS (1939–1970)
U.S. Maritime Commission, C2-S-AJ1, Ship Plans

Interviews by Author

WORLD WAR II VETERANS
Anthony, James W., Dec 4, 2002
Baker, James K., April 29, 2003
Borenski, John F., June 22, 2001
Bosarge, Wilmer J., Aug. 7, 2004
Bostic, J. C., Dec. 3, 2002
Buss, Earl W., Dec. 16, 2002
Buswell, Milton J., Dec. 10, 2002
Cecil, Rev. Ivo E., Feb. 28, 2003
Colley, Howard C., March 6, 2003
Comstock, Raymond M., March 9, 2003
Coslett, Alfred S., Jan. 3, 2003
Crew, Lewis A., June 29, 2001
Dorsey, Dr. Albert H. H., Jan. 7, 2003
Drake, W. T., March 7, 2003
Gries, Charles H., March 6, 2003
Johnson, Mark I., March 6, 2003
Joslyn, Alvin L., June 21, 2001
Kemske, Leroy W., Nov. 30, 2002
Keniry, Gerald J., March 6, 2003
Hathaway, Charles B., Aug. 28, 2004
Hokanson, Theron W., March 6, 2003
Lakes, Blaine, March 18, 2003
Larsen, Byron W., Jan. 13, 2003
Larsen, Morris D., April 21, 2003
Leahy, Paul R., Dec. 23–29, 2002
Maltese, Dewey, April 30, 2003
Maw, Alvin F., Sept. 13, 2003
McCaffrey, Ray A., March 6, 2003
Midgett, Zeblin V., Dec. 19, 2002
Newton, William G., Nov. 11, 2002
Nisen, Norman M., Dec. 18, 2002
Noga, Henry C., May 22, 2002
Norman, Arthur Lee, Sept. 11, 2004
Olkosky, Robert F., Dec. 19, 2002
Patrie, Donald L., April 23, 2003
Polikowski, William M., Dec. 16, 2002
Raynor, John C, Jan. 4, 2004
Righter, Norval W., Dec. 18, 2002

Russell, Harold R., Nov. 30, 2002

Salerno, Fortunate G., March 18, 2003

Six, Hubert J., Sr., March 18, 2003

Smith, Uel, March 27, 2002

Thompson, Dr. Warren C., July 12, 2003

Waller, David M., Feb. 8, 2003

Whitcome, Willard D., Dec. 20, 2002

Witte, Fredrick T., March 6, 2002

Worthington, John W., Aug. 26, 2004

WORLD WAR II VETERAN FAMILY MEMBER

Alexander, Timothy S., Nov. 19, 2003

Boland, Mary L., Feb. 4, 2003

Kampel, Lewis J., May 30, 2004

Milbourn, Linda O'Neil, Feb. 7, 2004

Munro, Cam, June 28, 2004

Toombs, Jon L., March 8, 2003

Published Material

Books and Articles

Alexander, Joseph H. *Storm Landings: Epic Amphibious Battles in the Central Pacific.* Annapolis: Naval Institute Press, 1997.

Ambrose, Stephen E. *To America.* New York: Simon and Schuster, 2002.

Anti-aircraft Training Center, U.S. Naval Operating Base, Guantanamo Bay, Cuba. *Anti-aircraft Gunnery.* [Training manual.] Guantanamo: U.S. Navy, 1944.

Appleman, Roy E., James M. Burns, Russell A. Gugeler, and John Stevens. *Okinawa: The Last Battle.* Washington, D.C.: Historical Division, Department of the Army, 1948.

Astor, Gerald. *Operation Iceberg: The Invasion and Conquest of Okinawa in World War II.* New York: Dell, 1995.

Becton, Julian F., and Morschauser, Joseph, III. *The Ship That Would Not Die.* Englewood Cliffs, N.J.: Prentice Hall, 1980.

Belate, James, and Belate William. *Typhoon of Steel: The Battle for Okinawa.* New York: Bantam, 1984.

Browning, Robert M., Jr. *U.S. Merchant Vessel War Casualties of World War II.* Annapolis: Naval Institute Press, 1996.

Carter, Worral Reed. *Beans, Bullets, and Black Oil: The Story of Fleet Logistics Afloat in the Pacific during World War II.* Washington, D.C.: USGPO, 1953.

Crowl, Philip A., and Edmund G. Love. *The War in the Pacific: Seizure of the*

Gilberts and Marshalls. Washington, D.C.: Center of Military History, U.S. Army, 1993.

Croizat, Victor J. *Across the Reef: The Amphibious Tracked Vehicle at War.* London: Blandford, 1989.

Defense Intelligence Agency. *Characteristics of U.S. Vessels, Vehicles, and Equipment for Amphibious Operations.* Washington, D.C.: Author, 1963.

Destroyer Escort Sailors Association. *Destroyer Escorts of World War Two.* Missoula, Mont.: Pictorial Histories, 2003.

Dodson, Kenneth. *Away All Boats.* Boston: Little and Brown, 1954.

Donnelly, Thomas J. *"Hey, Padre": The Saga of a Regimental Chaplain in World War II.* New York: 77th Infantry Division Association, undated.

Dyer, George C. *The Amphibians Came to Conquer: The Story of Admiral Richmond Kelly Turner II.* Washington, D.C.: USGPO, 1973.

Evans, Michael. *Amphibious Operations: The Projection of Power Ashore.* London: Brassey's, 1990.

Fane, Douglas F., and Moore, Dan. *The Naked Warriors.* Annapolis: Naval Institute Press, 1956.

Forrestal, E. P. *Admiral Raymond A. Spruance, USN: A Study in Command.* Washington, D.C.: Director of Navy History, 1966.

Francillon, René J. *Japanese Aircraft of the Pacific War.* Annapolis: Naval Institute Press, 1979.

Frank, Richard B. *Downfall: The End of the Imperial Japanese Empire.* New York: Random House, 1999.

Glantz, David M. *August Storm: Soviet Tactical and Operational Combat in Manchuria, 1945.* Leavenworth Papers, no. 7. Ft. Leavenworth, Kans.: Combat Studies Institute, 1983.

Goldman, Kenneth H. *USS* Charles Carroll, APA 28: *An Amphibious History of World War II.* Victoria, British Columbia: Trafford, 2004.

Heggen, Thomas. *Mister Roberts.* Boston: Houghton Mifflin, 1946.

Inoguchi, Rikihei, Tadashi Nakajima, and Roger Pineau. *The Divine Wind: Japan's Kamikaze Force in World War II.* Annapolis: U.S. Naval Institute Press, 1958.

Karig, Walter, Russell L. Harris, and Frank A. Manson. *Battle Report: Victory in the Pacific.* New York: Rinehart, 1949.

Kehl, James A. *When Civilians Manned the Ships: Life in the Amphibious Fleet during World War II.* White Stone, Va.: Brandylane, 1997.

López, Henry D. *From Jackson to Japan: The History of Company C, 307th Infantry, 77th Division, in World War II.* Self-published, 1977.

Lorelli, John A. *To Foreign Shores: U.S. Amphibious Operations in World War II.* Annapolis: Naval Institute Press, 1995.

MacGregor, Morris J., Jr. *Integration of the Armed Forces, 1940–1965.* Washington, D.C.: Center of Military History, 1985.

MacGregor, Wayne C., Jr. *Through These Portals: A Pacific War Saga.* Pullman: Washington State University Press, 2002.

Mayo, Lida. *The Ordnance Department: On Beachhead and Battlefront.* Washington, D.C.: Center of Military History, U.S. Army, 1991.

Meyers, Bruce F. *Swift, Silent, and Deadly: Marine Amphibious Reconnaissance in the Pacific, 1942–1945.* Annapolis: Naval Institute Press, 2004.

Miller, Francis T. *The Complete History of World War II.* Chicago: Reader's Service Bureau, 1948.

Miller, Lee G. *An Ernie Pyle Album: Indiana to Ie Shima.* New York: William Sloane Associates, 1946.

Mooney, James L., ed. *Dictionary of American Naval Fighting Ships.* Nine vols. Washington, D.C.: Naval Historical Center, Department of the Navy, 1959–1991.

Morison, Samuel Eliot. *Victory in the Pacific.* Boston: Little, Brown, 1960.

Naval Analysis Division. *The Offensive Mine-laying Campaign against Japan.* Washington, D.C.: Headquarters, Naval Material Command, 1969.

Nelson, Stewart B. *Oceanographic Ships Fore and Aft.* Washington, D.C.: Oceanographer of the Navy, 1971.

Nichols, Charles S., and Henry I. Shaw. *Okinawa: Victory in the Pacific.* Washington, D.C.: USGPO, 1955.

Nichols, David. *Ernie's War: The Best of Ernie Pyle's World War II Dispatches.* New York: Random House, 1986.

North Carolina Shipbuilding Company. *Five Years of North Carolina Shipbuilding.* Wilmington, N.C.: North Carolina Shipbuilding Company, 1972.

Pyle, Ernie. *Here's Your War.* New York: Henry Holt, 1943.

———. *Last Chapter.* New York: Henry Holt, 1946.

Randle, Edwin H. *Ernie Pyle Comes Ashore and Other Stories.* Clearwater, Fla.: Eldnar, 1972.

Roscoe, Theodore. *United States Destroyer Operations in World War II.* Annapolis: Naval Institute Press, 1953.

Rottman, Gordon L. "Japanese Suicide Boats at Okinawa, 1945." *Osprey Military Journal* 4(1) (2002): 51–57.

———. *Okinawa 1945: The Last Battle.* Oxford, UK: Osprey, 2002.

Sawyer, L. A., and W. H. Mitchell. *From America to the United States: The History of the Long-range Merchant Shipbuilding Programme of the United States Maritime Commission (1937–1952).* London: World Ship Society, 1981.

Shaw, Henry I., Jr. *The United States Marines in North China, 1945–1949.* Washington, D.C.: Historical Branch, G-3 Division, U.S. Marine Corps, 1968.

Sledge, E. B. *China Marine: An Infantryman's Life after World War II.* New York: Oxford University Press, 2003.

Stafford, Edward P. *Little Ship, Big War: The Saga of DE343.* New York: Morrow, 1984.

Tobin, James. *Ernie Pyle's War: America's Eyewitness to World War II.* Lawrence: University of Kansas Press, 1997.

U.S. War Department. *Handbook on Japanese Military Forces.* Baton Rouge: Louisiana State University Press, 1995.

Weaver, Victor E. *The 233d Engineer Combat Battalion, 1943–1945.* Washington, D.C.: Infantry Journal Press, 1947.

West, Charles O., Philip C. Wood, Neil F. Wender, Harold R. Butler, eds. *Second to None! The Story of the 305th Infantry in World War II.* Washington, D.C.: Infantry Journal Press, 1949.

Yahara, Hiromichi. *The Battle for Okinawa.* New York: Wiley, 1995.

77th Infantry Division Association. *Ours to Hold It High: The History of the 77th Infantry Division in World War II.* Washington, D.C.: Infantry Journal Press, 1947.

Cruise Books

USS *Goodhue (APA-107).* Self-published (undated [1946]).

USS *Mountrail (APA-213), November 16, 1944, to December 1, 1945.* Self-published (undated).

USS *Tazewell (APA-209). Two-O-Nine: A Ship's Biography.* Self-published (undated).

War-Time Log of the U.S.S. Tate, *AKA-70, 25 November 1944 to 12 December 1945.* Everett, Wash.: Kane and Marcus, 1947.

Newspapers and Magazines

Ann Arbor Press
Hot Tater
South Bend Tribune
Time
Wilmington Morning Star

Films

Empires of American Industry: Victory at Sea, Mass-producing Liberty. History Channel, 1996.

U.S. Navy. *Amphibious Warfare: The LCM-3.* Training film. 1944.

———. *Small Boat Landing Tactics and Supply.* 1944.

———. *The LST.* 1944.

Internet

American War Library. "WW2 Famous Quotations." (1988). http://
members.aol.com/forcountry/ww2/quo.htm.

Arikara 50s Association. "Story of the Seagoing Tug USS *Arikara* (ATF-98)."
(undated). http://ussarikara.com/war_diary.htm.

Hibbs, David L., Sr. "USS *Bunch* DE-694/APD-79." (2001). http://
www.informediate.com/USSBunch/History/Detail%20History.htm.

Naval Historical Center. "Japan Capitulates: Arrangements." (undated).
http://www.history.navy.mil/photos/events/wwii-pac/japansur/
js-3a.htm.

Princeton Union-Eagle. "WWII Veteran Injured in South Pacific Battle."
(2001). http://www.unioneagle.com/2001/may/24howard.html.

INDEX

Numbers in **bold** refer to maps; numbers in *italics* refer to photographs.